The Encyclopedia of HERBS, SPICES AND FLAVOURINGS

Arabella Boxer Jocasta Innes
Charlotte Parry-Crooke Lewis Esson

The Encyclopedia of

HERBS, SPICES AND FLAVOURINGS

Arabella Boxer   Jocasta Innes
Charlotte Parry-Crooke   Lewis Esson

First published in 1984 by Octopus Books Limited
59 Grosvenor Street
London W1

ISBN 0 8627 3122 4

Printed and bound by
Severn Valley Press Limited England

CONTENTS

SPICES

FLAVOURINGS

HERBS

INTRODUCTION

Over the past few decades few areas of British life have shown such a radical and dramatic change as our attitudes to good food and imaginative cookery. Cities up and down the country, not merely London, offer an extraordinary variety of national cuisines in restaurants to suit every pocket. Foodstores and markets provide an ever increasing range of exotic ingredients and to judge by the adventurous recipes in newspapers, magazines and television programmes, cooking in today's homes is of a completely different stamp from the timid, rather plain fare which makes up the bulk of recipes in most pre-war recipe books.

All sorts of factors have played their part in bringing about this revolution in our eating. Easier, cheaper travel must be one, since anyone who has sampled excitingly different food on holidays abroad is unlikely to remain uncritical of the lacklustre approach that was once so characteristic of meals in this country. The existance of immigrant minorities – West Indian, Indian, Middle Eastern, Chinese – meaning that specialised stores, markets and restaurants catering to their tastes makes economic sense, is another exciting influence. Where once a single run of the mill Chinese takeaway was the norm, there may now be two or three restaurants offering different Chinese regional specialities, indicating among other things that most people, given the chance to make comparisons, rapidly become more adventurous in their eating habits.

Information and knowledge are the key factors in exploring the fascinating and rewarding but unfamiliar territory of foreign cusines. *The Encyclopedia of Herbs, Spices and Flavourings* is intended to de-mystify and explain the role and relative importance of all the most important flavourings in cuisines the world over, taking the word flavourings in its widest sense of adding or modifying the taste of the basic ingredients. As such, a directory of all but the most obscure or dispensable spices, herbs and other flavour modifiers, it must become an invaluable and concise reference book; required reading for any adventurous cook.

Visual identification of unfamiliar ingredients is taken care of by the colour illustrations that accompany the short but informative entries for each of the 126 spices, flavourings and herbs listed in the A-Z sections. These give botanical information, describe their culinary uses, and give suggestions for growing, picking and storing where appropriate.

Herbal entries include all the herbs used at one time or another in cooking, including many less common ones such as purslane and marigold petals, which were important to medieval cooks and, of course, to physicians, for in those days the healing and calmative effects of herbs were more extensively developed than they are today. The spices section is the longest in the book, and contains many unfamiliar entries, since native spices are used the world over to enliven everyday dishes as well as the more elaborate feast day and special occasion food. The flavourings section deals with the many substances commonly added to food to strengthen its own flavour, to tenderize, to add sharpness, or richness, but which cannot properly be classified under herbs or spices. These include familiar ingredients like capers, dried mushrooms and tomato purée, as well as less known ones like tamarind, carob and blachan.

Background information of the sort contained in the A-Z section allows one to recognise unusual ingredients when shopping for a particular dish, and also to work out an approximate substitute where these are not available. Instead of using unfamiliar spices 'blind', in the sense of following a recipe dutifully, a few minutes spent looking them up will give the cook a much clearer idea of what the finished dish will taste like. This knowledge makes for confidence; another important ingredient in good creative cooking.

As well as being a directory, the encyclopedia is also an exciting recipe book. The way to get a 'feel' for any ingredient, herb, spice or flavouring is, of course, to cook with it. Every entry in the various sections has corresponding recipes, chosen to illustrate its own particular qualities. The number of recipes allotted to each entry varies, naturally enough, with its relative importance to cookery in general and to the dishes of its homeland in particular. Herbs are a familiar ingredient in European cookery, but it is all too easy to get into a rut, restricting them to stuffings and casseroles and overlooking the exciting possibilities of herbs used in unexpected ways – lovage soup, for instance, horseradish with duck breasts – or interesting combinations like coriander with avocado salad, or fresh ginger in watercress soup. The imaginative use of herbs is a distinctive feature of the *nouvelle cuisine* whose influence has changed restaurant menus so dramatically over the past few years, and the recipes in the herb section reflect a *nouvelle cuisine* concern for light, fresh distinguished flavours. Though many herbs dry well, and become still more pungent that way, there is a fragrant, delicate summery feel about many of the recipes which will be an inspiration to any cook planning a summer dinner party, or elegant picnic.

The recipes in the spice and flavourings section necessarily have a more international scope, since the most characteristic uses of most of these hot-country products occur in the dishes of their native countries. Reading through recipes from Indonesia, Malaysia, India, China, Japan and South America, is a little like taking a journey of the imagination. No one should let themselves be put off by the unfamiliar, however. The truly characteristic dishes of any country are invariably rewarding gastronomically, for the traditional wisdom and experience of countless generations of cooks and gourmets the world over are condensed into the recipes they have perfected over the years. Classic recipes, from anywhere, travel well, as the mushrooming development of ethnic and regional restaurants in recent years suggests.

Any adventurous cook must be stimulated by exploring, for instance, the subtle use of coconut milk (how many people still think that coconut milk is the thin fluid found inside a fresh coconut, rather than the richer liquid produced by infusing grated coconut meat in water?) in Indian and South East Asian cookery, or the complex ways in which Mexican cooks use their native chilli, which in Mexico is available in not one or two forms but in scores of different varieties, each one valued and used for its own special qualities of heat, pungency and flavour.

In their long history, spices and flavourings have been used in so many ways and combinations, in so many different culinary traditions, that following some of the many recipes using them is bound to provide cooks with many surprises, intriguing possibilities, and delicious meals. The difference between a routine use of spices and flavourings, and the more adventurous use of them, is a bit like the difference between black and white and colour photography, or between composing for a solo instrument and a symphony orchestra. The wider a cook's range, the more scope and confidence he or she will have in experimenting, adding a new twist to a familiar dish, or inventing a completely novel one.

Since locally grown ingredients are developed most intelligently as a rule in their countries of origin, and many of the spices and flavourings come from a distinct region, island or mountainous area, there is not just an international feel about many of the recipes in this section, but a strongly regional one. What food and flavourings are easily available inevitably affects the style and overall characteristics of the local food. It is one of the delights of motoring in a leisurely way through any European country, eating at restaurants along the way, to observe how changes in terrain and climate affect regional cooking. Cool, rainy mountain areas inland produce quite a different style of cookery – purer, understated, rich in dairy products – from the much more colourful, crude and pungent flavours developed in the dry, rocky coastal hill country. In just the same way, the rich Indian uplands of Kashmir and the Punjab have given a completely different feel to the typical dishes of the area – subtle, creamy kormas, and gently spiced 'dry' dishes like the celebrated tandoori chicken and fish – from the hotter cookery of coastal areas, with its reliance on coconut oil, milk, fish and sweet-sour combinations. To be acquainted with only one form of regional cookery is to miss out on a whole gastronomic journey of exploration, and to have a limited and fragmentary grasp of the richness and range of a country's culinary history. No lover of Chinese food should rest content with the regional cooking of Canton, or Peking, however rewarding, when there are the peppery pungent specialities of Szechuan, or the fishy delicacies of the Shanghai cuisine to be explored.

What an adventurous cook brings back from these culinary travels (even if he or she never leaves the kitchen) is not merely the discoveries, in the way of flavours and textures, that exotic new dishes provide, but – just as importantly – a sense of what these exciting new tastes can add to the everyday meals. As well as giving authentic native recipes for using spices and flavourings and herbs, *The Encyclopedia of Herbs, Spices and Flavourings* sets out to extend the scope of our everyday eating by including recipes that show how the imaginative use of a spoonful of caraway seeds, for instance, can transform plain buttered cabbage, or how a rich, relishing sauce, based on an Indonesian *saté* sauce, can give new interest to something as commonplace and familiar as fried bangers. Discriminatingly used, chefs' tricks like these (*nouvelle cuisine* gains much of its distinction from such experiments) make all the difference to everyday eating, for practically no extra expense and very little trouble.

If you have never experienced coriander seeds' orangey warm pungency in Middle Eastern dishes, you might never be led to try crushed coriander seeds with parsnips, and thereby miss one of the best, simplest and cheapest vegetable dishes to be found. Frozen New Zealand lamb, not a gourmet's treat unadorned, takes on a whole new dimension if the meat is coated with a spicy paste of crushed cumin seed, oil, garlic and salt before cooking, and served with a saffron coloured rice spiked with pine nuts and raisins.

Nowadays, as the raw materials of cookery – meat, fish, vegetables, fruit – tend increasingly towards a blandness and a certain tastelessness, due to intensive farming and cultivation methods, quick-freezing and all the other low-risk, short-cut approaches bound up with modern food retailing, it is more important than ever to develop a repertoire of tried and tested kitchen 'extras'; ways of enhancing or sharpening natural flavours or compensating for the flavours that mass production methods have removed. We are not talking here of crudely smothering plain-tasting sausages with a fierce proprietary sauce, but of something much more sensitive and subtle – a discriminating selection of complimentary flavours and fragrances from nature's own spice-box to make frozen battery chickens, farmed trout, frozen prawns, over-processed fruit and vegetables not merely palatable but memorable. There is nothing new or dishonest about this – herbs, spices and flavourings have always played a vital supportive role in cooking, making the best or the most of whatever ingredients were to hand, not merely from the point of view of enhancing flavours, but often helping to preserve food longer, neutralise rankness or staleness, add vital nutritional factors and to aid digestion. In fact it would be true to say that with our current interest in the imaginative use of herbs, spices and other flavourings, we are not so much turning over a new page as turning back to an old one, and rediscovering our culinary past.

Buying and Storing Herbs, Spices and Flavourings

The majority of ingredients listed in this book are at their best when freshest, though in some cases – such as dried fungi, herbs, mustards – the concentration of flavour and pungency in the dried versions results in what to all intents and purposes is another, specialized flavour. While most spices, many herbs and most flavourings, can be stored for some time without a serious loss of character, it still pays to buy them in prime condition, close enough to the harvesting and commercial processing for them to retain some of their more volatile, delicate and attractive scents and flavours.

Whether one is talking about Indian spices, Chinese sauces or Malaysian pickles, the most critical shoppers will always be the nationals concerned. The obvious place to look for good quality spices for use in Indian cookery will be in an Indian store, preferably in an Indian dominated residential district, because the demand there will justify a rapid turnover of imported ingredients, at a competitive price. The same applies to all exotic ingredients. Just as the best Chinese restaurant is likely to be the one where more Chinese than foreigners are eating, so the best store is likely to be the one catering to its native population. A Bengali or Pakistani run store in London's East End will sell a large plastic pack of black peppercorns, plump, fresh and wonderfully aromatic, for very little more than a small plastic drum of peppercorns past their best will cost in a supermarket rack.

The chief problem of shopping in foreign run stores is a language one, since not all foreign packers label their products clearly in English, but the A-Z directory included in this book should provide enough clues to identification to clear that hurdle. Many foreign products carry their Anglicized native name – *methi* instead of fenugreek, for instance – so it is wise to check on this under the appropriate entries before making out a shopping list. If you are uncertain about something, don't be shy of trying out your pronunciation on the store assistant – people love hearing their language mispronounced as a rule, and the enjoyment this gives them tends to endear you to them and make them immensely helpful.

Anyone who has entered at all seriously into Indian, Asian and Middle Eastern cooking, already knows that most spices bought whole, and ground as the recipe requires, have incomparably more fragrance and flavour than if they were bought pre-ground. Whole spices are obtainable readily and are not only gastronomically superior, and more authentic, but usually cheaper. Bulk buying, however, is only practicable for restaurants – buy a medium sized pack, store the contents in an airtight container in a dark, cool and dry place and they will retain their pungency for a year or so. Glass jars look attractive and help rapid identification (paste labels on all your more unusual spices, because many smaller seeds look remarkably alike) but unless they are stored in a cupboard, in the dark, the contents will be affected by the light. Whole spices can be ground, as needed, in the traditional style using a pestle and mortar (the heavier these are, the quicker the grinding), or much more rapidly, as Indian and Chinese housewives are discovering, in a small electrically powered grinder. Ideally a special grinder should be kept purely for spices, and carefully cleaned with kitchen paper after use. It can be an unpleasant shock to drink coffee which has been ground in the same machine as red chillies. The superiority of whole, as against processed, ground spices and flavourings, holds good too in the case of vanilla pods, which have a delicacy missing from the largely caramel based vanilla extract sold in small bottles, turmeric in its hard, root state (crack it with a hammer before grinding) and coconuts, which have a sweetness in their freshly ground flesh which is less apparent in the creamed or desiccated versions.

However, this is a counsel of perfection. Busy British cooks will find, as many busy foreign cooks already have, that with a little extra spicing, the convenience versions of such ingredients as ground peanuts for *saté* (crunchy peanut butter substitutes effectively), creamed for fresh coconut, proprietary garam masala blends for homemade, make all the difference in time and effort between trying recipes out and avoiding them on the grounds that they are too time consuming. Better to test out a new flavour combination, even approximately, than put it off because everything has to be exactly right. Once a new, or exotic blend of flavours has been tested, and appreciated, one is encouraged to repeat it, and increasing familiarity usually leads a cook to a greater concern for authenticity, hunting out lemon grass for instance, for Indonesian dishes, instead of substituting lemon peel, or the pungent blachan, in preference to anchovy paste.

Much the same applies to flavourings, as classified in this book. Buy them, where possible, in specialist shops, store them in a dark, cool place, and renew them from time to time. Some of these, like Chinese dried mushrooms, will be expensive wherever you buy them, but it only needs a few of these, soaked in water, to confer authenticity to any dishes where they are required – and don't make the mistake of throwing the soaking water away; it makes valuable stock in many Chinese dishes.

Freshness is more important with herbs than with any of the other ingredients mentioned in the encyclopedia. Since many herbs can be successfully grown in this climate, most people are familiar with them and with the difference they make to home cooking, as well as being aware of how easy it is to grow one's own. Since many herbs are as decorative as they are delicious it makes sense to grow them even where space is limited; bushy parsley or chives in windowboxes alongside geraniums and silver-leaved plants, spiky rosemary leaves against sheltered sunny walls in front of the house and creeping thymes in crevices in paving. With a little care and persistence, even a kitchen windowbox can produce enough snippings of chives, thyme or basil, to enrich salad dressings, chilled summer soups, pâtés, simple sauces and dishes of lightly cooked pasta.

Wonderful as fresh herbs are, and enlivening as their presence is in so many dishes, there are some which are no more than a pale shadow of themselves grown in our climate. To achieve the headily aromatic potential of which they are capable, they need to be grown in the hot, dry, often impoverished soil of the rocky Mediterranean coasts.

The dried herbs of Provence, blended together or singly, are a mindblowing addition to food, but remember – as with all dried flavourings – to use far less of the dried herb than you would of the fresh; no more than a third in most instances. The herbs containing volatile oils are those which dry most successfully – rosemary, thyme, marjoram, savory. Softer, sappier plants like basil, parsley, tarragon, lose much more in drying, though dried mint is a useful standby for Middle Eastern dishes. Many of these more fragile herbs are best preserved by steeping in vinegar, or oil, and adding a little of either to a dish instead of the herb itself.

Unlike spices, which usually work best used in combination (hence the number of spice blends developed in different national cuisines), herbs often taste freshest and most intriguing used on their own – a sprinkling of fresh basil over tomato salad, a few spoonfuls of sorrel purée added to egg or cheese dishes, a sprig of rosemary under a lamb roast, are all beautifully convincing examples of 'less is more' in cooking terms.

Many fresh herbs can be rapidly minced in a good grinder, but some cooks maintain that this bruises them more than is proper, thereby impairing the flavour, and that too much of the fragrance remains in the processor. Large bunches of parsley, or mixed herbs, will not suffer so much, but for more fragile herbs, a demi-lune chopper and small wooden bowl (available from specialist kitchen stores) is still probably the most satisfying implement.

SPICES

AJOWAN
Carum ajowan

Ajowan is a small annual of the parsley family, closely related to cumin and caraway; it grows between 30-60cm (1-2 feet) high. Its small, oval, reddish or greenish-brown striped seeds have a strong aroma and flavour of thyme and are used dried as a spice in parts of the Middle East and Asia, especially in their native India. Ajowan seeds are available whole or ground from Asian food shops and keep indefinitely in an airtight container.

Uses: Not much used in the West, ajowan seeds are useful for authentic Indian cooking; use them whole, lightly bruised, crushed or ground, according to recipe requirements. Occasionally a component of home-ground curry powders and other spicy mixtures, they are more frequently used in pulse dishes and in the many savouries and snacks so popular in India. Crispy, deep-fried snack dishes such as *pakoras* (small puffs of batter-coated vegetables, cheese or meat), many types of savoury biscuit, and *sev* (thin spirals of deep-fried spiced chick pea flour) often include them, as do *parathas* and *paratha* stuffings. In dire necessity, ajowan could be substituted for thyme in Western food, but experiment to test its strength first as the crushed seeds can have a very pungent and slightly acrid flavour.

Ajowan

Amchur

ALLSPICE
Pimenta dioica

Allspice berries are the small, round, dried fruit of a tall, aromatic evergreen of the myrtle and clove family, which can grow to over 12m (40 feet). Picked when green and unripe, they are dried in the sun to a rich, deep brown colour; they are similar in size and shape to large peppercorns, though less wrinkled. Native to the West Indies and parts of Latin America, allspice grows prolifically in Jamaica where it is widely used in native dishes. Its flavour, a mingling of the tastes of cloves, cinnamon and nutmeg, with cloves predominating, gives allspice its name. Buy the whole berries at any good grocer, and store in an airtight container; they will keep well for a long time. Use whole or grind as required; ground allspice does not store well.

Uses: Despite its combination of oriental flavours, allspice is a favourite Western spice, especially popular in Scandinavia – almost every dish in a Swedish *smörgäsbord* will be flavoured with allspice! It can be used in both savoury and sweet dishes; smoked and pickled foods such as raw fish, salamis and other Continental sausages, are frequently flavoured with it, as are traditional English pork or game pies. A few berries are often included in meat and game marinades and winter soups. As a sweet spice it is used ground in pies, cakes and puddings, especially in Christmas pudding recipes.

AMCHUR
Mangifera indica

Amchur is unripe fruit of the mango tree, a tropical evergreen which has been cultivated in India for over 4,000 years. The mango tree can reach a height of 39m (130 feet) and grows extensively in other tropical areas, especially South-East Asia, although amchur is associated primarily with India, where its uses are intimately interwoven with ritual, culture and cuisine. The sour green mangos are sliced and dried in the sun, turning a light brown; the powder made from them is similar but a paler colour. Amchur can be bought from good Indian or Asian grocers in sliced or powdered form. It is preferable to buy as required, but always store in an airtight container in a dark place. Lemon or lime juice, in double or treble quantities, can be used as a substitute for amchur, but will not supply the spice's sour-sweet, slightly resinous bouquet.

Uses: Amchur, powdered or sliced, features in a wide variety of savoury Indian dishes. Tart, with a sweet/sour taste, it is used, like tamarind, as a souring agent in curries, chutneys and pickles, and also to tenderize meat. Like lemon juice, it has a natural affinity with fish and chicken and is often included in spicy marinades for grilled or barbecued fish dishes, such as *tikkas* (fish chunks barbecued on skewers). Many fresh vegetables, aubergines and potatoes for example, are cooked with amchur, which is usually added towards the end of the cooking time or as part of a dry spice condiment sprinkled over the dish. Some pulse dishes also feature amchur, as can a variety of snacks such as *samosas*.

Allspice

ANISEED

Pimpinella anisum

The aromatic anise annual grows to about 60cm (2 feet) high and is similar to other small members of the parsley family. A native of the Middle East, the plant is now established in south-eastern Europe, North Africa, India and parts of Latin America. The small, oval, grey-green ribbed seeds should be bought whole in small quantities and stored out of the light.

Uses: Aniseed's spicy/sweet flavour combines well with both sweet and savoury foods. It is used in northern and eastern Europe in confectionery, desserts, biscuits, cakes and breads. Aniseed is a favourite seasoning in Indian fish curries and marinades, especially those from north-eastern areas; the seeds are often lightly dry roasted in a frying pan before use, to bring out their full flavour. Aniseed-flavoured alcoholic drinks are often used in cooking, in dishes such as Lobster à l'Anise and Oysters Rockefeller.

Aniseed

Annatto

ANNATTO

Bixa orellana

Annatto is a red seed, best known in the West as an orangey-red dye for food and fabric, but it is used as a spice in a number of tropical countries. Sometimes growing 10.5m (35 feet) high, the tree's leaves and prickly fruit pods are both heart-shaped. The latter contain a mass of small, deep red triangular seeds. Annatto is especially associated with the Philippines, having been brought there by seventeenth-century Spanish colonialists from Central America and the West Indies. Buy the seeds in West Indian grocers and store in an airtight container.

Uses: The rather peppery seeds are particularly effective with fish, rice and vegetable dishes. Annatto is used in Jamaica in a sauce for salt cod and ackee, and in the Philippines in *pipian*, a traditional dish of chicken and pork cubes braised in a spicy sauce. In Mexico annatto seeds give the characteristic colour and spiciness to stews, sauces and taco fillings. In the West the use of annatto is confined to colouring smoked fish and the rinds of cheeses such as Edam.

ASAFOETIDA

Ferula asafoetida

Asafoetida, or 'Giant Fennel', is a huge, odiferous member of the parsley family which grows to 3m (10 feet) high and is native to the Middle East, Afghanistan and north India. It is known colloquially as 'Stinking Gum' or 'Devil's Dung' and yields an equally evil-smelling spice. The spice asafoetida is made from the sap from the plant's stems and roots, which solidifies into grey-yellow lumps which then turn a reddish-brown with a crystal-like appearance. It is important to anyone interested in authentic Indian or Middle Eastern food. When used in minute quantities it is a remarkable enhancer of other tastes. Do not be put off by its appearance, or indeed its frightful smell, for this disappears in cooking. Indian or Asian shops usually stock asafoetida. Store in an airtight container.

Uses: Used very occasionally in France, asafoetida is used extensively in spicy Middle Eastern vegetable dishes and in regional Indian cooking. In Kashmir it appears in fresh vegetable dishes and in meat dishes like *kormas*, though only Hindu ones; Kashmiri Moslems will not touch it. In the western coastal states and in southern India, asafoetida features in pickles, soups, vegetarian and fish dishes.

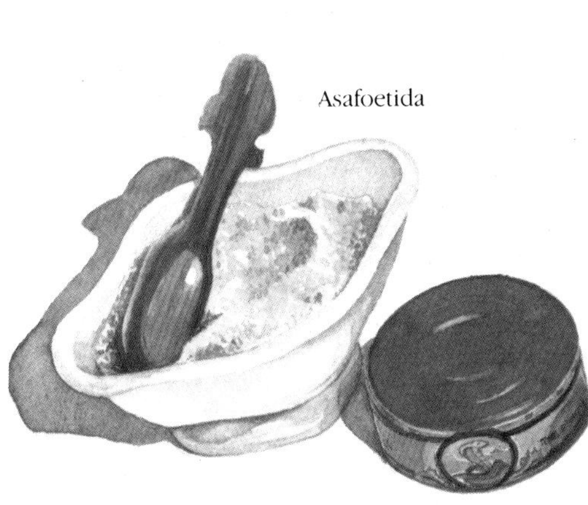
Asafoetida

CARAWAY SEEDS

Carum carvi

The small caraway annual is a member of the parsley family and closely related to fennel and dill, both of which it resembles. It grows to between 45-60cm (1½-2 feet) and is cultivated in many temperate regions, including parts of Europe, the southern Mediterranean and the USA. Caraway seeds are small, oval and ribbed, light to dark brown in colour. Strongly aromatic, they have a warming peppery undertone and should be bought as seeds which can be crushed if necessary. Store in an airtight container in a dark place.

Uses: Caraway successfully bridges the gap between sweet and savoury foods. Germany and Austria use more caraway than any other country; the rest of northern Europe, parts of eastern Europe and Scandinavia are also large consumers. Breads such as rye and pumpernickel frequently include caraway, as do German and Austrian seed cakes, dumplings, cheeses, noodle dishes, soups and goulashes. It is added to salads and vegetables, especially coleslaw and sauerkraut. Caraway is used to flavour *Kümmel, Schnapps* and other northern liqueurs.

Caraway seeds

CARDAMOM

Elettaria cardamomum

The cardamom bush is a relative of the ginger plant and grows nearly 3m (10 feet) high, its pod-bearing stalks sprawling along the ground. Native to India, the cardamom plant is now established in other tropical regions, including parts of Indonesia, China and Latin America. The whole seed-pod is used as the spice more often than the individual seeds it contains and three types of cardamom pod are available in the West. Most frequently seen is the small, oval, grey-green, ridged pod containing minute dark brown seeds. White cardamoms are merely bleached versions of the green, while the 'black' cardamom is actually brown and resembles a dark hairy beetle. The aroma of cardamom is unique and unmistakable; its flavour is sweet but clean with a hint of eucalyptus. Cardamom is an expensive spice. Green cardamom is widely available, and the black variety can be acquired from Indian grocers. Buy the pods whole and crush them to release the seeds if these are needed separately, but remember that the pods themselves cannot be eaten. Store pods in an airtight container.

Uses: Cardamom is one of the essential spices in Indian food, crucial in *biryanis, pilaus, dals* and curries, particularly those of northern India. Cardamom is an important component of spice mixtures such as garam masala, and also imparts its perfumed flavour to many Indian sweet dishes and beverages: ground cardamom is sprinkled on to *lassi*, the delicious yogurt drink. Cardamom is much used throughout the Middle East as well, and has been adopted by northern Europe and Scandinavia for use in cakes, pastries, mulling mixtures and pickles.

Cardamom

Cassia

CASSIA

Cinnamomum cassia

Cassia and cinnamon both come from the bark of closely related trees of the laurel family. The cassia of the spice trade is the bark of young shoots, sold as quills (small curled-up rolls of bark), pieces or as a powder. The rusty brown quills and pieces, about 7.5cm (3 inches) long, are thicker, rougher and altogether less delicate than cinnamon quills. Indigenous to Burma and parts of South-East Asia, different varieties of cassia grow in other tropical regions, including China, the East and West Indies and parts of Central America. Cassia tastes and smells very much like cinnamon, but is stronger and more bitter. The pieces are usually very hard, so it is useful to have at hand both pieces and powder, stored in airtight containers. Cassia can be acquired from good grocery stores.

Uses: Cassia is frequently used in the same manner as cinnamon but for preference reserve its stronger flavour for savoury foods and leave the more delicate cinnamon for sweet dishes. Spicy Indonesian curries can be flavoured with cassia, as can those from China, where it is considered one of the great spices and is a component of the Five Spice Powder (p 25). Indian curries and Middle Eastern stews can be flavoured with cassia, as can an English stew or casserole – but remember to remove it before serving. Cassia is a popular chocolate flavouring in Germany and the USA and may be used instead of cinnamon in spice mixtures for pastries, cakes and steamed puddings. Its flavour also blends well with cooked fruit, especially apples. See also: CINNAMON (p 16).

CAYENNE PEPPER

Capsicum frutescens

Cayenne pepper, paprika and Tabasco sauce are all made from varieties of capsicum, a vast collection of plants which range from small, searingly fiery chillies to the mild and much larger sweet bell pepper. Cayenne pepper is made from the flesh and seeds of the small slender fruits of the 'Bird chilli', ripened to a bright yellow or red, dried and ground to a fine powder. All chillis are indigenous to Latin America, although they now grow throughout the world in tropical and subtropical regions. Though the powerful 'heat' of cayenne is not as fierce as some chilli powders, it is nonetheless very pungent. Cayenne pepper should be stored in small quantities in an airtight container in a dark place; strong light will quickly rob it of its flavour.

Uses: Cayenne pepper is used as a spice, a seasoning and a condiment, and as a milder alternative to chilli powder. It is important in Indian, North African and Latin American dishes, to which it imparts a characteristic deep red colour and rich flavour. Cayenne has an affinity with fish and seafood and is used extensively as a seasoning in lobster, crab, prawn and oyster dishes. Potted crab or shrimps, grilled lobster, salmon soufflé, mousse and quiche all include it in small quantities, as do many Spanish seafood dishes. Cayenne teams well with cheese and eggs, and is used in devil sauces and spice mixes for deep-frying chicken, fish and vegetables. See also: CHILLI (p 15), PAPRIKA (p 21).

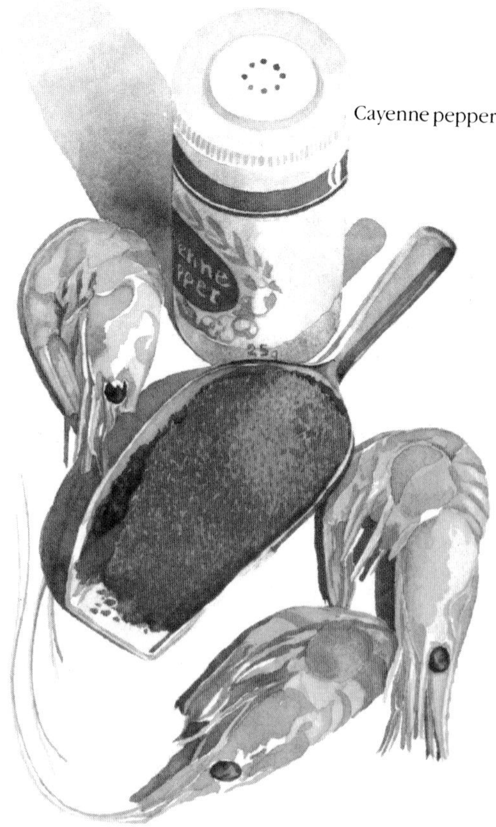
Cayenne pepper

Chilli

CELERY SEEDS

Apium graveolens

Celery is a member of the parsley family, related to both fennel and dill. The plant is familiar as a salad and stew ingredient, but the narrow, grey-green, ridged, oval seeds are also used in cooking in the West. The taste and aroma of celery seeds are similar to those of the plant, but more pungent and bitter. Buy seeds whole and crush as necessary. If you grow celery (p 137), allow the plants to flower, harvest the flower-heads in the autumn of their second year and hang them upside down to dry over a container to catch their seeds. Store celery seeds in an airtight container away from the light.

Uses: Celery seeds are popular in English, French and American cooking, and in dishes from the Balkans. They are often used with celery sticks (to accentuate the flavour), or as a substitute for them in soups, sauces, stuffings and vegetable dishes. Celery seeds and tomatoes are natural partners in pasta sauces, rice dishes and 'Bloody Mary' cocktails. They can be included in fish soups, marinades, stocks and seafood sauces and give zest to breads and biscuits. See also: CELERY LEAVES (p 137)

CHILLI

Capsicum annuum
Capsicum frutescens

Fiery chilli 'peppers' are a very ancient spice, their cultivation stretching back 10,000 years. Chillies originate in Latin America, they belong to the capsicum branch of the plant family which numbers among its members the tomato, the potato and the aubergine. The vast variety of different types of chilli defies consistent classification and indeed description (there are over a hundred different kinds in Mexico alone!); all varieties of chilli pepper do, however, bear certain common characteristics. With a preference for tropical or sub-tropical climates, the bushy chilli shrub grows to between 30cm-1.8m (1-6 feet) high, depending on variety; the various plants' berries, which become the spice, all share a smooth, shiny and taut skin which protects a hollow fruit containing several fleshy ribs, a central core and numerous tiny seeds, usually white in colour. Beyond these features the similarity ends, for the different fruits vary enormously in shape, size, colour and strength; ranging in size from 5mm-30cm (¼in to 1 foot) long, their shapes can be round and squarish, flattened, or long, narrow and tapering, with a pointed 'tail' and squared-off 'shoulders'. Colours, too, are diverse: from an unripe bright green the different types of fruit can turn to red, yellow, purple, brown, black or even creamy-white. The variety most commonly seen on our market stalls and in greengrocers are small, thin and tapering red or green fruits of about 7.5-10cm (3-4 inches) long. Pungency, too, is infinitely variable and spans a heat scale which ranges from relatively mild to furnace-like ferocity. As a very general rule (to which, needless to say, there are exceptions), the smaller, narrower and darker the chilli, the greater its pungency; unripe fresh chillies are usually less pungent than ripe fresh ones, and these in turn are milder than dried chillies.

The chilli is a crucial and essential culinary requisite in Latin America, Indonesia, South-East Asia, China, Japan, India, the Middle East and all parts of Africa.

Many different types of fresh and dried chillies are easily acquired; one can choose between fresh unripe or ripe whole chillies, dried whole chillies, chilli powders, and chilli seasonings. Two of the best known chilli powders, cayenne and paprika, come from particular types of chilli (see Cayenne (p 14) and Paprika (p 21)); chilli powder (as opposed to either of the former) is usually dried ground chillies of unspecified variety, while chilli seasoning is frequently a blend of dried ground chillies, with salt, garlic, cumin and oregano or other dried herbs. Whole pickled chillies can also be bought, and numerous chilli sauces are on offer; for example Tabasco.

For the unaccustomed it is better to err on the side of caution when trying and indeed preparing chillies. Wear rubber gloves during preparation and never touch eyes or mouth with fingers which have handled a hot chilli. Chilli seeds are invariably more pungent than the flesh, so discard them for less blistering results.

Uses: In many tropical areas chillies are used with the same frequency as true pepper is in Europe. Their uses are numerous and diverse, and they feature daily in one form or another in the majority of local savoury dishes in the regions where they grow. Crucial components of a host of spice mixtures (p 24) chillies also form the basis of a wide range of both pouring and dipping sauces (for example China's Hoisin, Tunisia's Harissa, the Caribbean's Hot Pepper Sauce and Latin America's Salsa Cruda). Many pickles, chutneys and other side dishes like fiery Indonesian sambals, frequently include chillies, too.

As a spicy fiery flavouring for main courses, chillies are used on their own (in poorer countries adding bite to bland diets or masking the taste of less than fresh meat), or combined with a few or numerous other spices. ***Chilli con carne*** is probably the world's best known example of the use of chillies. Numerous other Latin American meat, poultry and egg dishes are flavoured with chillies, as are fish and seafood. Similarly, chillies play an important part in much authentic Caribbean cooking (the traditional Trinidadian Pepperpot stew or Jamaican Pepperpot soup) and in the Creole food of the southern USA. Again, in many parts of Africa and the Middle East, chillies feature in all kinds of savoury dishes, as they do in India, where they are often included in the ginger and garlic paste used for meat cooking. The chilli addiction is also marked in Indonesia and South-East Asia, and they are essential favourites in hot and spicy Szechuan cooking, where they are put to good effect in stir fries, fiery sauces and pickles. See also: CAYENNE (p 14), PAPRIKA (p 21), SAUCES (p 84).

Celery seeds

CINNAMON

Cinnamomum zeylanicum

Cinnamon grows in many tropical areas, including its native Sri Lanka, southern India, Indian Ocean islands like the Seychelles, Brazil and the West Indies. The tropical cinnamon evergreen can reach a height of 9m (30 feet) or more, but it is from its young cultivated shoots that bark is harvested. The dried bark is eventually sold as a spice, in small quills usually 7.5-15cm (3-6 inches) long, or as a powder. The powder may seem more convenient to use, but fresh quills last longer and can be used whole in many dishes (and removed at the end of cooking), or ground in a robust grinder. Cinnamon has many qualities in common with cassia, its close relative, but is much more delicate in both form and flavour. Store all cinnamon in airtight containers in a dark place.

Uses: Cinnamon is a universally popular spice, but as a very general rule it is used to flavour sweet dishes in the West and savoury ones in the East. In India cinnamon is an important flavouring in curries, *biryanis* and *kormas*. Indonesian *gulés* (curries) include it and it is popular in China too. In the Middle East and Greece cinnamon is used in both spicy meat stuffings for baked aubergines and courgettes and in nutty, honeyed fillings for pastries. Many European cakes and puddings, especially those featuring apples, include it. Cinnamon is also a component of spice mixtures from all over the world (p 24). See also: CASSIA (p 14).

Cloves

CORIANDER SEEDS

Coriandrum sativum

Coriander is a member of the parsley family and grows in Asia, the Americas, Africa and Europe. The plant gives off a strong odour which disappears when the seeds are dried, to be replaced by a sweet orangey aroma. Coriander seeds are almost completely round and look like tiny ridged brown footballs. Buy them whole from any good grocer or Indian store. The seeds are much milder than many other spices, so can be used in comparatively large quantities. The taste, fresh and mild with a hint of bitterness, can actually improve with keeping; store in an airtight container away from the light.

Uses: Indian curries, Indonesian *gulés*, and numerous other spicy dishes almost invariably include coriander seeds, and ground coriander is an ingredient in garam masala and other spice mixtures (p 24). In Latin America coriander seeds are combined with chillies, and in Middle Eastern and North African food they are often combined with cumin in dishes such as *falafel, hummus, couscous* and in local breads. In Western food coriander seeds make an appearance in *à la grecque* dishes, pickling spice (p 24) and in smoked meats and sausages, such as the Italian Mortadella. Coriander seeds are also popular in fish, chicken and game dishes. See also: CORIANDER (p 138).

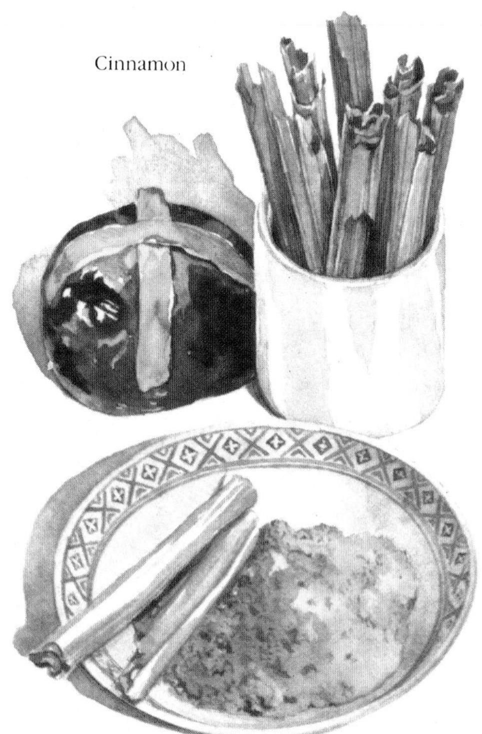

Cinnamon

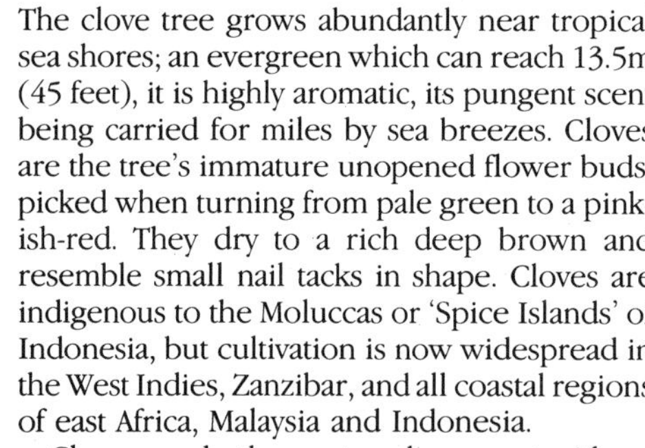

CLOVES

Eugenia caryophyllus

The clove tree grows abundantly near tropical sea shores; an evergreen which can reach 13.5m (45 feet), it is highly aromatic, its pungent scent being carried for miles by sea breezes. Cloves are the tree's immature unopened flower buds, picked when turning from pale green to a pinkish-red. They dry to a rich deep brown and resemble small nail tacks in shape. Cloves are indigenous to the Moluccas or 'Spice Islands' of Indonesia, but cultivation is now widespread in the West Indies, Zanzibar, and all coastal regions of east Africa, Malaysia and Indonesia.

Cloves are both sweet and pungent with an unmistakable aroma, but use them with restraint to avoid overwhelming other tastes. Buy them whole, in preference to powdered, and grind as necessary. Store in an airtight container.

Uses: Like cinnamon, cloves feature in both sweet and savoury dishes and in an endless number of international spice mixtures (p 24). European stocks and soups often contain a couple of cloves and a single clove makes an interesting addition to a bouquet garni. In traditional British cooking, a clove or two should flavour bread sauce, and they should be used to stud the outside of a 'honey roast' ham. They blend well with apples in pies and crumbles and should be included in mulled wines and liqueurs.

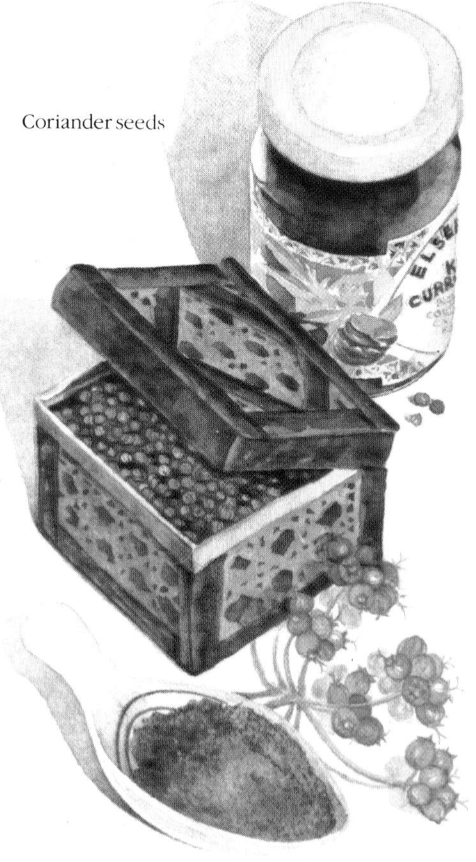

Coriander seeds

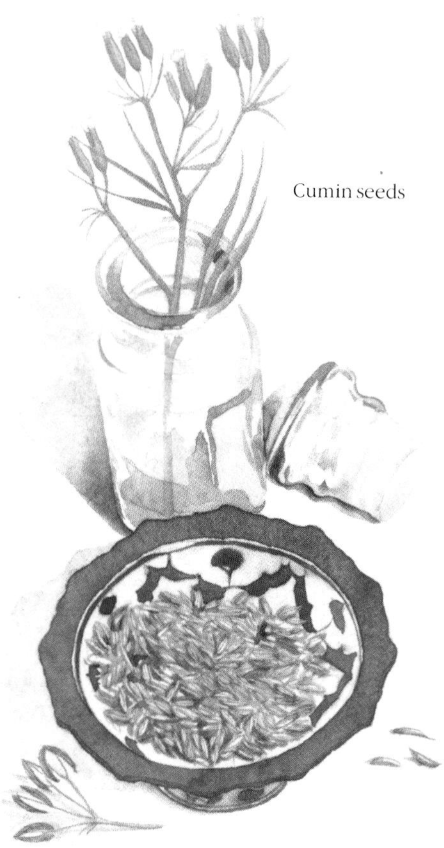
Cumin seeds

DILL SEEDS
Anethum graveolens

The dill plant is a member of the parsley family and the leaves and stalks, as well as the dried seeds, can all be used in cooking. A small, ridged oval in shape and light brown in colour, the seeds are flat on one side, rounded on the other. They have a fresh, sweet aroma but a slightly bitter taste, somewhat similar to caraway seeds. Dill seeds are widely available and will keep for a long time in an airtight container. Use them whole or lightly crushed and add to dishes towards the end of cooking, or once cooking is over, to best preserve their flavour.
Uses: Dill seeds are particularly associated with the cookery of northern climes, although both seeds and leaves are popular in Sri Lanka. They can be a convenient substitute for the fresh herb, and can be used instead of fennel, although dill has a much milder flavour. The seeds are good in pickled dishes, vinegars, marinades and dressings, as well as in fresh and braised cucumber dishes and winter salads of potatoes or shredded root vegetables. In Russia and Scandinavia dill is a 'basic' seasoning and features in pickling mixtures for fish, as well as in creamy soups and sauces. It is also much used in chicken and vegetable dishes. In Germany and Scandinavia bread can be sprinkled with dill seeds, rather than caraway, and dill is included in sauerkraut and other vegetable pickles including of course the famous dill pickles. See also: DILL (p 139)

Fennel seeds

CUMIN SEEDS
Cuminum cyminum

Like coriander, with which it is almost invariably paired in cooking, and caraway, which it closely resembles, cumin seed comes from a plant of the parsley family. A small and delicate annual, it is usually about 25cm (10 inches) high. Native to the Middle East, cumin now grows in most hot climates; India, North Africa, China and the Americas. The spicy seeds are small, boat-shaped, ridged and greenish-brown in colour; they have a strong and unmistakable aroma, sweetish and warming. Their flavour is similarly pungent and penetrating, and they should be used in moderation. Easily available in seed or powdered form, cumin's aroma is preserved by airtight storage. Cumin seed should not be confused with nigella (which is sometimes erroneously called 'black cumin') or fennel or anise (both sometimes called 'sweet cumin').
Uses: In India, most savoury spice mixtures and curry seasonings feature cumin seeds, as do Indonesian mutton *gulés*, Thai and Malaysian fish and chicken curries and *satés* (p 98). In the Middle East and North Africa cumin flavours fish dishes, casseroles, couscous and the 'Moroccan bean pot'. On the other side of the world, cumin is an authentic ingredient of Mexican *Chilli con carne*, Portuguese sausages and the Dutch semi-hard cheese, Leyden or Leiden.

Dill seeds

FENNEL SEEDS
Foeniculum vulgare

Fennel is best known in Europe, especially around the Mediterranean, as a herb, salad ingredient and vegetable, but its dried seeds are also valuable in cooking. Like dill and anise, fennel is a member of the parsley family. The seeds – curved, ridged and dullish yellow-green – are like plumper and larger versions of anise seeds. Fennel seeds are invariably found in Indian shops. They should be stored in an airtight container and used whole, crushed or ground, as recipes require.
Uses: Fennel seeds can often be used if the fresh herb is unavailable, and are a component of a number of spice mixtures (p 24). Fennel seeds are universally used with fish. In the West they are used in marinades, sauces and stuffings, or scattered over oily fish like mackerel and sardines before grilling. In India, Malaysia and Indonesia, they are used in fish curries, with spicy grilled lobster or giant prawns, and in batters and spiced breadcrumbs for fried fish. In both the West (especially Italy) and the East fennel seeds also have a traditional affinity with pork and poultry. Like caraway and dill seeds, fennel seeds are also often sprinkled on bread and cakes, especially in France and Italy. See also: FENNEL (p 140).

FENUGREEK

Trigonella foenum-graecum

The 30-60cm (1-2 foot) high fenugreek plant belongs to the bean and pea family; its flowers and pods resemble those of the pea. Each long narrow pod contains ten to twenty ochre-brown seeds which resemble tiny pebbles both in appearance and texture. Native to the eastern Mediterranean and India, fenugreek has grown wild and in cultivation in Europe, Africa and Asia for thousands of years. Only when roasted do the seeds give off their pungent aroma; their taste is bitter-sweet and powerful so they should be used in moderation. Fenugreek seeds are easy to come by. Roast the whole seeds lightly until just golden, then grind to a powder. Ready-ground powder can also be bought and stored in an airtight container.

Uses: Fenugreek is used most frequently in Indian food. Most curry powders include it, both commercial and home-prepared, as do other mixtures such as panchphoran (p 27). A wide variety of spicy vegetable and pulse dishes feature fenugreek, which is often used in conjunction with fennel seeds, giving a delicious tangy taste. It is used in innumerable pickles and chutneys and in *halva*, the sesame-based sweetmeat found in India, Greece and other countries of the Middle East.

Fenugreek

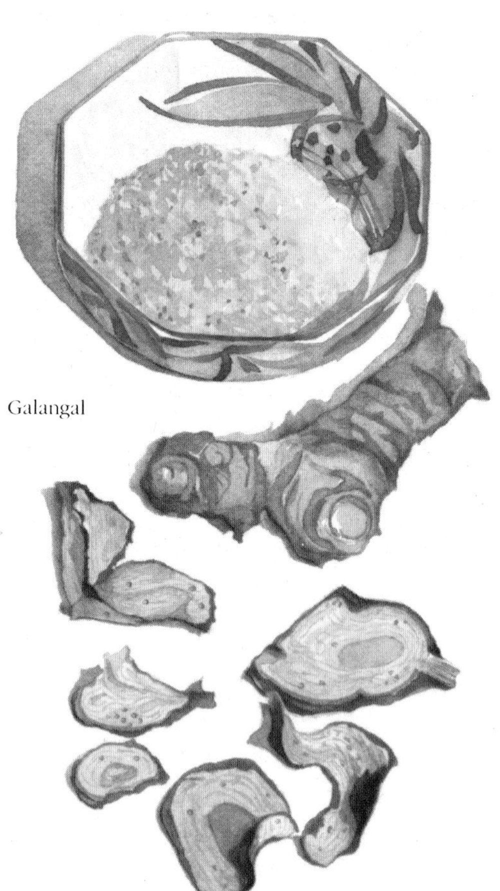
Galangal

GALANGAL

Languas galanga
Languas officinarum
Kaempferia galanga

The tropical galangals are members of the same family as ginger, with which they have much in common both in form and flavour: it is their gingery-tasting and ginger-like rhizomes that are used in cooking. Greater galangal's knobbly rhizomes are orange-brown outside, yellow-white inside; Lesser's are rusty brown outside and a paler brown inside; Kaempferia's are reddish outside and white inside. The galangals grow in Indonesia, South-East Asia and southern China; they are a predominant spice in the cooking of Indonesia, Malaysia, Thailand and Indo-China. Ask for them by their local names in stores which stock Indonesian or Malaysian products: *laos* or *lengkuas* for Greater Galangal, *kencur* for Lesser, which has the most powerful flavour, and *kentjur* for Kaempferia, which is sweeter-tasting. The fresh rhizomes are not obtainable in the UK although the dried root is available in sliced or powder form. Store galangal in an airtight container.

Uses: The inclusion of some form of galangal, together with other typical South-East Asian ingredients and seasonings, such as blachan (p 78) distinguishes Indonesian hot and spicy dishes like *gulés* and *sambals* from the curried preparations of other countries. Like ginger, galangal frequently features in fish and seafood dishes of Indonesia and Malaysia, whether fiery or delicately aromatic, and in spicy chicken, egg and vegetable dishes from the same areas.

GINGER

Zingiber officinale

In its many forms, ginger is an important spice in both East and West. Like other tropical plants of the same family, such as the galangals and turmeric, it is the rhizome or knobbly root of the ginger plant which is used as a culinary spice.

Fresh ginger root, essential for the exotic cuisines of many Eastern lands, is easily acquired (see p 141). It is very different to dried ginger and the latter cannot be used as a substitute for it in Asian dishes. Dried ginger root, similarly, comes whole, in pieces or slices; it is sold in two forms: 'black' with its outer layer intact, or 'white' without. It is prepared from the tougher, more fibrous parts nearer the root and must be firmly bruised with a hammer or similar instrument before use to break up the fibres. The beige powder sold commercially is the dried ground root. Crystallized ginger is a sweetmeat. Fresh ginger has a distinctive smell and strong taste, the fieriness of which is diminished in the crystallized and powdered versions. Keep dried ginger of all forms in airtight jars. Fresh ginger does not keep well; buy in small quantities and store

Ginger

JUNIPER BERRIES

Juniperus communis

A small coniferous and prickly evergreen, the juniper tree ranges in height from 120cm-10.5m (4-35 feet) and grows throughout Europe. The small spherical berries turn from an unripe green to a ripe blue-black; when dried, they are a purplish-black and light brown inside. The berries' spicy pine aroma and sweet, resinous flavour varies according to where they grow; those from southern regions are far more pungent than the northern varieties. Juniper berries can be bought at good grocers; if you pick your own – remember they take up to three years to ripen – select only complete ripe blue berries

excess in the refrigerator, wrapped in foil.
Uses: Ginger is one of the most widely used spices, though certain of its forms and uses are more popular in certain areas; the broadest division being between its use in sweet dishes in the West and savoury ones in the East. In Asia and the East fresh ginger is used in numerous savoury dishes of meat, poultry and fish, while thin delicate slices of pickled ginger (preserved in brine or vinegar) are a favourite side dish or garnish in China and Japan. Ground dried ginger is an important and traditional baking and pudding spice in the West, ginger puddings, ginger cake, ginger nuts, ginger snaps, gingerbread to name but a few examples. Dried ginger root can be bruised and ground to a powder (its fibres removed) and used as ground ginger, or bruised and infused in the cooking liquid of savoury dishes. Stem ginger in syrup and crystallized ginger can be roughly chopped and used in breads (p 74), cakes, confectionery and puddings; sweet ginger pancakes are delicious, as is ginger ice cream (p 129). Pickling spice (p 24) often calls for the inclusion of a piece of ginger, and it is popular as a drink flavouring: in ginger ale and ginger beer. See also: GINGER (p 141).

in the autumn. Store the berries in a spice jar and use them whole, or gently crushed.
Uses: Juniper berries have a particular affinity with robust meat dishes, and can be included in marinades and stuffings for game, pork and poultry and in hearty beef stews. Traditionally used in English spiced salt beef and in the curing of Welsh and York hams, juniper berries feature in many other traditional European salted meats as well as in pâtés, terrines and potted meats. In Germany, cold meats are often served with a juniper berry conserve. Juniper berries blend well with many of the stronger culinary flavourings popular in Europe: wines and spirits, spices and herbs such as bay, garlic, marjoram, thyme and fennel, and are indispensable as the traditional flavouring for gin.

KOKUM

Garcinia indica

The solitary tall and slender kokum tree grows exclusively along the paradise-like coast of tropical south-western India; related to the mangosteen, it can reach a height of 15m (50 feet). Its round, purplish, plum-like fruit contains eight seeds, but it is the skin of the fruit that is used in cooking. Stripped from the fruit, flattened and dried, the skins turn a deep black-brown and have a sour and rather salty taste; like tamarind, with which it has much in common, kokum is often used as a souring agent. Kokum may be bought from good Indian grocers and should be kept in an airtight container, for use according to recipe instructions: either whole or as an infused liquid.
Uses: Kokum is a uniquely Indian flavouring, used especially in its native region. Fresh fish and seafood abound, and three or four skins are often included in marinades for grills and kebabs, in curries and other spiced fish dishes. Like tamarind and amchur, kokum is also used in fresh tangy chutneys, pickles and butters.

MACE

Myristica fragrans

Mace and nutmeg are two completely distinct but uniquely related spices: they are both parts of the fruit of a towering tropical evergreen tree which grows in the Moluccas and the rest of Indonesia, the Philippines, Malaysia and the Caribbean. Mace is the crimson, lacy 'cage' at the centre of the fruit which encloses a dark brown shell containing the seed or kernel (nutmeg). When the fruit is harvested, the mace is removed from the nutmeg, flattened and dried in the sun to become hard and brittle, ochre-orange, 2.5-4cm (1-1½ inch) long blades. Mace is available both as blades and ready-ground, although ground mace deteriorates rapidly. Store both blades and ground mace in an airtight container.
Uses: Mace tastes and smells rather like nutmeg but is much more powerful and should be used in moderation. Because of its warm pungency, mace is best suited to savoury dishes; use the blades in sauces, soups, chowders and casseroles and other liquids from which they can be removed after cooking. Mace is a component of some pickling mixtures and spiced peppers and is a traditional seasoning for English spiced beef. Potted meat dishes and savoury pies invariably include mace. Like nutmeg, ground mace can also be used to boost sweet dishes, particularly milk puddings. See also: NUTMEG (p 20).

MUSTARD SEEDS

Brassica nigra
Brassica juncea
Brassica alba

Mustard is famous throughout the world as a condiment and flavouring. The whole seeds are the basis of all prepared mustards, and the pungent mustard oil, much used in India, is extracted from them; they are also used as a cooking spice, especially in India and neighbouring countries. There are three main varieties of mustard: Black, Brown (or Indian), and White; all three plants are similar in looks and grow to about 75-105cm (2½-3½ feet); all bear tiny, spherical, hard seeds contained in long pods. Mustard is an important commercial crop in many areas of the world, but it is the seeds of Brown mustard that are the typical Indian cooking spice. They are easily acquired from Asian grocers, although they are sometimes wrongly referred to as 'black mustard'. If used raw, in pickling for instance, mustard seeds are powerfully hot, but if they are fried quickly in hot oil before use their pungency diminishes and they become deliciously sweet and nutty.

Uses: Mustard seeds are used primarily in Indian food, but the White variety are sometimes used in the West, as a component of pickling spice, for example. The Brown seeds are used in a wide range of Indian, Sri Lankan and Malaysian dishes, and they blend well with other spices. Used raw they flavour pickles and chutneys, and combine with other spices in the Bengali panchphoran mixture (p 27) and several other spicy mixes for fish and meat. Whole and roasted, they are best known for their successful partnership with vegetables. See also: MUSTARD (p 82)

Mustard seeds

Nutmeg

NIGELLA SEEDS

Nigella sativa

The nigella plant, which grows to about 60cm (2 feet), is a small herbaceous annual of the buttercup family. Nigella grows wild and in cultivation in parts of central and southern Europe and Asia; it is also cultivated in the Middle East and extensively in India. Its tiny black teardrop seeds, rough on the outside and oily white inside, are used as a cooking spice. The seeds' earthy aroma, faint until they are rubbed or bruised, is slightly reminiscent of carrots or nutmeg and they are peppery, bitter and crunchy to taste. Ask for them by their Indian name, *kalonji*, in Indian food stores, to avoid confusion with black onion seeds. Store in an airtight container.

Uses: Nigella seeds are important in the cookery of India and the Middle East. Often lightly roasted before use, they play the role of both spice and condiment, their peppery flavour making them an ideal pepper substitute. They give flavour and texture to bread doughs, cakes and pastries; in northern India they are sprinkled on tandoori-cooked *nans* (p 58) before baking. Some Indian spice mixtures include nigella seeds, notably panchphoran (p 27). They are used in many Bengali vegetable dishes, especially those containing aubergines and tomatoes, and in recipes for curried, fried or breaded fish. Vegetarian curries, especially kormas, often include them too.

NUTMEG

Myristica fragrans

The nutmeg kernel is dried in its seedcoat, which is then removed. Oval in shape and about 4cm (1½ inches) long, the nutmeg has a hard, brown, uneven surface and a paler interior. Nutmeg is milder than mace but has a similar though more nutty flavour; warm and sweetish, it also has a light bitter undertone. Nutmegs are widely available, both whole and ready-ground, but the ground powder deteriorates rapidly, so buy whole nutmegs and store in an airtight container. Grate nutmeg with a special nutmeg grater or other fine grater directly over the mixing bowl or cooking pot.

Uses: Nutmeg is widely used in both Western and Eastern cooking. In India and South-East Asia it is an important meat seasoning; in the West it features in sweet and savoury dishes alike. It harmonizes with other spices, and enhances and blends with a wide variety of flavours. Often found in spice mixtures (p 24), nutmeg is also used to flavour a wide range of sauces such as béchamel, mornay, onion and bread sauce. In Italy nutmeg is frequently used to flavour spinach, and it is a typical French charcuterie spice, used in saucissons, terrines and galantines; it is used similarly in the Italian sausage Mortadella, German wursts and Scottish haggis. Like mace, nutmeg is a traditional ingredient of English pies and puddings, such as steak, kidney and oyster pudding, baked custard and junket. A grating of nutmeg is an essential ingredient in an authentic West Indian rum punch. See also: MACE (p 19).

Nigella seeds

Pepper

PEPPER

Piper nigrum

Pepper is undoubtedly the most familiar and indispensable of all cooking spices in the West. It comes from the tropical trailing vines of the Piperaceae family. Native to southern India and South-East Asia, pepper vines are now cultivated in many tropical areas such as Brazil, the East and West Indies, Indonesia and Malaysia. The vines grow to heights of 3.6m (12 feet) and bear long 'strings' of 20-30 small berries which ripen from green to reddish-yellow. Black peppercorns are the dried, unripe berries of the Piper nigrum vine; white peppercorns are the riper red berries, washed, fermented, de-husked and dried; green peppercorns are the fresh, unripe berries, pickled or freeze-dried. Black pepper is stronger than white, while green peppercorns have a milder, fresh taste. It is always preferable to buy whole peppercorns as opposed to ready-ground powders to avoid adulteration and an almost instant loss of aroma. Peppercorns store well in airtight containers: the fresh green variety should be kept in their preserving liquid in the refrigerator and used soon after opening.

Uses: Pepper is a universal seasoning and condiment. Whole or crushed peppercorns are an important component in a wide range of spice mixtures (p 24) and whole peppercorns are frequently added to marinades, stocks and *court bouillons*. Crushed peppercorns are used in comparatively large quantities in several classic French recipes, notably *poivrade* (pepper) sauce, which is served with duck or venison (p 45) and *Steak au Poivre*. Fresh green peppercorns are used to make sauces to serve with both fish and chicken. Roughly ground or crushed peppercorns are important charcuterie seasonings and some German salamis have an outer coating of roughly ground pepper, as do some creamy cheeses. Surprisingly, pepper may also be used in sweet dishes: as part of pudding or mixed spice for cakes, puddings and pies: and in French *nouvelle cuisine* a very light milling of pepper over fresh strawberries and pineapple is recommended to enhance the flavour.

PAPRIKA

Capsicum annuum

Brick-red paprika is a very familiar spice in the West, especially in Spain and Hungary. Like cayenne pepper, it is a finely ground powder made from the fruits of several different chilli plants. The ripe flesh is used for mild and sweet paprikas; for more pungent versions the seeds are included. Paprika chillies are widely grown in Spain as well as in a number of eastern European countries and the USA. Both Spain and Hungary (where paprika is considered the national spice) produce several types, graded according to quality and pungency. The mildest kind is best known and most widely sold in Britain, it has a light, sweet smell and almost no pungency; the most pungent paprika is as powerful as cayenne. All paprikas impart a wonderful rich, reddish-brown colour to food. Like cayenne and all chilli powders, paprika is affected by light, so buy small amounts and store in an airtight container away from the light.

Uses: In Hungary, paprika flavours a profusion of savoury foods – from meat stews, such as goulash (p 50), fish and poultry to vegetables, cheeses and soured cream. Paprika is particularly good with fish and shellfish and is traditional in many Spanish seafood stews such as *zarzuela*. See also: CAYENNE (p 14), CHILLI (p 15).

Paprika

Poppy seeds

POPPY SEEDS

Papaver somniferum

The pretty opium poppy is the source not only of a highly narcotic drug but also of the harmless and delicious poppy seeds used in cooking. The plant is related to both the common field poppy and garden varieties. It grows to anything from 30-120cm (1-4 feet) and bears white, pink or lilac flowers and erect oval seedpods which contain a mass of hard, minuscule seeds. The lilac-flowered Asian variety has creamy-coloured seeds, while those of the European variety are blue-grey. Both types are very mild and sweetish and acquire a bitter-sweet, nutty flavour when cooked. The blue-grey seeds are easily bought, the creamy ones found mainly in Indian grocers; store them in a very cool place in airtight containers to prevent them going rancid.

Uses: Blue-grey poppy seeds are most commonly used in the West and the creamy version in the East, but they can be interchanged without alteration of flavour. In the West, poppy seed is best known for its association with baking; it is especially popular in Poland and Germany, and in traditional Jewish baking. The seeds decorate many types of bread, buns and rolls, including bagels and platzels, and are used as a filling in some east European cakes. In southern Germany and other Alpine regions poppy seeds are used in savoury noodle dishes and to flavour or garnish vegetables. In the East, poppy seeds are used in India and Japan (where their oil is popular too), either whole in a variety of vegetable dishes and chutneys, or crushed or ground in certain varieties of spice mixtures for *kormas*, *masalas* and tandooris.

SAFFRON
Crocus sativus

Saffron is the world's most expensive spice and unique in its origin, for saffron is the dried stigmas of the flowers of the saffron crocus. The stigmas are extracted from the freshly harvested flowers and dried to become irregular, deep orange-red threads about 4cm (1½ inches) long. It takes about 50,000 stigmas to make up 100g (4oz) saffron, and every bloom must be individually picked, and every stigma individually extracted by hand. Saffron flourishes in the hot but not tropical climates of the south of France, the Middle East, Kashmir and China; the best saffron is said to come from Valencia in Spain. It imparts a distinctive aroma, a bitter, honey-like taste and a strong, yellow colour to food. Buy threads in preference to powder, which can easily be tampered with, and store in an airtight container away from the light.

Uses: To use saffron, either infuse a few threads in a cup of hot water and add the coloured liquid towards the end of cooking, or crumble the threads and add directly to the pot. Alternatively, dry roast, crumble and then steep the crumbled threads as done in India. Ready-ground powder can be added directly to the pot. A pinch will suffice to colour most dishes, but as its flavour is important too, saffron should not be replaced with other yellow colorants, such as turmeric. Saffron is important in the cooking of Spain and other Mediterranean countries, the Middle East and India: in all these areas it is particularly associated with rice dishes, both savoury and sweet. It is traditional in Spain's famous *paella Valenciana* and in southern France's renowned *bouillabaisse*.In Britain, saffron has been used for centuries to flavour cakes and bread.

Saffron

Sassafras

SASSAFRAS
Sassafras albidum

Sassafras is one of the few true North American spices, well known to the indigenous American Indians. The tall North American sassafras tree grows to a height of 13m (43 feet); its flowers are yellow and its berries dark blue. A member of the laurel family, it is a common wayside tree, of which the aromatic leaves, roots, root bark, pith and shoots are used as a spicy flavouring, though neither the berries nor the flowers, as might be expected. In cookery, the leaves are generally the most important sassafras product: oval and up to 18cm (7 inches) long, these are dried and powdered to form what is known as *filé* powder. Look for proprietary brands of *filé* powder at specialist spice suppliers and store it in an airtight container.

Uses: Sassafras is primarily associated with the exotic, highly seasoned Creole cooking of the American 'deep south'. Here, *filé* powder appears in soups, sauces, meat and fish stews and casseroles, and especially *gumbo*, a thick soup or stew of okra, sweet peppers, onions, tomatoes and chillies served with rice. The shoots, roots and sassafras oil are widely used in the production of traditional sassafras cordials, beers and other bottled and carbonated drinks.

SESAME SEEDS
Sesamum indicum

Sesame is a tropical annual with a pungent smell and foxglove-like flowers. The sesame plant grows to anything between 60-180cm (2-6 feet), and its seedpods contain a large number of small, flat, oval seeds in a variety of colours; the most commonly on sale are black and beige (unhulled) or white (hulled and polished). Sesame is native to India, but it is also grown extensively in the hot climates of Africa, parts of the Americas, China and the Middle East. Dried sesame seeds have a mildly nutty aroma and a stronger nutty flavour and are widely available. Dry roast before use or fry lightly in a little oil until they just turn colour, begin to jump and give off a roasted aroma.

Uses: Sesame seeds are extensively used in most lands east of southern Europe. They are popular in both Chinese and Japanese cooking, in which their nutty oil is also a favourite flavouring. In Indian cookery, sesame seeds flavour aubergines and beans, and make deliciously nutty fried potato dishes and potato salads. In their crushed, ground form, sesame seeds are well known as the cream paste, *tahini*. Throughout the Middle East and neighbouring countries like Greece, *tahini* flavours savoury dips such as *hummus*. Whole sesame seeds are used in Middle Eastern breads and biscuits, and in *halva*, a favourite sweetmeat.

Sesame seeds

Star anise

STAR ANISE

Illicium verum

Star anise is an attractive oriental spice, especially associated with Chinese cookery. It is the dried fruit of an oriental evergreen of the magnolia family which can reach a height of 7.3m (24 feet) and is a native of China and Japan, where it still mainly grows, though it is also established in parts of Indo-China and the Philippines. Harvested when unripe and dried in the sun, each reddish-brown star-shaped fruit contains 8 small brown oval seeds. The dried stars have a pungent but harsh aniseed aroma and are available whole or ready-ground from good grocers, especially those which stock Chinese provisions. Whole stars store well in an airtight container for a long time and are preferable to the powdered form.

Uses: Star anise is an important component in spice mixtures, it is included in Chinese Five Spice (p 25). Chinese and Malay curry mixtures (which are 'sweeter' than Indian ones), and in some Chinese spiced salts. In Chinese cookery it is used in stocks and marinades, soups and sauces. 'Red-cooked' Chinese dishes often include star anise, and it partners both red and white meat; it has a natural affinity with duck, pork and chicken. Like other aniseed-flavoured spices, star anise combines excellently with fish, and it can be used instead of Pernod in Western fish dishes and sauces for fish and shellfish: it is especially good with mussels and oysters.

SUMAC

Rhus coriaria

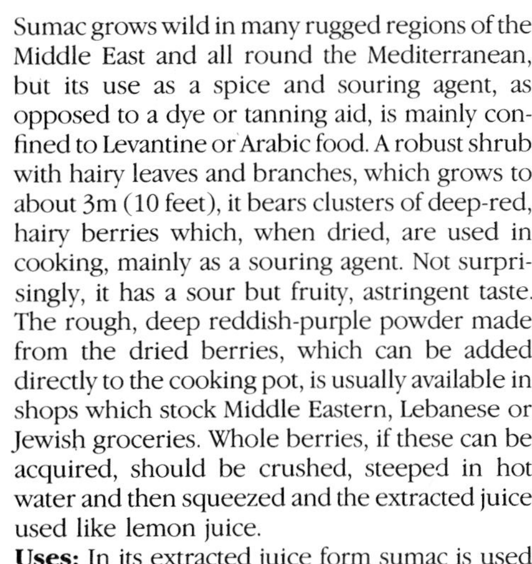

Sumac grows wild in many rugged regions of the Middle East and all round the Mediterranean, but its use as a spice and souring agent, as opposed to a dye or tanning aid, is mainly confined to Levantine or Arabic food. A robust shrub with hairy leaves and branches, which grows to about 3m (10 feet), it bears clusters of deep-red, hairy berries which, when dried, are used in cooking, mainly as a souring agent. Not surprisingly, it has a sour but fruity, astringent taste. The rough, deep reddish-purple powder made from the dried berries, which can be added directly to the cooking pot, is usually available in shops which stock Middle Eastern, Lebanese or Jewish groceries. Whole berries, if these can be acquired, should be crushed, steeped in hot water and then squeezed and the extracted juice used like lemon juice.

Uses: In its extracted juice form sumac is used extensively as a dressing for salads and as a marinade for meat, poultry and fish, especially when these are to be grilled or barbecued. Sumac powder flavours meat, fish and vegetable stews and many chicken dishes; it also seasons kebabs. Its taste blends well with that of yogurt and it is part of the sour and aromatic Middle Eastern spice mixture known as *zathar* (equal parts of thyme and sumac).

Sumac

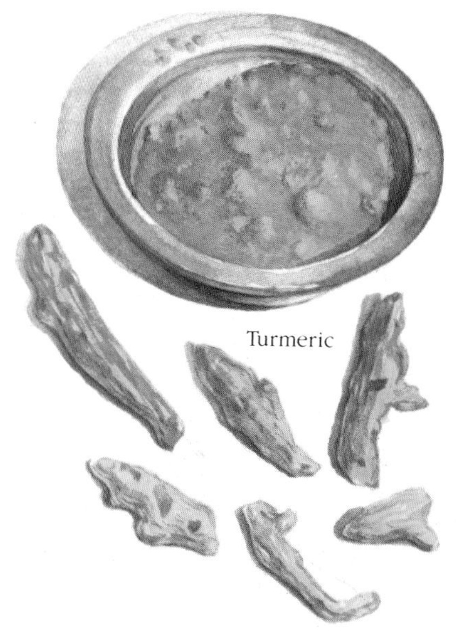

Turmeric

TURMERIC

Curcuma longa

With its spiky yellow flowers and long, shiny, pointed leaves, the tropical turmeric can reach a height of 1m (3½ feet) and grows profusely in the tropical climates of many parts of the world – from India and the Far East to Africa and Latin America. It is a typical member of the ginger family, and like both ginger and galangal, it is the rhizomes, or knobbly roots, which form the cooking spice. It has a strong woody aroma and distinctive, pungent flavour; because of this it should not be used as a cheap substitute for saffron, despite its similar yellow colouring property. In its powdered form it is widely available. Buy in small amounts and store the powder in an airtight container in a dark place.

Uses: Turmeric is used for flavour and colour in Malaysian, Indonesian, Indian and Middle Eastern food; it is best known for its partnership with fish and rice, and its inclusion in numerous curried dishes. Most Indian curry powder mixes for both 'wet' and 'dry' dishes feature turmeric, as do *korma* and other spice mixtures. In addition, it is frequently added to pulse dishes like *dhal*, and used as a condiment with vegetables. Certain festive rice dishes take their colour from turmeric as opposed to saffron, and it is a must in the traditional English kedgeree. Turmeric is just as popular in the Middle East and North Africa, where it is included in sweet and savoury *pilaus*, sauces for other rice dishes and couscous, rich meat casseroles and vegetable dishes. A staple spice in Morocco, it is a component of the La Kama mixture (p 25). Commercially, turmeric is inevitably a component of mass-produced curry powders, English powdered mustard, and sour chutneys and pickles such as the bright yellow piccalilli.

Every corner of the world has its own particular spice mixtures; and this includes not only the exotic Orient and other far-flung areas, but also the West, where many traditional spice mixtures are a legacy of centuries past. The mixtures described here are among the better known and most useful of the literally hundreds of different national and regional spice combinations.

A word of warning: many of these mixtures include whole or ground chillies; for unaccustomed Western palates, their fiery 'heat' will be far too much, so lessen the chilli content according to taste or substitute cayenne or paprika.

Ground spices lose their aroma and pungency more quickly than whole spices, so it is fine to store a ground mixture for 2-3 days, but its strength will diminish the longer it is kept. A freshly ground spice mixture should not be kept for more than one month. If you do make too much of a mixture for your immediate requirements, store excess 'dry' mixtures in airtight jars and 'wet' ones in bottles in the refrigerator.

Although many individual spices are available ready-ground as proprietary brands, it is always preferable to grind your own, as the strong fresh aromas of home-ground spices bear little relation to the smell of a commercial powder. Commercial powders may seem more convenient (and are useful as a stand-by), but an electric grinder is efficient and quick and the results will handsomely repay that little bit of extra effort.

DRY CHILLI MIXTURE OR CHILLI SEASONING

Latin America and the Caribbean

If the mixture is for immediate use, fresh garlic is preferable; if it is to be stored, choose the garlic powder or granules.

1-3 teaspoons ground dried chillies
1½-2 teaspoons ground coriander seeds
1 teaspoon ground cumin seeds
½ teaspoon garlic powder or granules or
5 garlic cloves, peeled and crushed
1½-2 teaspoons dried crushed oregano
¾ teaspoon ground cloves (optional)

Combine all ingredients together.

Uses: Numerous savoury Latin American dishes are seasoned or garnished with dry chilli mixtures including all types of egg dishes, meat, poultry, fish and seafood dishes. It is essential in Mexican and Texan *chilli con carne* and can be used in Indian and Caribbean dishes.

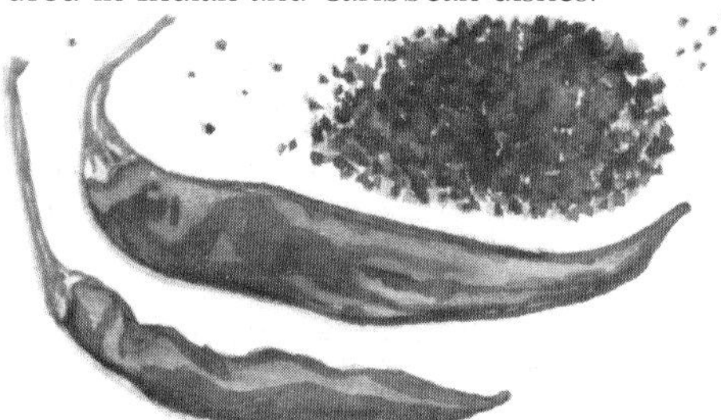

WET CHILLI MIXTURE OR SALSA CRUDA

Latin America and the Caribbean

For an authentic Caribbean flavour add a couple of tablespoons of chopped papaya to this mixture and use fresh lime juice instead of vinegar.

2 tablespoons skinned, seeded and chopped tomatoes
1-2 tablespoons finely chopped onion
1 tablespoon chopped fresh coriander
2 teaspoons chopped seeded fresh chillies, or according to taste
sea salt, to taste
4 tablespoons water or 2 tablespoons olive oil plus 2 tablespoons wine vinegar
4 garlic cloves, peeled and crushed (optional)

For a rough textured 'salsa', mix all ingredients together in a bowl, for a smooth 'salsa', combine all the ingredients in an electric blender. Store in the refrigerator if not required immediately.

Uses: Salsa cruda is the standard table sauce throughout much of the Caribbean and Latin America; it accompanies almost anything, from chicken to meat, vegetables to tacos, and tortillas to eggs. *Huevos rancheros* (fried eggs drenched in salsa cruda) is popular for breakfast or as a reviving snack.

MIXED SPICE

The West

Mixed spice is a traditional British 'seasoning' for many types of sweet food. Ready-mixed powders are widely available as proprietary brands.

1 teaspoon ground allspice
¾ teaspoons ground cinnamon
1 teaspoon ground cloves
1¼ teaspoons ground ginger
¾ teaspoon grated or ground nutmeg
pinch of black pepper

Mix the ground spices together and use immediately. Vary this basic mixture according to taste with other 'sweet' spices such as ground anise, ground cardamoms or ground coriander.

Uses: Mixed spice is *the* sweet spice mixture; it is frequently called for in traditional recipes for cakes and biscuits and in those for old-fashioned puddings and pies; it is a crucial component of many a traditional pudding mixture.

PICKLING SPICE

The West

Pickling spice is another traditional Western spice mixture, the contents of which are much open to personal interpretation. Here is a basic mixture which can be adjusted or altered according to taste and the items chosen for pickling.

1 litre (1¾ pints) wine vinegar
15-18 whole allspice berries
1 whole fresh green chilli
1 × 2.5cm (1 inch) piece cinnamon stick
10-12 whole cloves
1 teaspoon whole coriander seeds
1 × 2.5cm (1 inch) piece fresh root or dried and bruised ginger
2 mace blades
25-28 whole peppercorns
1 whole bay leaf (optional)
1-3 teaspoons whole mustard seeds (optional)

Just as there are many different pickling mixtures, so too are there many methods of using them. Choose one of the following options:

Method 1
Bring all the ingredients to the boil; strain and immediately pour the pickling liquid over the items to be pickled already packed in their jar; allow to cool and then seal and store.

Method 2
Bring all the ingredients to the boil; allow the mixture to cool, then strain and use the resulting pickling liquid as before.

Method 3
Include the whole spices in the jar with the items to be pickled.

Method 4
Steep the spices in the vinegar in a closed jar for 4-8 weeks; strain and use the resulting liquid.

Uses: A number of vegetables are suitable for pickling. Pickled cabbage, especially red cabbage, is excellent, as are pickled onions, shallots and gherkins. Firm fruits such as pears and apricots can also be pickled.

QUATRE EPICES

France and the Middle East

The quatre epices spice mix is a favourite seasoning not just in France, but also in many parts of the Middle East and the Arab world, especially North Africa. You may be able to find proprietary brands in specialist shops which sell continental or Middle Eastern provisions.

1 teaspoon ground cloves
3½ teaspoons ground ginger
3¼ teaspoons grated or ground nutmeg
4 tablespoons ground white pepper

Mix all ingredients together; store any excess for short periods in an airtight container.

Uses: Quatre epices is a favourite French charcuterie spice, much used in terrines, galantines and other charcuterie products. In the Middle East and Arab countries, many meat stews, meatball dishes and casseroles of meat and dried fruit are seasoned with local versions of it.

MIDDLE EASTERN MIXTURES

Spice mixes abound in the Middle East, especially in North Africa, where each country has at least one or two favourite and characteristic mixes. Here are just two of this 'clutch' of mixtures: an Egyptian dukkah and the la kama mixture from Morocco, both quite mild by comparison to some of the other combinations!

DUKKAH

10 tablespoons whole coriander seeds
8 tablespoons whole cumin seeds
25g (1oz) whole hazel or other nuts, to taste
9 tablespoons brown sesame seeds
salt and pepper, to taste

Lightly crush ingredients together. Mint or other herbs can be included instead of cumin, and cinnamon can be added to taste.

Uses: Dukkah mix is a delicious and favourite Egyptian snack for all times of day. Bread is first dunked into olive oil and then into the mixture.

LA KAMA

1 ½ teaspoons ground cinnamon
4 teaspoons ground ginger
⅓ teaspoon ground or grated nutmeg
3 ⅓ teaspoons ground black pepper
4 ⅓ teaspoons ground turmeric

Mix all the ingredients together, and store any excess in an airtight jar.

Uses: La kama seasons and flavours Moroccan soups and stews, especially those from Tangier.

SEVEN FLAVOUR SPICE OR SCHICHMI TOGARASHI

Japan

Schichmi togarashi (or togarashi) is a favourite Japanese mixture of seven spices. It will be necessary to adjust the chilli content to suit Western palates as it is very hot. The quantities of other ingredients are also variable. Several different types of this spice mixture are available as proprietary brands from Japanese suppliers, as are the individual ingredients.

4 tablespoons ground chillies, or to taste
1 ¼ teaspoons whole poppy seeds
20g (¾oz) sansho pepper (ground anise pepper leaves)
1 ¾ teaspoons whole black sesame seeds
3 ½ teaspoons ground white or brown sesame seeds
20g (¾oz) ground dried tangerine peel
5g (⅛oz) whole rape seeds (optional)

Mix the ingredients together. Other ingredients such as mustard seeds, pepper or even crushed toasted *nori* (Japanese seaweed) can be included. Use sparingly.

Uses: Seven flavour spice is used in Japanese cooking as both a seasoning and as a condiment. It accompanies many noodle dishes or noodles with vegetables; potatoes and aubergines and other vegetables are also good with it. As a 'dry' dip it is served with *sukiyaki*.

CHINESE FIVE SPICE OR FIVE SPICE POWDER

China

This mixture is a crucial spice not just for many authentic Chinese dishes, but also for much Malay and Indo-Chinese food. Available ready-made in Chinese stores, it is increasingly found in general grocers and supermarkets. The mixture is often only part of the seasoning of a particular dish and used in small amounts, so store any excess in an airtight container, away from the light.

1 teaspoon ground anise (Szechuan) pepper
½ teaspoon ground cassia or cinnamon
½ teaspoon ground cloves
1 ¼ teaspoons ground fennel seeds
1 teaspoon ground star anise

Either mix all ingredients together or mix the whole spices together before grinding to allow their aromatic oils to mingle during grinding.

Uses: Chinese five spice is used especially in marinades and sauces and in 'red cooked' dishes (meat, poultry or fish slow-braised with soy sauce and other flavourings). Many other Chinese meat and poultry dishes also include it, and it is excellent with both crisp roasted duck and fried or barbecued pork. It is particularly used in Szechuan, home of spicy Chinese cooking, notably in Szechuan smoked duck.

SEVEN SEAS SPICE

Indonesia and Malaysia

This mixture's chilli content can be adjusted to taste without any loss of flavour; for an authentic version, try using cassia instead of cinnamon.

2 ½ teaspoons ground cardamom
1 ¾ teaspoons ground cassia (or cinnamon)
1 teaspoon ground celery seeds
2 ½ teaspoons ground dried chillies, chilli powder or cayenne
1 teaspoon ground cloves
2 tablespoons ground coriander seeds
2 ½ teaspoons ground cumin seeds

Mix together all ingredients and use as soon as possible; store any excess in an airtight jar.

Uses: This spice mixture can form part of marinades, bastes or seasonings for many Indonesian and Malay dishes, including *gulés* from the former and curries from the latter.

VIRGIN ISLAND SPICE

The West Indies

This aromatic spice mixture is ideally suited to English palates because of its somewhat uncharacteristic lack of chillies. It can also be found ready-made in West Indian shops, or those which stock West Indian provisions. This fresh-tasting dry spice mix is very popular in the Caribbean, especially in the Virgin Islands, from where it originates.

1 teaspoon whole celery seeds
1 ¾ teaspoons crushed cloves
1 ½ teaspoons garlic powder or granules
¾ teaspoon ground or crushed mace
¾ teaspoon grated or ground nutmeg
2 teaspoons crushed dried parsley
2 teaspoons ground black pepper
¾ teaspoon roughly ground sea salt

Thoroughly combine the ingredients and use immediately. Excess mixture can be stored in an airtight container for up to 3 months.

Uses: A natural partner to any dish featuring tomato sauce or juice, or to vegetable juices prepared in a blender or juice extractor. It is an excellent seasoning for meat and is often used instead of a salt and pepper in salad dressings. Also good with cheese and egg dishes. The mixture could also be used as the seasoning for a barbecue marinade.

CURRY MIXTURES

India

Curry powder, despite its popular association with India, is a Western, and specifically British invention; some brands may be produced in India, but it is almost never used there. The idea of resorting to a commercially mass-produced powder, as opposed to a careful selection of specific spices chosen to complement a particular food, is unthinkable. The better proprietary brands of curry powder are useful and convenient but no commercial blend, however good, can take the place of freshly ground spices or provide the seasoning for a host of dishes which should all taste different. The word curry, which derives from *kari*, a Tamil word for sauce, refers not to the name of a dish but to the technique of stewing with water and spices to form a sauce. Currying is not the ubiquitous cooking method of India; it is just one of the many different Indian cooking techniques. Many areas of India use different characteristic spice mixtures; the mixtures given here represent only a minute selection of the many Indian spice combinations used for currying, but they do exhibit regional variations in terms of heat and emphasis of ingredients.

BOMBAY MIXTURE

4-5 small dried chillies
(to make 1 teaspoon when ground)
1 × 4-5cm (1½-2 inch) piece cinnamon stick
4½ tablespoons whole coriander seeds
1 teaspoon whole cumin seeds
½ teaspoon whole fennel seeds
⅔ teaspoon whole fenugreek seeds
½ teaspoon garlic powder or granules
2⅔ teaspoons ground turmeric
2 kokum skins (p 19)
2 crushed curry leaves

Lightly roast together the first six ingredients; then grind and mix with the garlic and the turmeric. Use according to recipe instructions, adding the kokum skins and the crushed curry leaves directly to the cooking pot, removing the kokum skins before serving.

MADRAS MIXTURE

1-3 teaspoons ground chilli
8½ tablespoons ground coriander seeds
3 tablespoons ground cumin seeds
⅛ teaspoon ground ginger
1 teaspoon ground black mustard seeds
1 teaspoon ground fenugreek seeds
1 teaspoon ground black pepper
1⅔ teaspoons ground turmeric
4 whole curry leaves

Mix together all ground dry spices; then proceed according to recipe instructions, adding the curry leaves directly to the cooking pot.

VINDALOO MIXTURE

This is a classic and historic Goan vindaloo mixture: choose the appropriate method for the individual recipe concerned.

1 teaspoon whole cardamom seeds
1 × 7.5cm (3 inch) piece cinnamon stick
1 teaspoon whole cloves
2 teaspoons whole cumin seeds
1 teaspoon whole fenugreek seeds
1½ teaspoons whole black mustard seeds
1 teaspoon whole black peppercorns
3 teaspoons whole coriander seeds
10 garlic cloves, peeled and chopped, or to taste
1 × 2.5cm (1 inch) piece fresh ginger, finely chopped (or ¼ teaspoon ground ginger)
½ teaspoon ground turmeric
1-5 teaspoons ground chilli, to taste
1½ teaspoons salt
1 teaspoon brown sugar (optional)
65-120ml (2½-4fl oz) vinegar
175g (6oz) onions, peeled, chopped, fried and puréed (optional)

Method 1
Lightly roast the first ten ingredients together, then grind and add the turmeric, chilli, salt, sugar, vinegar and onion to make a Vindaloo paste marinade. Use according to the recipe.

Method 2
Lightly roast together the first seven ingredients, then grind and add the chilli, salt, sugar, vinegar and the onions. Use this as the Vindaloo paste marinade. Then, blend together the garlic and fresh ginger, adding a little water if necessary; fry this and add the turmeric and coriander. Use according to recipe instructions.

CHINESE/MALAY MIXTURE

1½ teaspoons whole anise (Szechuan) pepper
1 × 4-5cm (1½-2 inch) piece cassia or cinnamon stick
5 small dried chillies
¾ teaspoon whole cloves
6⅓ tablespoons whole coriander seeds
3½ teaspoons whole fennel seeds
1½ teaspoons grated or ground nutmeg
2 teaspoons ground star anise
2½ teaspoons ground turmeric

Lightly roast all the first six ingredients, then grind and mix the remaining ingredients. Use according to recipe instructions.

Uses: The currying technique of cooking can be applied to meat, poultry, fish and seafood. Eggs and vegetables, too, can be curried; indeed, most south Indian curries are vegetarian ones. The Vindaloo mix is traditionally used with pork, though it can do just as well with other meats or poultry; try the Bombay version with chicken and the Madras with fish or mixed vegetables. In the West curry powder (as opposed to mixtures) can be used as a flavouring for mayonnaise (for coronation chicken), cream sauces (for fish), in quiches and savoury mousses and soups (like curried parsnip). It can also be used to good effect in kedgeree (the Raj version of the Indian *kitcheri*).

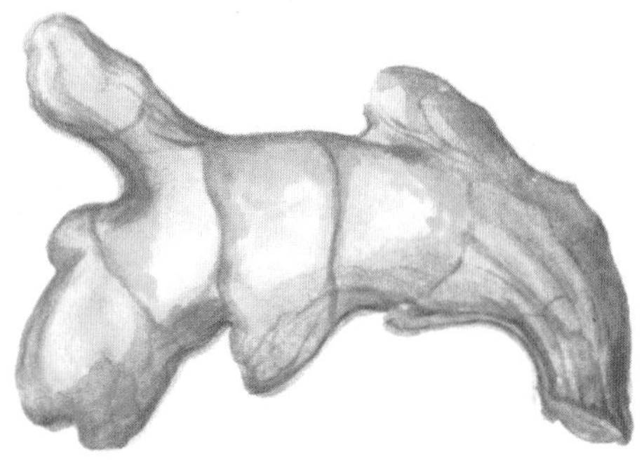

GARAM MASALA

India

Masalas are frequently only a part of the seasoning for a particular dish and usually added towards the end of the cooking process, or they can be used on their own like a condiment. The best known masala is Garam Masala (meaning 'hot spices'): it is a finely ground aromatic mixture. Here are two versions to try, the former more complex than the latter. Both mixtures can be adapted according to personal taste.

Mixture 1

¾-2 teaspoons ground cardamom seeds, according to taste
½-1 teaspoon ground cinnamon
½ teaspoon ground cloves
1½ teaspoons ground black cumin seeds
1¾ teaspoons ground black pepper
½ teaspoon ground bay leaves (optional)
1¾ teaspoons ground coriander seeds (optional)
1½ teaspoons ground whole cumin seeds (optional)
¼ teaspoon ground mace (optional)
¼-1 teaspoon grated or ground nutmeg (optional)

Mix the chosen ground spices together, according to taste; mace and nutmeg will give a fresh fragrance.

Mixture 2

1 ½-3 teaspoons ground cardamom seeds
1 × 2.5-5cm (1-2 inch) piece cinnamon stick, ground
½-1 teaspoon ground cloves
1-1 ⅓ teaspoons ground black cumin seeds
1 teaspoon grated or ground nutmeg (or 2 teaspoons ground pomegranate seeds)
1-1 ½ teaspoons ground black pepper

Mix the chosen ingredients together. For a sharper, tarter garam masala, use the pomegranate seeds and the lower limit of the other ingredients.

Uses: Garam masala is an essential Indian spice mix for the kitchen. It is used frequently with meat, poultry and fish cooking, in curried dishes, *kormas*, tandooris and grills and also with eggs, vegetables, rice and pulses. *Pakoras* and *samosas* can also call for its inclusion. Its aromatic character also blends well with yogurt and it makes an excellent garnish for *raitas*.

KORMA

India

Rich and substantial, milder and more delicate than curried dishes, there are numerous different types of korma, but they all share a common cooking method: braising. Korma spice mixes characteristically include almonds or coconut, and use yogurt, cream or stock as the braising medium. Most types of meat and poultry are suited to the korma technique. Here is a basic korma mixture using ground spices, but follow individual korma recipes for instructions on using the mixture and the braising medium required.

2 teaspoons ground almonds or 4 teaspoons desiccated coconut
1 ¼ teaspoons ground cardamoms
½-¾ teaspoon ground chilli, chilli powder or cayenne, to taste
½ teaspoon ground cinnamon
½ teaspoon ground cloves
3-4 garlic cloves, peeled and chopped
¾ teaspoon ground ginger or 1 × 6cm (2 ½ inch) piece fresh ginger root, finely chopped
1 ¼ teaspoons ground turmeric or saffron (optional)
1-2 teaspoons ground coriander (optional)

For a simple korma, combine the spices with yogurt, but for authentic results follow individual recipe instructions, since cooking methods vary. Some recipes will combine all the spices, others will mix the ginger and garlic (or ginger, garlic and almond) to a paste which is used separately from the rest of the spices.

Uses: Chicken, lamb, mutton, pork and beef (even meatballs) are all suited to the korma cooking technique and will result in some of the most delicious and sophisticated Indian dishes; not too 'hot', but rich and creamy, they are excellent for special occasions.

PANCHPHORAN OR BENGALI FIVE SPICES

India

This spice mixture originates from Bengal in north-eastern India. Like various other Indian mixes (such as khara masala and khara korma), the panchphoran spices are used whole as opposed to ground. It is available as a proprietary brand from Indian grocers, but it may be marketed under 'Five Spices' or 'Five Spice Mixture', so do not confuse it with the Chinese 'Five Spice' mixture.

2 teaspoons whole cumin seeds
2 ¾ teaspoons whole fennel seeds
1 teaspoon whole fenugreek seeds
1 ¾ teaspoons whole black mustard seeds
1-2 teaspoons whole nigella (kalonji) seeds

Mix ingredients together.

Uses: Panchphoran makes an excellent frying spice and can be used to good effect with fish and seafood (crunchy fried prawns, for example), and with meat and poultry. It is sometimes included in curried dishes, especially those of Bengali origin and it is excellent with vegetables, particularly aubergines.

TANDOORI AND TIKKA MIXTURES

India

The name tandoori refers to the large traditional oven called a tandoor, in which tandoori foods are cooked on a spit. Whole or large pieces of food like chicken are usually referred to as 'tandooris', while smaller skewered cubes are known as 'tikkas'. Anything to be cooked in a tandoor is first prepared by lengthy marinating in a mixture seasoned with the spices given here; this moistens, flavours and penetrates the food. Approximate a tandoor oven by pre-heating an ordinary domestic oven to its highest temperature and using the items to be cooked in pieces rather than whole. Alternatively use a barbecue or grill (this is especially good for tikkas). When placed in the tandoor, the high heat seals the juices of the food and the marinade and subsequent bastings form the outside crust.

TANDOORI MIXTURE

1 teaspoon ground chilli
1-4 teaspoons ground coriander seeds, to taste
1-2 teaspoons ground cumin seeds, to taste
2 teaspoons Garam masala
2 garlic cloves, peeled and crushed
1 × 2.5cm (1 inch) piece fresh ginger root, chopped (or ⅛-¼ teaspoon ground ginger)
½ teaspoon red food colouring
pepper to taste
4-5 tablespoons lemon juice (optional)
150ml (¼ pint) plain unsweetened yogurt

TIKKA MIXTURE

¼ teaspoon ground chilli or cayenne
¼-1 teaspoon Garam masala, to taste
3 garlic cloves, peeled and chopped
1 × 2.5cm (1 inch) piece chopped fresh ginger root
2 teaspoons chopped fresh coriander leaves (optional)
1 teaspoon ground cumin seeds (optional)
½ teaspoon red food colouring (optional)
1 teaspoon turmeric (or yellow food colouring; both optional)
pepper to taste
1 ¼ teaspoons salt
2-3 tablespoons lemon juice
6 tablespoons plain unsweetened yogurt

Check individual recipes to see whether lemon juice or salt needs to be used in advance of marinading, whether food needs to be scored and whether colouring should be added at a later stage. Otherwise, combine all ingredients (for either mixture) and mix together thoroughly. Brush this marinade all over items to be cooked and leave to marinade for 6 hours or more, depending on size of item. Then follow individual recipe instructions.

Uses: Chicken is certainly the favourite food chosen for tandoori or tikka cooking; although lobster and prawns are also superb. Both chicken and fish *tikkas* are exceptionally good and often eaten as snacks with evening drinks. Serve both tandooris and tikkas on a bed of lettuce, garnished with onion rings, tomato quarters and slices of lemon.

SWEDISH SPLIT PEA SOUP

1.75 litres (3 pints) cold water
1 gammon knuckle
500g (1lb) yellow or green split peas
2 large onions, peeled and chopped
3 large carrots, scraped and grated
1 teaspoon cumin seeds

Preparation time: 10 minutes
Cooking time: 2½ hours
Serves 6-8

1. Put the water and gammon knuckle in a large saucepan and bring to the boil. Skim, then cover and simmer for 1 hour.
2. Pick over the split peas, discarding any black ones. Rinse under cold running water and add to the saucepan with the onion, carrot and cumin seeds. Cover and simmer for 1½ hours.
3. Remove the gammon knuckle and liquidize the contents of the pan. Cut the gammon into small chunks. Serve the soup, sprinkling each bowl with a little chopped gammon and serving the remaining meat as an accompaniment.

BEETROOT AND TOMATO SOUP WITH CUMIN

4 medium raw beetroots, peeled and cubed
450ml (¾ pint) water
½ teaspoon whole cumin seeds
10 whole black peppercorns
4 cloves
2.5cm (1 inch) piece cinnamon stick
½ tablespoon butter plus ½ tablespoon vegetable oil
1×225g (8oz) can peeled tomatoes, sieved
1 teaspoon salt
4 tablespoons single or soured cream
4 sprigs fresh sage or parsley, to garnish

Preparation time: 10 minutes
Cooking time: 30 minutes

1. Put the beetroot with the water in a food processor or blender for 1 minute, turn into a fine sieve set over a bowl and extract as much of the juice as possible, pressing with the back of a wooden spoon.
2. Tie the spices together in a piece of muslin and crush lightly. Heat the fats in a saucepan over a moderate heat and add the spice bag and the tomatoes with their juice. Stir well to mix, then stir in the beetroot juice. Bring to the boil, cover and simmer for 25 minutes. Remove and discard the muslin bag.
3. Liquidize the contents of the pan in a food processor or electric blender, if liked. Just before serving, add the salt, then the cream. Stir well to mix, then reheat over a very gentle heat, without boiling.
4. Ladle the soup into warmed soup bowls or cups, garnish with sage and serve with hot pitta bread.

LENTIL SOUP

225g (8oz) lentils, soaked for 1 hour, drained
2 onions, peeled and chopped
2 cloves garlic, peeled and crushed
1 teaspoon Chinese/Malay curry mixture (p 26)
1 teaspoon celery seeds, bruised
1 litre (2 pints) chicken stock
salt
freshly ground black pepper
2 tablespoons chopped fresh parsley
hot croûtons, to serve

Preparation time: 5 minutes
Cooking time: 1½ hours
Serves 4-6

1. Put the lentils, onions, garlic, curry powder and celery seeds in a large saucepan. Pour in the stock and bring to the boil. Cover, then lower the heat and simmer for about 1½ hours or until the lentils are soft. Process in a food processor or blender for 1 minute until smooth.
2. Return the soup to the pan and taste and adjust the seasoning. Reheat gently and serve in warmed soup bowls, garnished with croûtons.

FENNEL AND SCALLOP SOUP

25g (1oz) butter
3 shallots, peeled and finely chopped
3 bulbs fennel, chopped
300 ml (½ pint) dry white wine
8 scallops, cleaned
600 ml (1 pint) homemade chicken stock
salt
white pepper
1 bouquet garni
3 egg yolks
3 tablespoons dry white wine

Preparation time: 35 minutes
Cooking time: 50 minutes
Serves 6

1. Melt the butter in a pan, add the shallots and cook for 5 minutes, without browning, until softened. Add the fennel and cook for a further 5 minutes.
2. Remove the corals from the scallops, cut these and the white flesh into small pieces. Heat the wine in a small saucepan and poach the scallops for 1 minute, drain well and reserve the liquor.
3. Add the wine liquor to the vegetables, with the stock, salt and pepper to taste and the bouquet garni. Bring to the boil, cover and simmer for 30 minutes.
4. Remove the bouquet garni, cool the soup slightly, and blend until smooth. Sieve the soup.
5. Return the soup to the pan, add the reserved scallops, reheat the soup to just below boiling point, remove from the heat, and set aside for 5 minutes.

6. Lightly beat the egg yolks and remaining wine together with a few tablespoons of the hot soup. Stir into the soup and serve at once.

PARSNIP SOUP

75g (3oz) butter
1 medium onion, peeled and chopped
1 clove garlic, peeled and crushed
225g (8oz) parsnips, peeled and chopped
1 tablespoon plain flour
1 ½ teaspoons Korma mixture (p 27)
450ml (¾ pint) stock
salt
white pepper
300ml (½ pint) milk
150ml (5fl oz) single cream
1 tablespoon chopped fresh thyme or 1 teaspoon dried thyme
1 tablespoon fresh thyme, to garnish

Preparation time: 20 minutes
Cooking time: 50 minutes

1. Melt the butter in a large saucepan, add the onion and fry over a gentle heat for 5 minutes until soft and lightly coloured.
2. Add the garlic and parsnip and stir to coat all the parsnip pieces in butter. Cover the pan and cook gently for 5 minutes.
3. Sprinkle in the flour and Korma mixture, stir well and cook gently for 2 minutes.
4. Gradually pour in the stock, stirring constantly, and simmer for 20-30 minutes.
5. Liquidize the contents of the pan in a food processor or electric blender, then sieve. Season to taste with salt and pepper. Stir in the milk and cream and reheat very gently. Do not allow to boil.
6. Serve the parsnip soup in warmed individual soup bowls, sprinkled with thyme.

From top left, clockwise: *Swedish split pea soup; Beetroot and tomato soup with cumin; Lentil soup; Parsnip soup*

MUSSEL AND SAFFRON SOUP

1kg (2lb) fresh mussels
3 tablespoons vegetable oil
2 medium onions, peeled and chopped
3 cloves garlic, peeled and chopped
1 × 400g (14oz) can peeled tomatoes
1 sachet powdered saffron
1 sprig fresh thyme
150ml (¼ pint) dry white wine
salt
freshly ground black pepper
150ml (5fl oz) single cream
1 tablespoon chopped fresh parsley

Preparation time: 30 minutes
Cooking time: 20 minutes

Be sure to buy heavy, tightly closed mussels – a sign that they are still alive, and fresh. The liquid released by the mussels makes up the basic stock for this flavourful soup.

From the top: *Mussel and saffron soup; Fennel and scallop soup (recipe p 28)*

1. Tip the mussels into clean cold water and scrub each shell well, removing any beard. Rinse in clean cold water. Turn into a large saucepan and set over a high heat for 2-3 minutes, or until the shells have just opened, but the mussels are still firmly compacted and not fully opened out. Discard any mussels that do not open. Remove from the heat, rapidly remove the mussels from their shells and reserve. Strain the liquor into a bowl.
2. Heat the oil in a deep flameproof casserole, add the onions and garlic and fry over a gentle heat for 5 minutes until soft and lightly coloured. Add the tomatoes with their juice, breaking them up with a wooden spoon. Simmer for 3 minutes.
3. Add the saffron, thyme and wine and stir to mix, then cover and simmer for 5 minutes. Stir in the mussel liquor and taste and adjust the seasoning, using salt sparingly as mussels usually contain some salt water.
4. Five minutes before serving add the reserved mussels to the soup with the cream. Stir to mix, then reheat very gently without boiling until the mussels are heated through.
5. Sprinkle with the parsley and serve ladled into heated soup bowls, with plenty of French bread.

SEAFOOD GRATIN

450g (1lb) Pacific prawns, cooked unshelled
25g (1oz) butter
3 shallots or 1 onion, peeled and finely chopped
1 tablespoon plain flour
150ml (¼ pint) double cream
salt
½ teaspoon cayenne pepper
3 tablespoons dry white breadcrumbs
25g (1oz) butter

Preparation time: 10 minutes
Cooking time: 20 minutes
Oven: 200°C, 400°F, Gas Mark 6

1. Peel the prawns and put the shells in a saucepan. Pour in enough water just to cover, then bring to the boil, lower the heat and simmer for 5 minutes.
2. Melt the butter in a frying pan, add the shallot or onion and fry over a gentle heat for 5 minutes or until soft and lightly coloured. Sprinkle in the flour, stir to mix and cook over a gentle heat for 2 minutes.
3. Strain the liquid from the boiled prawn shells and measure – if necessary add hot water to achieve 150ml (¼ pint). Pour into the pan and bring to the boil. Cook for 2-3 minutes, then remove from the heat and stir in the cream. Season with salt and cayenne pepper.
4. Arrange the prawns in a shallow ovenproof dish and pour over the sauce. Sprinkle with the breadcrumbs, dot with butter and bake in a preheated hot oven for 15 minutes or until lightly browned and bubbling. Serve immediately with melba toast.

From the bottom, clockwise: *Prawn pâté; Seafood gratin; Devilled crabs*

PRAWN PÂTÉ

100g (4oz) butter
1 garlic clove, peeled and crushed
1 teaspoon crushed coriander seeds
100g (4oz) peeled prawns, defrosted if frozen
3 tablespoons double or whipping cream
salt
cayenne pepper
TO GARNISH
unpeeled prawns
parsley sprigs

Preparation time: 5 minutes, plus chilling

1. Melt the butter in a heavy frying pan over a low heat, add the garlic and coriander and fry for 2-3 minutes.
2. Add the prawns and turn to coat with the butter.
3. Transfer the contents of the pan to a food processor or electric blender and process until smooth. Add the cream and process again briefly. Season to taste with salt and cayenne pepper.
4. Spoon the prawn paté into individual pots and chill. Garnish with prawns and parsley and serve with toast and lemon wedges.

DEVILLED CRABS

450g (1lb) crabmeat, defrosted if frozen
8 tablespoons fresh white breadcrumbs
4 tablespoons milk
½ teaspoon cayenne pepper
½ teaspoon English mustard powder
2 egg yolks
1 teaspoon tomato purée
50g (2oz) butter, melted
lemon slices or butterflies, to garnish

Preparation time: 10 minutes
Cooking time: 15 minutes
Oven: 220°C, 425°F, Gas Mark 7

1. Put the crabmeat into a large bowl. Soak the breadcrumbs in the milk, then squeeze out the excess milk and mix the crumbs with the crabmeat.
2. Add the cayenne, mustard powder, egg yolks, tomato purée and melted butter to the crab mixture. Stir to mix thoroughly, then spoon the mixture into 4 scallop shells, dividing it equally among them.
3. Dot with butter and bake in a preheated hot oven for 15 minutes, until lightly browned. Garnish with lemon butterflies and serve at once.

MUSHROOMS A LÀ GRECQUE

2 tablespoons lemon juice
2 tablespoons olive oil
150ml (5fl oz) dry white wine
1 teaspoon coriander seeds
1 sprig parsley
1 sprig thyme
1 small celery stalk with leaves
1 bay leaf
12 black peppercorns
225g (8oz) button mushrooms, washed, unpeeled
½ head curly endive, to serve

Preparation time: 2-3 minutes, plus cooling
Cooking time: 5 minutes

1. Combine all the ingredients but the mushrooms in a small saucepan and bring to the boil.
2. Add the mushrooms to the pan and simmer for 5 minutes over a gentle heat.
3. Remove from the heat, cover and leave to cool completely in the liquid – about 2-3 hours.
4. Discard the parsley, thyme, celery stalk and bay leaf. Arrange a bed of curly endive leaves in a shallow serving dish. Spoon the chilled mushrooms and the liquid into the centre and serve with crusty french bread.

RILLETTES

750g (1½lb) pork belly, as lean as possible, rinded, boned and cut into 2cm (¾ inch) cubes
1 clove garlic, peeled and bruised
1 sprig fresh thyme
½ teaspoon Quatre epices (p 24)
salt
2 tablespoons water
gherkin fans, to garnish

Preparation time: 10 minutes, plus cooling
Cooking time: 2½-3 hours
Oven: 140°C, 275°F, Gas Mark 1

An excellent example of the French talent for making a delectable dish from a cheap cut of meat, rillettes are a garlicky form of potted pork, very lightly spiced and cooked long and slowly. Rillettes make good picnic food or a lunchtime snack. The mixture keeps well - left-over rillettes can be covered with cling film and kept in the refrigerator for up to a week.

1. Place the pork belly cubes in a heavy casserole with the garlic, thyme, Quatre Epices, a pinch of salt and the water.
2. Cook in a preheated slow oven for 2½-3 hours until the pork belly cubes are lightly coloured and

From the left: *Rillettes; Mushrooms à la grecque*

swimming in their own fat. If they show signs of overbrowning add more water.
3. Tip the contents of the casserole into a sieve placed over a bowl, to catch the melted fat. Remove the thyme sprig then turn the pieces of pork belly in the sieve on to a board. Using two forks, shred the pork belly finely until no lumps remain.
4. Mix the shredded pork belly with the fat in the bowl. Add a little salt to taste. Pack into individual earthenware pots and leave to cool completely, or chill for 2-3 hours in the refrigerator. Garnish each one with a gherkin and serve with crusty bread.

GRUYÈRE DELICES

350ml (15fl oz) milk
slice of onion
1 blade of mace
1 parsley stalk, crushed
1 bay leaf
6 whole peppercorns
75g (3oz) butter
100g (4oz) plain flour
175g (6oz) Gruyère cheese, finely grated
1 egg yolk
freshly ground black pepper
freshly grated nutmeg
salt
1 egg, beaten
2 tablespoons dried breadcrumbs
vegetable oil, for frying
lime slices, to garnish

Preparation time: 5 minutes, plus infusing and chilling
Cooking time: 8-10 minutes
Makes 20

1. Put the milk into a saucepan with the onion, mace, parsley stalk, bay leaf and peppercorns. Warm over gentle heat, then remove from heat and leave to infuse for 20 minutes. Strain.
2. Lightly oil a 25×20cm (10×8 inch) baking sheet.
3. Melt the butter in a saucepan and stir in the flour. Cook for 2 minutes, stirring, then remove from the heat and gradually stir in the milk. Return to the heat and bring to the boil, stirring, then lower the heat and simmer for 2 minutes, stirring from time to time.
4. Remove from the heat and beat in the cheese and egg yolk. Season to taste with pepper and nutmeg, and a little salt if necessary.
5. Pour the mixture evenly over the prepared baking sheet, chill in the refrigerator for 2-3 hours.
6. When firm, cut into 20 squares. Dip them first in beaten egg, then in breadcrumbs, to coat evenly. Heat some oil in a deep fryer, add the cheese squares and fry for 3 minutes until golden brown. Drain on crumpled absorbent paper and sprinkle immediately with a little salt. Transfer to a warmed serving dish, garnish with lime slices and serve at once.

From the top: *Creamy turbot vol au vents; Gruyère delices*

CREAMY TURBOT VOL AU VENTS

100g (4oz) butter
150ml (¼ pint) double cream
½ teaspoon ground mace or nutmeg
salt
white pepper
50g (2oz) peeled prawns, defrosted if frozen, chopped
350g (12oz) cooked turbot or other white fish, skin and bones removed, flaked
1 tablespoon chopped fresh parsley
4 large or 8-10 medium vol au vent cases

Preparation time: 4 minutes
Cooking time: 3 minutes, plus heating
Makes 4 large or 8-10 medium vol au vents

A simple but sumptuous way of making a small amount of fish go a long way. A good way to use up cooked leftover fish.
1. Melt the butter in a small pan, add the cream, mace and salt and pepper and heat through briefly. Stir in the prawns, turbot and chopped parsley.
2. Spoon into the vol au vent cases and serve.

VARIATION
Any firm white fish, such as cod or haddock, may be substituted for turbot.

GIPSY EGGS

3 tablespoons olive oil
1 teaspoon powdered saffron
1 teaspoon ground cumin
1 teaspoon ground cinnamon
2 slices bread
2 garlic cloves, peeled and chopped
1 tablespoon blanched almonds
4 large eggs

Preparation time: 2-3 minutes
Cooking time: 20 minutes
Oven: 180°C, 350°F, Gas Mark 4

This is a medieval Spanish dish which combines fried bread with almonds and saffron. It makes an interesting hors d'oeuvre garnished with salad, or it could be served as a lunch or supper dish with French Beans in Tomato Sauce (p 57) and warm crusty bread.

1. Heat 2 tablespoons of the oil in a frying pan, add the saffron, cumin and cinnamon and fry for 1 minute, then add the bread and fry on both sides until crisp and golden. Remove the fried bread and allow to cool slightly.
2. Add the remaining oil to the pan, add the garlic and almonds and fry for 1-2 minutes without allowing either to brown.
3. Pound the contents of the pan with the fried bread in a mortar and pestle, or process in a food processor or electric blender, to make a smooth paste.
4. Lightly oil a shallow ovenproof dish and spread the paste over the bottom. Break the eggs on top and bake in the oven for about 15 minutes until the whites are set and the paste is crunchy and golden but not browned.
5. Remove and serve immediately.

Below, from the top: *Gypsy eggs; French beans in tomato sauce (recipe p 56)*
Opposite, from the top: *Sesame seed dip with raw vegetables; Spinach rolls; Spiced empanadas*

SPICED EMPANADAS

vegetable oil, for frying
350g (12oz) lean chuck steak, finely minced
8 spring onions, trimmed and finely chopped
12 pimiento-stuffed green olives, sliced
2 tablespoons seedless raisins
½ teaspoon chilli powder
salt
freshly ground black pepper
1 egg, beaten
450g (1lb) shortcrust pastry, defrosted if frozen
1 egg yolk, beaten

Preparation time: 15 minutes
Cooking time: 40-45 minutes
Oven: 220°C, 425°F, Gas Mark 7
then: 180°C, 350°F, Gas Mark 4
Makes 8 small empanadas

Empanadas, or spiced meat pasties, are very popular in the Argentine; small ones are served as cocktail snacks, and larger ones for picnics or a quick lunch. Different regions have their distinctive fillings. This is a sophisticated version, which contrasts the slight bitterness of green olives with the sweetness of raisins in a chilli-flavoured meat filling.

1. Heat the oil in a heavy frying pan over a moderate heat. Add the steak and spring onions and fry for about 10 minutes, stirring from time to time, until the beef is lightly cooked but not browned. Drain off any fat and mix the beef with the olives, raisins, chilli powder and salt and pepper to taste. Leave to cool then mix in the beaten egg.
2. Roll the pastry out thinly on a lightly floured board, cut out 8×20cm (8 inch) circles.
3. Spoon a portion of filling into the centre of each circle. Moisten the edge of each circle with water, then fold over the pastry and pinch the edges firmly to seal, to make semi-circular pasties. Brush with egg yolk to glaze. Arrange the pasties on an oiled baking sheet leaving enough space in between to allow for a little spreading.
4. Bake in a preheated hot oven for 10-15 minutes, then reduce the oven temperature and bake for a further 20 minutes, or until the pastry is crisp and lightly browned. Serve hot, warm or cold.

SPINACH ROLLS

175g (6oz) frozen chopped spinach
50g (2oz) butter
freshly grated nutmeg
salt
freshly ground black pepper
6 eggs
2 tablespoons water
6-8 crusty rolls or soft baps
175g (6oz) cream cheese with herbs and garlic

Preparation time: about 5 minutes
Cooking time: about 10 minutes
Makes 6 rolls

These rolls make delicious picnic fare. They are equally nice warm or cold.

1. Cook the spinach according to packet instructions, then drain in a sieve, pressing out as much moisture as possible with the back of a wooden spoon.
2. Return the spinach to the pan and add half the butter. Season to taste with nutmeg, salt and pepper.
3. Beat the eggs lightly with the water and season with salt and pepper. Stir in the spinach.
4. Melt the remaining butter in a large frying pan over a brisk heat, swirling the butter over the base and sides. Pour in the egg and spinach mixture and once the edge starts to set, lift it with a spatula or small fish slice and allow the liquid from the centre to run underneath. Cook for 2-3 minutes or until set.
5. Halve the rolls and spread each half with the cream cheese. Cut the omelette into strips and arrange these on the bottom half of each roll. Replace the tops on the rolls and serve.

SESAME SEED DIP

5 tablespoons sesame seeds
1 tablespoon sesame oil or olive oil
1 tablespoon light soy sauce
2 tablespoons dry sherry
1 teaspoon sugar
1 teaspoon malt vinegar
1 teaspoon chopped fresh coriander, to garnish

Preparation time: 5 minutes

The Chinese use this dark, aromatic dip as a sauce for boiled noodles but it makes an unusual dip for crisp vegetables too.

1. Heat the sesame seeds over a low heat in a heavy frying pan until they begin to colour.
2. Grind the seeds finely in a coffee grinder.
3. Combine the ground sesame seeds with all the remaining ingredients in a small serving bowl. If too thick stir in a little more sherry.
4. Sprinkle with chopped coriander and serve with pieces of raw cucumber and mooli (Japanese radish), and blanched mangetout and French beans.

CARIBBEAN STUFFED CRAB

350g (12oz) crabmeat, defrosted if frozen
75g (3oz) fresh white breadcrumbs
2 tablespoons coconut milk (p 80) or double cream
1 fresh green chilli, seeded and finely chopped
3 tablespoons finely chopped chives
2 tablespoons finely chopped fresh parsley
2 garlic cloves, peeled, crushed and finely chopped
1 tablespoon fresh lime or lemon juice
½ teaspoon Virgin Island spice (p 25)
2 tablespoons dark rum
25g (1oz) butter
TO GARNISH
lime wedges
sprigs of fresh rosemary or parsley

Preparation time: 10 minutes
Cooking time: 20 minutes
Oven: 180°C, 350°F, Gas Mark 4

1. Mash the crabmeat in a bowl with a fork. Add 50g (2 oz) breadcrumbs, the coconut milk, chillis, chives, parsley, garlic, lime juice, spice and rum. Stir very thoroughly to mix.
2. Spoon the mixture into a trimmed and cleaned crab shell or ovenproof dish. Sprinkle the remaining breadcrumbs on top and dot with the butter.
3. Bake in a preheated moderate oven until lightly browned on top. Garnish with lime wedges and sprigs of rosemary and serve at once.

CHICKEN CALYPSO

5 tablespoons olive oil
1.75kg (4lb) oven-ready chicken, jointed into 8
450g (1lb) long-grain rice
1 onion, peeled and finely chopped
1 garlic clove, peeled and finely chopped
1 green pepper, cored, seeded and finely chopped
1 fresh green chilli, seeded and finely chopped
225g (8oz) mushrooms, sliced
1.2 litres (2 pints) hot chicken stock
½ teaspoon powdered saffron
1 strip finely pared lime or lemon peel
1 tablespoon fresh lime or lemon juice
½ teaspoon Virgin Island spice (p 25)
½ teaspoon Angostura bitters
salt
freshly ground black pepper
3 tablespoons rum
banana slices, to garnish

Preparation time: 30 minutes
Cooking time: 45 minutes
Serves 8

A paella-type party dish, but with a Caribbean flavour, which features chicken cooked with spiced rice and vegetables.

1. Heat 3 tablespoons of the oil in a large, heavy-based frying pan, add the chicken pieces and fry over a moderate heat, turning from time to time, until browned on all sides. Remove the chicken pieces and place in a large flameproof casserole.
2. Add a tablespoon of the oil to the frying pan, add the rice, onion, garlic and green pepper and chillies and fry over a gentle heat for 4-5 minutes, stirring. Transfer to the casserole with the chicken.
3. Heat the remaining oil in the pan, and add the mushrooms and fry over a gentle heat for 5 minutes. Transfer to the casserole.
4. Pour the stock into the casserole, add the saffron, lime peel, lime juice, spice, bitters and salt and pepper to taste. Stir well to mix, then cover and simmer over a low heat for about 30 minutes, or until the chicken is tender and cooked through and the liquid is absorbed.
5. Stir in the rum and cook over the lowest possible heat, uncovered, for a further 5 minutes. Serve hot, garnished with banana slices.

PRAWN PIE

350g (12oz) stale white breadcrumbs
300ml (½ pint) dry white wine
½ teaspoon ground mace
½ teaspoon freshly grated nutmeg
½ teaspoon cayenne pepper
salt
freshly ground black pepper
500g (1¼lb) peeled prawns
1 tablespoon finely chopped fresh parsley
50g (2oz) butter, diced
SAUCE
1×225g (8oz) can tomatoes, sieved
1 tablespoon celery leaves
300ml (½ pint) fish stock
TO GARNISH
100g (4oz) unpeeled prawns
1 sprig fresh coriander

Preparation time: 20 minutes
Cooking time: 45 minutes
Oven: 190°C, 375°F, Gas Mark 5

1. In a large bowl, combine the breadcrumbs with the wine, and season with mace, nutmeg, cayenne, salt and pepper, then add the peeled prawns, with the parsley, and stir well to mix.
2. Transfer the prawn mixture to a buttered ovenproof dish, dot with the butter and bake in a preheated medium-hot oven for about 30 minutes, until the top is lightly browned.
3. Meanwhile, put the sauce ingredients into a saucepan and season with salt and pepper. Bring to the boil, cover and simmer for 30 minutes.
4. Garnish the prawn pie with the unpeeled prawns and a sprig of coriander. Serve with a green salad and the tomato sauce handed separately.

From the bottom, clockwise: *Fish with Creole sauce; Chicken calypso; Caribbean stuffed crab; Prawn pie*

FISH WITH CREOLE SAUCE

4 tablespoons olive oil
4 red mullet, cleaned and scaled
1 large onion, peeled and finely chopped
1 green pepper, cored, seeded and finely chopped
1×225g (8oz) can tomatoes
1 tablespoon finely chopped coriander or parsley
½ teaspoon dried thyme
1 teaspoon Tabasco sauce
½ teaspoon sassafras (filé) powder (p 22)
4 tablespoons rum
½ teaspoon salt

Preparation time: 15 minutes
Cooking time: 25 minutes
Oven: 190°C, 375°F, Gas Mark 5

1. Heat 3 tablespoons of the oil in a large frying pan, add the mullet and fry for 2-3 minutes on each side to brown lightly. Transfer to a flat baking dish.
2. Heat the remaining oil, add the onions and green pepper and fry over a gentle heat for 5 minutes until soft, then add the tomatoes with their juice. Stir and simmer for 2-3 minutes. Add all the remaining ingredients and cook for 2 minutes. Pour over the fish.
3. Bake in a preheated moderately hot oven until the mullet flesh is white and flakes easily. Serve hot, with plain boiled rice and fried bananas.

VARIATION

For a simpler dish, fry the mullet for 7-8 minutes on each side and keep warm. Prepare the sauce and cook for 5 minutes longer than in the main recipe. Spoon the sauce on to a heated serving platter and arrange the mullet on top.

Above: *Curried Chicken mayonnaise*

CURRIED CHICKEN MAYONNAISE

1 tablespoon olive oil
1 onion, peeled and finely chopped
2 teaspoons Bombay curry mixture (p 26)
2 teaspoons lemon juice
1 teaspoon apricot jam
2 tablespoons red wine
300ml (½ pint) thick mayonnaise
500g (1 ¼lb) cold poached chicken, cut into pieces
salt
freshly ground black pepper
TO GARNISH
finely chopped fresh coriander
½ avocado, peeled, sliced and dipped in lemon juice

Preparation time: 10 minutes
Cooking time: 10 minutes

1. Heat the oil in a frying pan. Add the onion and fry over a gentle heat for 5 minutes until soft and lightly coloured. Stir in the curry powder. Cook for a further 2 minutes.
2. Add the lemon juice, jam and wine and simmer for 2 minutes. Remove from the heat and leave to cool for 5 minutes. Remove the kokum skins (if using curry mixture on p 26).
3. Put the mayonnaise in a large bowl and add the curry mixture, stirring very thoroughly to mix. Add the chicken and turn in the curried mayonnaise until thoroughly coated. Garnish with chopped coriander and avocado slices.

NORMANDY CHICKEN

50g (2oz) butter
450g (1lb) dessert apples, peeled, cored and sliced
1.5kg (3 ¼lb) roasting chicken
1 tablespoon Calvados or brandy
150ml (5fl oz) dry white wine
150ml (5fl oz) double cream
sugar
salt
white pepper
pinch of ground cinnamon
COATING
25g (1oz) butter
¼ teaspoon powdered saffron
25g (1oz) caster sugar
1 tablespoon white wine vinegar
1 egg yolk
TO GARNISH
1 dessert apple, peeled cored and sliced
sprigs of fresh chervil

Preparation time: 25 minutes
Cooking time: 2 hours

1. Wash the chicken and dry with absorbent paper.
2. Melt the butter in a roasting tin. Arrange the apple slices in the bottom and place the chicken on top. Pour the calvados over the chicken and set alight.
3. When the flame subsides, cover the chicken with foil and roast in a preheated hot oven for 40 minutes.
4. Remove the apples and reserve. Roast the chicken for a further 40 minutes, uncovered, until the breast is browned and the chicken is cooked through.
5. Meanwhile sieve or liquidize the apples and put them in a saucepan. Stir in the white wine and simmer over a gentle heat for 5 minutes, stirring from time to time. Remove from the heat, stir in the cream and season to taste with sugar, salt, pepper and cinnamon.
6. Prepare the coating mixture: put the butter in a small saucepan with the saffron and heat gently until the butter has melted. Stir in the sugar and vinegar and cook, stirring, until syrupy. Remove from the heat and cool for 3 minutes; stir in the egg yolk.
7. Pat the chicken dry with absorbent paper and brush it all over with the coating mixture. Place the chicken on a carving dish and return to the turned off oven for 10 minutes to settle.
8. Pour off all the fat from the roasting tin and add the juices to the sauce. Reheat the sauce very gently.
9. Garnish the chicken with apple slices and chervil and accompanied by the sauce handed separately in a warmed sauceboat.

CHICKEN WITH PRUNES

50g (2oz) butter
1.5kg (3 ¼lb) chicken, jointed into 4
2 teaspoons plain flour
½ teaspoon ground allspice
450g (1lb) prunes, soaked overnight in 350ml (12fl oz) dry white wine and stoned
1 tablespoon redcurrant jelly
200ml (⅓ pint) double cream
salt
freshly ground black pepper

Preparation time: 20 minutes, plus soaking overnight
Cooking time: 45 minutes

In south-west France, prunes are often included in poultry and game recipes. If unavailable dried apricots may be used instead.

1. Melt the butter in a large flameproof casserole, add the chicken pieces and fry over a moderate heat, turning from time to time, until the chicken is browned on all sides.
2. Sprinkle in the flour with the allspice. Add the prunes and the wine, cover the casserole and simmer very gently for 30 minutes or until the chicken is cooked through and the juices run clear when the thickest parts of the chicken joints are pierced with a skewer.
3. Using a slotted spoon, transfer the chicken pieces and prunes to a warmed serving dish and keep warm. Measure the cooking liquid and reduce by boiling briskly or add water to achieve 200ml (7fl oz). Lower the heat and stir in the redcurrant jelly until it is melted. Stir in the cream, reheat gently and season to taste with salt and pepper.
4. Pour the sauce over the chicken joints and serve immediately, with new potatoes and a crisp green salad to follow.

From the left: *Normandy Chicken; Chicken with prunes*

JAPANESE CHICKEN

2 tablespoons sesame seeds
5 tablespoons light soy sauce
2 teaspoons cornflour
2 teaspoons caster sugar
4 spring onions, finely chopped
1×1.5kg (3 ¼lb) chicken, boned and cut into 8×5×10cm (2×4inch) pieces
1 tablespoon vegetable oil
1 teaspoon Seven flavour spice (p 25)
8 thin lemon slices
TO GARNISH
radish roses
carrot slices

Preparation time: 20 minutes
Cooking time: 30 minutes
Oven: 190°C, 375°F, Gas Mark 5

A very simple, delicious way of cooking chicken, highly recommended for battery birds.

1. In a dry frying pan heat the sesame seeds until they begin to jump. Remove from the pan and process to a coarse powder in a blender.
2. In a bowl, combine the sesame seed powder with the soy sauce, cornflour, sugar and spring onions.
3. Cut 8 pieces of cooking foil each large enough to contain a chicken piece. Lightly brush each piece of foil with the oil. Coat each chicken piece in the sesame seed mixture, sprinkle with Seven Flavour Spice, and lay a thin slice of lemon on top of each chicken piece. Wrap the chicken pieces in the foil, sealing the edges to make neat parcels.
4. Lay the parcels on an ovenproof dish and cook in a preheated oven for 30 minutes or until the chicken is cooked through.
5. Serve 2 parcels per person, garnished with radish roses and carrot slices and accompanied by hot bread rolls, removing the slices of lemon before eating.

Below: *Japanese chicken*

PARTRIDGE WITH CABBAGE

1 large cabbage, about 1.25kg (2 ½lb), cored and finely shredded
75g (3oz) butter
2 young partridges
225g (8oz) bacon cut into 2.5cm (1 inch) pieces
2 garlic cloves, peeled and crushed
6 juniper berries, crushed
1 tablespoon finely chopped sage or 1 teaspoon dried sage
1 tablespoon finely chopped thyme, or 1 teaspoon dried thyme
½ teaspoon freshly grated nutmeg
salt
freshly ground black pepper
450ml (15fl oz) chicken stock
20g (¾oz) plain flour
2 tablespoons orange juice

Preparation time: 20 minutes
Cooking time: 4 hours
Oven: 160°C, 325°F, Gas Mark 3

1. Blanch the cabbage in boiling salted water for 2 minutes. Drain and refresh under cold water, then drain again.
2. Melt 50g (2oz) of the butter in a frying pan, add the partridges and fry over a brisk heat, turning, to brown on all sides.
3. Butter a large casserole and lay half the cabbage in it. Cover with the bacon and add the garlic, juniper berries, sage, thyme, nutmeg, salt and pepper.
4. Lay the partridges on top and cover with the rest of the cabbage. Pour over the stock. Cover and cook in a preheated oven for 4 hours, adding a little extra stock if the casserole shows signs of drying out.
5. Remove the partridges from the casserole and strip the meat from the bones, discarding the skin.
6. Strain the cabbage and bacon, reserving the cooking liquid. Mix the partridge meat with the cabbage and place in a warmed serving dish. Keep warm.
7. Make the cooking liquid up to 300ml (½ pint) with extra stock, white wine or cider. Melt the remaining butter, stir in the flour and gradually add the reserved cooking liquid, stirring all the time. Simmer for 2-3 minutes, stirring. Stir in the orange juice and taste and adjust the seasoning. Hand the sauce separately in a warmed sauceboat.

From the left: *Pheasant in gin; Partridge with cabbage*

PHEASANT IN GIN

100g (4oz) butter, diced
2 pheasants
salt
freshly ground black pepper
12 juniper berries, crushed
4 rashers streaky bacon, rinded
600ml (1 pint) game stock or cider
1 tablespoon flour
2 tablespoons gin
2 tablespoons orange juice
2 teaspoons redcurrant jelly

Preparation time: 5 minutes
Cooking time: 1 hour
Oven: 200°C, 400°F, Gas Mark 6

1. Put half the butter into the body cavities of the pheasants and rub the remainder over the bird.
2. Place the pheasants in a large casserole and season with salt and pepper and the crushed juniper berries. Arrange the bacon rashers over the breasts of the birds.
3. Pour on half the stock. Cover and cook in a preheated hot oven for 45-60 minutes, until the pheasants are tender and cooked through.
4. Remove the pheasants to a warmed serving dish and keep warm. Skim off the fat from the casserole and stir the remaining stock into the juices. Whisk in the flour and the gin, orange juice and redcurrant jelly. Bring to the boil and simmer for 2-3 minutes, stirring.
5. Taste and adjust the seasoning. Carve the pheasants and serve with carrot purée and the gravy handed separately in a warmed sauceboat.

CHEESE AND EGG BOREK

4 hard boiled eggs, finely chopped
100g (4oz) Feta or Cheddar cheese, grated
1 small onion, peeled and finely chopped
1 tablespoon finely chopped fresh mint or 1 teaspoon dried mint
salt
1 teaspoon dukkah (p 25)
½ teaspoon Cayenne pepper or paprika (optional)
1 egg, beaten
6 sheets filo pastry, defrosted if frozen
100g (4oz) melted butter

Preparation time: 30 minutes
Cooking time: 12-15 minutes
Oven: 200°C, 400°F, Gas Mark 6
Makes 24

Borek is the Middle Eastern name for these small savoury parcels of paper-thin filo pastry, which make delicious appetizers. Sheets of filo pastry can be bought in rolls from Greek or Middle Eastern food stores. Wrap filo pastry that you are not working with in a damp cloth to prevent it drying out.
1. Put the chopped eggs, cheese, onion, mint, salt, dukkah and Cayenne into a bowl. Mix thoroughly, then stir in the beaten egg to bind.
2. Cut each sheet of filo pastry into 4 rectangles, and brush each one with melted butter.
3. Place one teaspoonful of filling on one end of a filo pastry rectangle. Fold both long sides over, then roll up to make a small rectangular parcel. Repeat until all the pastry rectangles are used up.
4. Brush the boreks all over with melted butter and arrange on oiled baking sheets.
5. Bake in a preheated moderate oven for 12-15 minutes, or until crisp and golden brown. Serve hot.

STUFFED TROUT WITH SUMAC

50g (2oz) butter
2 tablespoons finely chopped fresh parsley
2 tablespoons finely chopped fresh basil
4 large spring onions, trimmed and chopped
2 tablespoons finely chopped fresh mint
2 tablespoons radish leaves, finely chopped (optional)
1 teaspoon ground sumac or lemon juice
½ teaspoon ground turmeric
2 tablespoons stale breadcrumbs
½ teaspoon salt
4 medium trout, cleaned, washed and dried
2 tablespoons olive oil
TO GARNISH
lime wedges
fresh basil or thyme

Preparation time: 10 minutes
Cooking time: 25 minutes
Oven: 200°C, 400°F, Gas Mark 6

A fragrant Middle Eastern dish of baked fish, with a herby stuffing to which sumac lends a pleasant astringency.
1. Melt the butter in a small frying pan. Add the chopped herbs and onion and fry over a gentle heat for 2-3 minutes, stirring constantly.
2. Add the sumac, turmeric, breadcrumbs and salt to the pan and fry for a further 2-3 minutes, stirring until all the fat is absorbed and the stuffing is well mixed.
3. Divide stuffing into four portions and use to fill the cavity in each fish. Close with wooden cocktail sticks.
4. Heat the oil in a large flameproof baking dish over a fierce heat, add the fish and brown lightly on both sides over a moderate heat.
5. Bake in a preheated hot oven, basting once or twice, until the flesh is white and flakes easily. Serve on a warmed serving dish, garnished with lime wedges and fresh basil.

MOROCCAN CHICKEN PIE

FILLING
1.5kg (3¼lb) oven-ready chicken, jointed
1 onion, peeled and roughly chopped
3 garlic cloves, peeled and sliced
1 × 7.5cm (3 inch) piece cinnamon stick
½ teaspoon ground ginger
½ teaspoon ground cloves
½ teaspoon ground allspice
½ teaspoon ground turmeric
4 tablespoons chopped fresh parsley
salt
freshly ground black pepper
2 tablespoons lemon juice
4 eggs, lightly beaten
PASTRY
16 sheets filo pastry, defrosted if frozen
100g (4oz) butter, melted
100g (4oz) almonds, toasted and coarsely chopped
1 tablespoon caster sugar
1 teaspoon ground cinnamon
½ teaspoon ground allspice
1 teaspoon salt
egg yolk, to glaze

Preparation time: 30 minutes
Cooking time: 2 hours
Oven: 180°C, 350°F, Gas Mark 4
Serves 8-10

A rich, suble party dish.
1. Put the chicken pieces and all the filling ingredients except the lemon juice and eggs in a large, heavy-based saucepan. Pour in water to cover, bring to the boil, cover and simmer for 45 minutes.
2. Lift out the chicken and remove and discard the skin and bones. Cut the flesh into neat small pieces.
3. Strain the stock into a saucepan, add lemon juice

and boil rapidly to reduce to approximately 300ml (½ pint). Season well with salt and pepper. Pour half the stock into a bowl. Add the eggs to the stock in the pan and stir over a low heat until soft curds form.
4. Grease a rectangular 25 x 20cm (10×8 inch) ovenproof dish and line with a layer of filo pastry leaving a 2.5cm (1 inch) overlap. Brush with melted butter. Repeat the layers 5 times, brushing the layers with butter. Sprinkle with half the almonds, half the sugar and half the allspice and spoon in half the egg curd mixture.
5. Over this arrange 4 layers of filo pastry, brushing each with melted butter as it is laid down. Arrange the chicken meat on top, then spoon over the remaining egg curd mixture and sprinkle over the remaining almonds, sugar and spice. Pour in stock.
6. Fold the edges of the filo pastry in over the filling. Layer the remaining sheets of filo pastry on top, brushing each layer with melted butter and tucking the edges into the sides of the dish.
7. Brush with egg yolk and bake in a preheated moderate oven for 45-60 minutes.

From the right, clockwise:
Moroccan chicken pie;
Cheese and egg borek;
Stuffed trout with sumac

GARLIC SAUSAGE EN BRIOCHE

15g (½oz) fresh yeast
2 tablespoons tepid milk
200g (7oz) strong plain white flour
½ teaspoon salt
1 teaspoon caster sugar
2 eggs
100g (4oz) butter, at room temperature
1 tablespoon oil
2 garlic cloves, peeled and finely chopped
450g (1lb) pork sausagemeat
1½ teaspoons Quatre epices (p 24)
1½ teaspoons chopped fresh sage or a large pinch of dried sage
1 tablespoon top of the milk or single cream, for glazing

Preparation time: 30 minutes, plus proving
Cooking time: 1 hour 10 minutes
Oven: 190°C, 375°F, Gas Mark 5

1. Cream the yeast with 2 tablespoons tepid milk in a small bowl.
2. Sift the flour into a warmed mixing bowl with the salt and sugar. Make a well in the centre.
3. Break the eggs into the well, add the yeast mixture and gradually draw the flour into the liquid, beating vigorously with a wooden spoon.
4. Cream the butter and gradually stir into the mixture. Process in a food processor for 2-3 minutes, by hand for 10 minutes.
5. Place the dough in a large clean bowl, cover with a cloth and leave in a warm place to prove for 2 hours.
6. Knock back the dough, knead for 5 minutes and cover the bowl again. Leave in a warm place until required.
7. Heat the oil in a frying pan, add the garlic and sausagemeat and fry over a moderate heat for 10 minutes. Drain off the fat if necessary and leave to cool slightly, then sprinkle with the Quatre epices and sage.
8. Place the dough on a buttered baking sheet and flatten out roughly into a rectangle 25×15cm (10×6 inches). Place the sausage mixture in the middle, wet the fingers and draw the edges together, pressing lightly to seal. (Do not worry if the dough seems sticky and unmanageable.) Leave in a warm place for 10 minutes.
9. Brush the brioche all over with the milk and bake in the oven for 30 minutes. Serve warm, cut into slices, with a crisp green salad of lettuce, cress and cucumber.

Below: *Garlic sausage en brioche*
Opposite from the top: *Venison au poivre; Peppered lamb's liver*

PEPPERED LAMB'S LIVER

450g (1lb) lamb's liver, cut into very thin slices, about 5× 2.5cm (2×1 inches)
2 tablespoons lemon juice
salt
2 tablespoons black peppercorns, coarsely crushed
25g (1oz) butter
1 tablespoon vegetable oil
1 tablespoon Cinzano or white wine
1 tablespoon mild mustard
4-5 tablespoons soured cream
finely chopped fresh parsley, to sprinkle

Preparation time: 10 minutes
Cooking time: about 5 minutes

1. Pat the liver dry with absorbent paper and sprinkle with lemon juice and a little salt.
2. Turn the liver slices in the crushed peppercorns to coat lightly.
3. Heat the butter and oil in a large, heavy-based frying pan. Add the liver slices and fry over a moderate heat, for about 3 minutes, turning once, until the liver is cooked but still slightly pink inside.
4. Transfer the liver to a warmed dish. Stir the Cinzano then the mustard into the pan juices, stir well to mix, add the cream and heat through gently, but do not allow to boil.
5. Pour the sauce over the liver, sprinkle with parsley and serve at once, with mashed potatoes and garden peas, if wished.

VENISON AU POIVRE

1kg (2lb) lean venison, cut into 8 equal pieces about 2cm (¾ inch) thick
2 teaspoons black peppercorns, crushed
3 tablespoons fresh orange juice
600ml (1 pint) beef stock
1 carrot, scraped and grated
1 onion, peeled and finely chopped
2 garlic cloves, peeled and crushed
1 celery stick, finely chopped
1 sprig thyme
1 tablespoon red wine vinegar
25g (1oz) plain flour
25g (1oz) butter, softened
4 tablespoons vegetable oil
3 tablespoons redcurrant jelly
2 tablespoons port
salt
freshly ground black pepper

Preparation time: 30 minutes, plus marinading
Cooking time: 45 minutes
Serves 6

Venison is a lean meat with little fat and therefore is greatly improved by being marinated for several hours. This softens the fibres of the meat, making it more tender and juicy and better suited to a quick cooking method. The rich flavour of venison is delicious with this peppery sweet and sour sauce. This recipe is especially suitable for frozen venison. If venison is unavailable veal may be used instead.

1. Arrange the venison pieces in a shallow dish, sprinkle with half the peppercorns and the orange juice and leave to marinate for 2 hours, turning once or twice.
2. Put the stock, carrot, onion, garlic, celery and thyme into a saucepan and bring to the boil. Lower the heat, cover and simmer for 30 minutes, skimming the pan occasionally.
3. Strain into a bowl, pressing with the back of a wooden spoon to extract all the liquid. Return to the pan, add the vinegar and the remaining peppercorns and bring to the boil.
3. Work together the flour and butter and whisk it into the pan in small pieces, whisking well between each addition until the sauce is thick and glossy. Season to taste with salt and pepper, remove from the heat and keep hot.
4. Heat the oil in a preheated frying pan, add the venison pieces with the peppercorns, and fry over a high heat for 2 minutes on each side. Remove from the pan and keep warm.
5. Add the strained hot sauce to the pan with the redcurrant jelly and port. Season to taste with salt and pepper and stir over a moderate heat until the redcurrant jelly is melted. Return the venison pieces to the pan and cook over a gentle heat for 5 minutes until tender. Serve with creamy mashed potatoes and a crispy vegetable.

MUTTON HAM

2.25kg (5lb) leg of lamb
225g (8oz) sea salt
75g (3oz) soft light brown sugar
15g (½oz) saltpetre
25g (1oz) whole allspice crushed (p 12)
25g (1oz) black peppercorns, crushed
15g (½oz) coriander seeds, crushed
TO GARNISH
watercress sprigs
fresh orange segments

Preparation time: 10 minutes, plus curing
Cooking time: 2½ hours
Serves 6

Lamb cured like ham has a rich, spicy flavour and an attractive reddish-brown colour. It is especially good eaten cold.

1. Pat the lamb dry with absorbent paper. In a bowl combine the salt, sugar and spices and generously rub the lamb all over with the mixture. Put the lamb in a large bowl and leave for one week in a cool larder or in the bottom of the refrigerator. Turn the lamb every day, spooning over it the dark liquid which will accumulate in the bowl.
2. Remove the lamb and wipe all over with a damp cloth. Place the lamb in a large saucepan and pour in cold water to cover. Bring very slowly to the boil, then cover and simmer for about 2½ hours, until thoroughly cooked.
3. Remove the lamb, wipe again with a damp cloth, then wrap tightly in a clean tea-towel. Place between two chopping boards, on a large platter, and weight down. Leave overnight.
4. The following day unwrap the lamb, place on a large serving platter and garnish with watercress sprigs and orange segments. Serve in thin slices, with fresh crusty bread and accompanied by a bowl of peach or mango chutney.

Below: *Mutton ham*

ROAST LAMB WITH SPICY STUFFING

1.75kg (4lb) leg of lamb, boned and trimmed
4 tablespoons long-grain rice
3 tablespoons vegetable oil
1 onion, peeled and finely chopped
2 garlic cloves, peeled and chopped
1 sachet powdered saffron
25g (1oz) flaked almonds, lightly roasted
2 tablespoons seedless raisins
½ teaspoon ground allspice
½ teaspoon powdered cinnamon
salt
freshly ground black pepper
4 tablespoons fresh orange juice

Preparation time: 25 minutes
Cooking time: 1 hour 35 minutes
Oven: 180°C, 350°F, Gas Mark 4

1. Open out the boned leg of lamb and rub the skin side lightly with a little of the oil.
2. Cook the rice in boiling salted water for 10 minutes, then drain thoroughly.
3. Heat the remaining oil in a large frying pan, add the onion and garlic and fry over a gentle heat for 5 minutes until soft and lightly coloured. Remove from the heat. Add the saffron and almonds, and stir over a gentle heat for 2 minutes, until the mixture is golden.
4. Add the cooked rice, raisins, and spices to the pan and stir well to mix. Leave to cool for 5 minutes.
5. Spoon the stuffing into the hollow in the boned leg of lamb, spreading it out evenly. Roll up the lamb and secure in several places with string or meat skewers and transfer to preheated oven.
6. Place the lamb in a roasting tin and roast in a preheated moderate oven for 45 minutes. Pour over

From the left: *Roast lamb with spicy stuffing; Lamb with cumin and garlic*

half the orange juice and cook for a further 30 minutes, or until the lamb is done to your liking. Pour over the remaining orange juice.
7. Transfer the lamb to a heated carving dish and keep warm. Add a little water to the juices in the tin and heat through on top of the cooker, scraping the base and sides of the tin with a wooden spoon.
8. Serve the lamb carved into thick slices, with baked potatoes, a green salad and the gravy.

LAMB WITH CUMIN AND GARLIC

1.75kg (4lb) shoulder of lamb
4 tablespoons olive oil
4 garlic cloves, peeled and cut into slivers
4 cloves garlic, peeled and crushed
2 tablespoons ground cumin
salt
freshly ground black pepper

Preparation time: 15 minutes
Cooking time: about 1¾ hours
Oven: 180°C, 350°F, Gas Mark 4

In this oven-cooked version of Arab *mechoui,* traditionally cooked over an open fire, the powerful taste of garlic blends with cumin to make a delicious crusty coating over the slowly roasted lamb.
1. Pat the lamb dry with absorbent paper and rub with ½ tablespoon of the oil. Make small cuts in the surface and insert a sliver of garlic into each.
2. Mix the crushed garlic with the cumin and the remaining oil, to make a thick paste. Season with salt and pepper. Spread over the meat, rubbing it in well.
3. Place the lamb in a roasting tin on a rack and roast in the centre of the oven for about 1¾ hours, basting from time to time with the pan juices.
4. Serve the lamb carved into thick slices, accompanied by new potatoes, sliced cucumber and a dressing of plain yogurt flavoured with mint.

VARIATION

A less pungent dish can be prepared using finely ground onion instead of garlic. For best results onion juice (made by squeezing chopped onion in a garlic press) should be rubbed over the meat, which is left to stand for an hour before cooking. Onion pulp is then mixed with cumin and salt and pepper and rubbed over the lamb before roasting.

LAMB CUTLETS WITH ORANGE JUICE AND ANISEED

8 lamb cutlets, approximately 150g (5oz) each, trimmed of fat
450ml (¾ pint) fresh orange juice
1 tablespoon aniseed, crushed
2.5cm (1 inch) piece fresh ginger root, grated
2 tablespoons soft light brown sugar
salt
½ teaspoon freshly ground black pepper
1 tablespoon cornflour
2 tablespoons medium sherry
orange slices, to garnish

Preparation time: 10 minutes, plus marinading
Cooking time: 1 hour 20 minutes
Oven: 170°C, 325°F, Gas Mark 3

Braising lamb chops in spicy orange juice gives them an excitingly different flavour; pungent and warming.

1. Arrange the cutlets in a single layer in a shallow baking dish. Combine the orange juice, aniseed, ginger, sugar and salt and pepper and pour over the chops. Leave to marinade for 2 hours.
2. Cover the dish with a lid or foil and cook in a preheated oven, basting frequently, for about 1¼ hours, until the lamb chops are tender.
3. Transfer the chops to a warmed serving dish and keep warm. Skim the fat from the cooking juices and pour into a small saucepan. Boil fast to reduce for 10-15 minutes, then stir in the cornflour, sherry, reheat and pour over the chops.
4. Garnish with orange slices and serve.

PORK CHOPS WITH ORANGE JUICE AND GINGER

4 large pork chops, about 225g (8oz) each, trimmed
1 tablespoon vegetable oil
salt
freshly ground black pepper
1 garlic clove, peeled and crushed
a strip thinly pared orange rind, blanched and cut into fine shreds
juice of 2 oranges
1 small piece preserved stem ginger, chopped
1 tablespoon ginger syrup
1 tablespoon cornflour

TO GARNISH

1 small piece preserved stem ginger, finely sliced
sprigs of fresh rosemary

Preparation time: 10 minutes
Cooking time: 15 minutes
Oven: 110°C, 225°F, Gas Mark ¼

1. Pat the pork chops dry with absorbent paper. Brush the chops with oil and season with salt, pepper and garlic.
2. Grill the pork chops for 2-3 minutes on each side under a preheated hot grill to seal and brown. Reduce the grill to moderate and grill for a further 5 minutes on each side, until the chops are browned and cooked through. Transfer the pork chops to a heated serving dish and keep warm in a preheated low oven.
3. Put the orange rind and juice with the ginger and ginger syrup into a small saucepan, stir in the juices from the grill pan and the cornflour and bring to the boil. Simmer for 1 minute then pour over the chops.
4. Transfer to individual plates. Garnish each plate with ginger and a sprig of fresh rosemary and serve.

PORK WITH SWEET PEPPERS

50g (2oz) butter
1 tablespoon vegetable oil
500g (1¼lb) pork fillet, cut into strips 2cm (¾ inch) wide
1 large Spanish onion, peeled and finely sliced
1×350g (12oz) can sweet red peppers, drained and cut into 2cm (¾ inch) squares
1 teaspoon coriander seeds
pinch of sugar
salt
freshly ground black pepper
150ml (5fl oz) white or rosé wine
150ml (5fl oz) soured cream
paprika, to sprinkle

Preparation time: 15 minutes
Cooking time: 1 hour 10 minutes
Oven: 190°C, 375°F, Gas Mark 5

1. Heat the butter and oil in a large heavy-based pan and when sizzling add the pork strips a few at a time. Fry over a moderate heat for 2-3 minutes, turning frequently, to seal and brown on all sides. Using a slotted spoon, transfer the pork to a casserole and fry the remaining pork in batches in the same way.
2. Lower the heat, add the onions to the pan and fry over a gentle heat for about 10 minutes, until soft and light golden.
3. Add the peppers to the pan, stir well to mix, then add the onions and peppers to the casserole. Add the coriander and sugar and season to taste with salt and black pepper.
4. Pour the wine into the pan, bring to the boil and allow to bubble over a moderate heat for 1-2 minutes, stirring and scraping the sides and base of the pan to remove any sediment. Pour into the casserole, cover and cook in a preheated low oven for 1 hour, until the pork is tender and cooked through.
5. Using a slotted spoon, transfer the pork and vegetables to a warmed serving dish and keep warm. Stir the soured cream into the sauce in the casserole. Reheat gently on top of the stove without boiling and pour over the pork and vegetables. Sprinkle with paprika and serve with buttered noodles.

From the top, clockwise: *Pork chops with orange juice and ginger; Pork with sweet peppers; Lamb cutlets with orange juice and aniseed*

BEEF STROGANOV

50g (2oz) butter
1 medium Spanish onion, peeled, or 2 bunches spring onions, trimmed and chopped
100g (4oz) mushrooms, sliced
150ml (5fl oz) red wine
1 teaspoon German mustard
150ml (5fl oz) soured cream
½ teaspoon caraway seeds
pinch of sugar
salt
freshly ground black pepper
750g (1½lb) fillet or sirloin steak, cut into strips

Preparation time: 10 minutes
Cooking time: 20 minutes

1. Melt 20g (¾oz) of the butter in a saucepan, add the onion and fry over a gentle heat for 5 minutes until soft and lightly coloured.
2. Push the onions to one side of the pan. Melt a further 10g (¼oz) butter in the pan, add the mushrooms and stir to coat.
3. Add the wine, cover the pan and simmer for about 10 minutes or until almost all the liquid is absorbed. Stir in the mustard, soured cream, caraway seeds, sugar, salt and pepper. Heat through gently, but do not allow to boil.
4. Melt the remaining butter in a large frying pan, add the steak strips and fry for 2 minutes on each side for fillet steak and 3 minutes for sirloin.
5. Transfer the steak strips to a warmed serving dish, pour over the sauce and serve accompanied by buttered new potatoes with an orange and watercress salad to follow.

HUNGARIAN POTTED CHEESE

150g (5oz) unsalted butter
225g (8oz) cream cheese
1 teaspoon German mustard
4 teaspoons paprika
2 tablespoons beer
1 teaspoon grated onion
½ teaspoon caraway seeds
1 teaspoon finely chopped fresh parsley
1 teaspoon finely chopped chives
salt
freshly ground black pepper
sprigs of fresh mint, to garnish

Preparation time: 5 minutes, plus chilling

1. Cream the butter in a mixing bowl, or food processor and then work in the remaining ingredients.
2. Pack the mixture into individual pots and chill. Garnish with sprigs of fresh mint and serve with crackers or fingers of buttered toast.

PICKLED HERRINGS

200g (7oz) sea salt
1.75 litres (3 pints) cold water
8 herrings, boned and filleted
PICKLING LIQUID
1.75 litres (3 pints) white wine or cider vinegar
50g (2oz) soft light brown sugar
4 tablespoons pickling spice
2 teaspoons whole black peppercorns
2 teaspoons dill seeds
1 bay leaf
½ Spanish onion, peeled and thinly sliced
fresh dill, to garnish
SOURED CREAM DRESSING
2 teaspoons French mustard
1 tablespoon chopped fresh dill
300ml (½ pint) soured cream

Preparation time: 15 minutes, plus soaking and pickling

1. Dissolve the salt in the water in a bowl. Add the herrings and leave to soak for at least 3 hours.
2. Bring the vinegar, sugar and spices to the boil in a saucepan, then remove from the heat and leave to infuse and cool completely. Strain when cold.
3. Pat the herrings dry with absorbent paper. Place onion slices on each fillet, then roll up and secure with cocktail sticks. Place them in sterilized jars with non-metallic lids and pour in the pickling liquid to cover. Leave in the refrigerator for 3-4 days.
4. Combine the mustard, dill and soured cream in a bowl, whisking with a fork until smooth. Arrange the rolled herring fillets on a serving dish and pour the dressing over. Garnish with fresh dill and serve with rye bread.

Opposite, from the top: *Beef goulash; Pickled herrings with soured cream dressing; Beef stroganov (recipe previous page); Hungarian potted cheese*

BEEF GOULASH

1kg (2lb) lean stewing beef, trimmed of fat, cut into 5cm (2 inch) cubes
2 tablespoons plain flour
½ teaspoon salt
freshly ground black pepper
4 tablespoons vegetable oil
225g (8oz) onions, peeled and roughly chopped
2 carrots, scraped and sliced
1 × 400g (14oz) can tomatoes
½ tablespoon caraway seeds
1 tablespoon paprika
150ml (5fl oz) soured cream

Preparation time: 20 minutes
Cooking time: 2¾-3 hours
Oven: 180°C, 350°F, Gas Mark 4

Although traditionally made with beef, pork, veal and chicken can also be used for goulash. Each region of Hungary has its own special version of this recipe: some include fresh tomatoes, others include caraway seeds or marjoram. Paprika and caraway seeds give this rich, warming dish its typically Hungarian flavour, as does the last-minute addition of soured cream.

1. Pat the beef cubes dry with absorbent paper. Mix the flour with the salt and pepper and dust the beef cubes lightly but thoroughly on all sides.
2. Heat the oil in a large heavy-based frying pan. Add the beef cubes and fry over a brisk heat for 3-4 minutes, turning frequently, to seal and brown on all sides. Using a slotted spoon, transfer the beef cubes to a large casserole. Add the onions to the pan and fry gently for 5 minutes until soft and lightly coloured, then add to the casserole.
3. Add the carrots and the tomatoes with their juice to the casserole. Stir in the caraway seeds and paprika. Cover the casserole with foil, then with the lid. Cook in a preheated moderate oven for 2 hours, until the beef is tender and cooked through.
4. Stir in the soured cream, taste and adjust the seasoning and cook for a further 15 minutes, uncovered, stirring occasionally.
5. Serve the goulash with buttered noodles or plain boiled potatoes and a crisp winter vegetable such as buttered cabbage.

VARIATION

Boiled suet dumplings can be served with the goulash for a typically Central European touch, instead of potatoes or noodles.

To make the dumplings, sift 225 g (8 oz) self-raising flour, and a pinch of salt into a bowl. Stir in 100 g (4 oz) shredded suet and add enough cold water to make a light dough. Divide the dough into small pieces and roll into balls with the palms of the hands. Drop into boiling salted water or beef stock and cook for 15-20 minutes. Add to the goulash with the soured cream.

CABBAGE WITH SOURED CREAM

salt
1 large green cabbage, about 750 - 2 kg (1 ½-2 lb), roughly chopped
50 g (2 oz) butter
½ teaspoon caraway seeds
freshly ground black pepper
½ teaspoon paprika
150 ml (¼ pint) soured cream
½ teaspoon caraway seeds, to garnish

Preparation time: 3 minutes
Cooking time: 12-15 minutes
Serves 6

Serve this hot cabbage dish as an unusual accompaniment to pork or lamb roasts.

1. Bring 2.5 cm (1 inch) salted water to the boil in a large saucepan, add the cabbage, cover and cook over a moderate heat for 6-8 minutes, or until barely tender. Drain well.
2. Melt the butter in the rinsed out pan, add the drained cabbage, with the caraway seeds and stir well. Season to taste with salt and pepper, then stir in the paprika and soured cream. Cook over the lowest possible heat, without boiling, for 3 minutes until cooked through.
3. Transfer to a warmed serving dish, sprinkle with caraway seeds and serve.

Below: *Cabbage with soured cream*

POTATOES AND ARTICHOKE HEARTS, MIDDLE EASTERN STYLE

1 teaspoon salt
juice of 3 lemons
1 teaspoon coriander seeds
1 teaspoon fennel seeds
1 teaspoon whole black peppercorns
3 cloves garlic, peeled and bruised
450ml (¾ pint) water
5 tablespoons olive oil
½ teaspoon caster sugar
4 large fresh artichokes, stems removed
2 medium potatoes, peeled and cut into 2.5cm (1 inch) pieces
1 medium onion, peeled and quartered
1 orange, peeled and segmented
8-10 black olives
½ teaspoon coriander seeds, crushed
1 lettuce, to serve

Preparation time: 10 minutes
Cooking time: 35 minutes

This aromatic salad makes a delicious first course. Unlike many salads, it can be made all year round; when fresh artichokes are out of season, canned ones can be used instead.

1. Bring a large pan of water to the boil. Add the salt and juice of 1 lemon and the artichokes. Simmer for 20-25 minutes until a leaf pulls out easily. Remove the artichokes and leave upside down to drain. Leave to cool.
2. Meanwhile tie the coriander and fennel seeds, peppercorns and garlic in a piece of muslin. Place in a saucepan with the water and bring to the boil. Simmer, covered, for 20 minutes. Remove the spice bundle with a slotted spoon and allow to cool slightly, then squeeze well to extract the flavour. Add the juice of 1 lemon, the oil, and sugar to the pan, stir well and set aside.
3. Using a teaspoon carefully remove the hairy choke from the base of each artichoke heart. Cut each heart into quarters and rub all the cut surfaces with the remaining lemon juice to prevent discoloration.
4. Bring the spiced liquid to the boil and add the artichoke hearts, potatoes and onions. Cover the pan, lower the heat and simmer for about 12 minutes or until the potatoes and artichoke hearts are tender. Taste and adjust the seasoning.
5. Leave for 2-3 hours to cool in the liquid. Stir in the orange segments, olives and coriander and toss gently. To serve, arrange a bed of lettuce on a serving dish and spoon the vegetables on top.

From the left: *Potatoes and artichoke hearts, Middle Eastern style; Turkish stuffed courgettes*

TURKISH STUFFED COURGETTES

750g (1 ½lb) whole courgettes
150g (5oz) long-grain rice
4 tablespoons olive oil
1 tesaspoon ground turmeric
1 large onion, peeled and finely chopped
3 garlic cloves, peeled and crushed
25g (1oz) flaked almonds or pine nuts
2 tablespoons finely chopped fresh parsley
½ teaspoon paprika
salt
freshly ground black pepper
6 tablespoons lemon juice

Preparation time: 8 minutes
Cooking time: 45 minutes
Oven: 180°C, 350°F, Gas Mark 4

These courgettes make an attractive accompaniment to fish or chicken. Or they can be served alone, as a starter, with a sauce of plain unsweetened yogurt whisked up with salt, a little crushed garlic and a tablespoon of lemon juice.

1. Cook the whole courgettes in a large saucepan of boiling salted water for 10 minutes, then drain and cool. Cut in half lengthways and carefully scoop out the seeds.
2. Cook the rice in a large saucepan of boiling salted water for 12 minutes, then drain and cool.
3. Heat the oil in a frying pan, add the turmeric, onion and garlic and fry over a gentle heat, stirring, for 2 minutes. Add the almonds and fry for a further 30 seconds.
4. Add the cooked rice to the pan and mix gently to heat through. Remove the pan from the heat and stir in the parsley, and paprika, with salt and pepper to taste.
5. Spoon the stuffing into the halved courgettes and arrange them close together in a medium roasting tin. Pour enough water into the tin to come 1 cm (½ inch) up the sides of the courgettes. Sprinkle the stuffed courgettes with the lemon juice. Cover with foil and cook in a preheated moderate oven for about 30 minutes, or until tender. Serve hot or allow to cool, transfer to a serving dish and serve cold.

Below, from the top: *Purée of Brussels sprouts; Braised onions*
Opposite, from the top: *Red cabbage with chestnuts; Franklin's potatoes*

BRAISED ONIONS

500g (1 ¼lb) onions, peeled and finely sliced
2 garlic cloves, peeled and finely chopped
2 tablespoons olive oil
1 tablespoon white wine or cider vinegar
1 tablespoon paprika
2 teaspoons sugar
salt
freshly ground black pepper
TO SERVE
2 teaspoons finely chopped fresh parsley
150ml (¼ pint) soured cream

Preparation time: 5 minutes
Cooking time: 2 hours
Oven: 160°C, 325°F, Gas Mark 3

1. Lightly oil a large casserole and put in the onions, garlic, oil, vinegar, paprika, sugar, salt and pepper.
2. Cover the casserole and cook in a preheated moderate oven for 2 hours, stirring occasionally.
3. Transfer the onions to a warmed serving dish and sprinkle with parsley and serve accompanied by soured cream.

PURÉE OF BRUSSELS SPROUTS

salt
750g (1 ½lb) Brussels sprouts, trimmed
50g (2oz) butter
1 garlic clove, peeled and crushed
¼ teaspoon freshly grated nutmeg
freshly ground black pepper
2 tablespoons double cream
1 tablespoon double cream, to garnish

Preparation time: 5 minutes
Cooking time: 12 minutes

A familiar vegetable gets a new look when puréed and flavoured with garlic.
1. Bring 2.5cm (1 inch) salted water to the boil in a large saucepan. Add the sprouts and cook, uncovered, for 6-8 minutes, or until the sprouts are very tender. Drain.
2. Purée the sprouts by hand or work in a food processor for 30 seconds, depending on whether a coarse or fine purée is wanted.
3. Melt the butter in the rinsed out pan, add the garlic and fry for 1 minute, then return the sprouts, and stir well to coat in butter. Add the nutmeg and salt and pepper to taste. Heat through over a low heat for 2 minutes, shaking the pan once or twice. Stir in the cream and transfer to a warmed serving dish, garnished with a spoonful of double cream.

FRANKLIN'S POTATOES

450ml (¾ pint) milk
½ onion studded with 4 cloves
blade of mace
bay leaf
parsley stalk
6 whole black peppercorns
100g (4oz) fresh soft breadcrumbs
25g (1oz) butter
2 tablespoons double cream
salt
freshly ground black pepper
butter, for greasing
750g (1 ½lb) new potatoes, thinly sliced
1 sprig fresh bay, to garnish

Preparation time: 10 minutes, plus infusing
Cooking time: about 2¼ hours
Oven: 150°C, 300°F, Gas Mark 2

This is a very adaptable dish. If the potatoes are to be cooked alone, follow the cooking time and oven temperature given below. If however you wish to serve the potatoes as an accompaniment to a roast, the cooking time and oven temperature can be adapted as convenient, for example to 1¼ hours at 190°C, 375°F, Gas Mark 5.

1. Put the milk into a saucepan with the onion, mace, bay leaf, parsley stalk and peppercorns. Warm over a gentle heat, then remove from the heat and leave to infuse for 20 minutes. Strain.
2. In a bowl, combine the breadcrumbs, butter and cream with the milk. Beat well with a wooden spoon until the sauce is smooth, then season to taste with salt and pepper.
3. Grease a small casserole. Arrange layers of potatoes in the casserole, pouring a little sauce between each layer and finishing with sauce.
4. Bake in a preheated oven for about 2 hours or until the potatoes are tender when pierced with a sharp knife.
5. Garnish with a sprig of bay and serve.

RED CABBAGE WITH CHESTNUTS

450g (1lb) chestnuts
175g (6oz) prunes, soaked overnight, stoned and roughly chopped
175g (6oz) cooking apples, peeled, cored and chopped
1 medium onion, peeled and finely chopped
1 × 1kg (2lb) red cabbage, shredded
salt
freshly ground black pepper
1 tablespoon soft light brown sugar
2 tablespoons cider vinegar
200ml (7fl oz) beef stock
1 teaspoon ground coriander

Preparation time: 30 minutes
Cooking time: 2 hours
Oven: 150°C, 300°F, Gas Mark 2
Serves 8

Red cabbage is never boiled or steamed, but cooked slowly in a casserole with plenty of spices and flavourings. Vinegar helps to preserve the cabbage's bright colour during cooking and adds a welcome sharpness to the finished dish. This should be cooked in a glazed earthenware or enamelled iron casserole; an enamelled one would be too thin and might cause the cabbage to stick or burn.

1. Prick the chestnuts and cook in a saucepan of boiling water for 20 minutes. Drain and leave until cool enough to handle, then peel and halve.
2. In a casserole, make layers of the chestnuts, prunes, apples, onion and red cabbage. Season with salt and pepper.
3. Combine the sugar, vinegar, stock and coriander and pour over the vegetables.
4. Cook in a preheated low oven for 2 hours, stirring occasionally. Taste 30 minutes before serving. If too bland add a little more vinegar and sugar. Transfer to a heated serving dish and serve with pork or game.

ORANGE AND CELERY SALAD

4 oranges, peeled and separated into segments, all pith and membrane removed
1 head celery, finely sliced
1 mild onion, peeled and coarsely chopped
1 teaspoon coriander seeds, lightly crushed
DRESSING
2 tablespoons red wine vinegar or lemon juice
5 tablespoons olive oil
salt
freshly ground black pepper
celery leaves, to garnish

Preparation time: 10 minutes

This refreshing, juicy salad goes well with most cold meats.

1. Place the orange segments, celery and onion in a salad bowl. Fork through lightly to mix. Sprinkle with the coriander seeds.
2. Combine all the dressing ingredients and whisk together with a fork to blend thoroughly. Pour over the salad, toss gently and garnish with celery leaves.

COLESLAW

225 g (8 oz) white cabbage, finely shredded
175 g (6 oz) red cabbage, finely shredded
1 small onion, peeled and thinly sliced
50 g (2 oz) walnuts, chopped, or canned chestnuts, drained and chopped
½ teaspoon caraway seeds, lightly crushed
1 tablespoon sultanas
DRESSING
2 tablespoons cider vinegar or lemon juice
4 tablespoons olive oil
1 teaspoon clear honey
1 teaspoon Dijon mustard
½ teaspoon salt
6 tablespoons soured cream
1 teaspoon paprika, to sprinkle

Preparation time: 10 minutes, plus standing
Serves 4-6

Pungent caraway seeds add flavour to this nutty and colourful salad. Coleslaw will keep well for a couple of days in the refrigerator.

1. Combine the cabbage, onion, walnuts, caraway seeds and sultanas in a large salad bowl.
2. Combine all the dressing ingredients except the soured cream in a jug, whisking with a fork until thoroughly blended. Pour over the salad and toss well. Leave to stand for 30 minutes.
3. Just before serving stir the soured cream briskly with a fork until smooth, then pour over the dressed salad and toss again. Sprinkle the salad with the paprika and serve with sausages or gammon steaks and jacket potatoes.

RED CABBAGE WITH SOURED CREAM DRESSING

1 small red cabbage, about 350 g (12oz) shredded
1 small mild onion, peeled and finely sliced
1 large tart dessert apple, peeled, cored and sliced
1 teaspoon cumin seeds, crushed to a powder
1 tablespoon poppy seeds
DRESSING
150 ml (5 fl oz) soured cream
2 teaspoons Dijon mustard
1 tablespoon wine vinegar or lemon juice
2 teaspoons sugar
salt

Preparation time: 5 minutes, plus standing

1. Put the cabbage, onion and apple in a large salad bowl and fork through to mix. Sprinkle with the cumin and poppy seeds.
2. Combine all the dressing ingredients and whisk with a fork to blend thoroughly. Pour over the salad and toss with 2 salad spoons to distribute evenly.

FRENCH BEANS IN TOMATO SAUCE

450g (1lb) stringless French beans, topped and tailed
salt
3 tablespoons olive oil
1 onion, peeled and roughly chopped
2 garlic cloves, peeled and chopped
1 tablespoon chopped fresh parsley
1 × 400g (14oz) can tomatoes, chopped
1 teaspoon ground cumin
1 tablespoon wine vinegar
freshly ground black pepper
pinch of sugar
fresh celery leaves or parsley, to garnish

Preparation time: 10 minutes, plus infusing
Cooking time: about 50 minutes

1. Cook the beans in boiling salted water for about 10 minutes until they are tender but still slightly crunchy. Drain, rinse and drain again.
2. Heat 2 tablespoons of the oil in a large saucepan; add the onion, 1 garlic clove and the parsley and fry over a gentle heat for about 5 minutes.
3. Stir in the tomatoes with their juice, the cumin and wine vinegar. Cook over a gentle heat for about 30 minutes, then pass through a sieve. Season to taste with salt, pepper and the sugar.
4. Heat the remaining tablespoon of olive oil in the rinsed out pan, add the remaining garlic clove and and fry over a gentle heat for 2-3 minutes until softened. Toss the beans in the oil, using wooden spoons so as not to break them up.
5. Transfer the beans to a warmed serving dish, pour over the tomato sauce, forking it through the beans. Garnish with celery leaves or fresh parsley and serve.

Opposite, clockwise from the bottom: *Orange and celery salad; Red cabbage with soured cream dressing; Coleslaw*

LOBSTER TANDOORI

100g (4oz) plain unsweetened yogurt
1 teaspoon cumin seeds, roasted and ground
1 teaspoon coriander seeds, roasted and ground
1 garlic clove, peeled and crushed
1cm (½ inch) piece fresh ginger, peeled and grated
½ teaspoon saffron strands, soaked in 1 tablespoon hot water
4 tablespoons lemon juice
1 large cooked lobster, about 1kg (2lb), halved
½ teaspoon salt
40g (1½oz) butter or ghee, diced
fresh coriander, to garnish

Preparation time: 10 minutes, plus marinating
Cooking time: 8-10 minutes
Serves 4 as part of an Indian meal

Ask your fishmonger to halve the lobster and remove the spongy gills and intestinal vein.
1. Put the yogurt in a blender with the spices, garlic, ginger, saffron and soaking water and process until smooth.
2. Sprinkle the lemon juice over the cut sides of the lobster halves, sprinkle with salt, then spread with the yogurt mixture and leave to marinate for 2-8 hours.
3. Dot the lobster halves with the butter and grill under a preheated moderate grill until the lobster meat is white and firm, and the tandoori mixture is beginning to brown.
4. Garnish with coriander and serve sizzling hot with nan bread.

NAN

1kg (2lb) plain flour
¾ teaspoon baking powder
¼ teaspoon bicarbonate of soda
½ teaspoon salt
1 teaspoon sugar
1 egg
75ml (6fl oz) milk
100ml (4fl oz) water
25g (1oz) sesame seeds or 1 tablespoon nigella seeds

Preparation time: 25 minutes, plus proving
Cooking time: 7-10 minutes
Oven: 220°C, 425°F, Gas Mark 7
Makes about 12

Traditionally cooked in a tandoor oven, this soft bread is unusual among Indian breads in being made from a raised dough. It is good with curries or tandoori chicken and fish, or as an Indian version of a hamburger bun.
1. Sift the flour with the baking powder, bicarbonate of soda, salt and sugar into a mixing bowl. Make a well in the centre and add the egg. Mix well together.
2. Combine the milk and water, then gradually mix into the flour mixture. Knead the dough lightly for 5 minutes until soft and smooth.
3. Transfer the dough to a bowl, cover with cling film and leave in a warm place for about 45 minutes.
4. Knead the dough again for 5 minutes on a lightly floured board or work surface. Divide into 12 equal pieces and roll out into 12.5cm (5 inch) rounds.
5. Place the rounds on greased baking sheets, brush with milk and sprinkle with sesame or nigella seeds. Bake in a preheated hot oven until puffed up but firm. Serve hot.

POTATO SAMOSAS

PASTRY
450g (1lb) plain flour
½ teaspoon baking powder
1 teaspoon salt
25g (1oz) butter, melted
4 tablespoons plain unsweetened yogurt
about 4 tablespoons tepid water
FILLING
50g (2oz) butter
2 small onions, peeled and finely chopped
675g (1½lb) cooked potatoes, peeled and cut into small dice
2 fresh green chillies, seeded and finely chopped
2 teaspoons Garam masala (p 26)
3 teaspoons desiccated coconut
salt
vegetable oil, for deep frying

Preparation time: 30 minutes
Cooking time: 10 minutes
Makes 40

A classic Indian snack, made from the simplest ingredients, spicy and hot with chillies.
1. Sift the flour with the baking powder and salt into a mixing bowl. Make a well in the centre and add the melted butter and yogurt. Draw the flour into the liquid, using a wooden spoon, adding water as necessary to make a smooth dough. Knead until free from cracks and set aside.
2. Make the filling: melt the butter in a frying pan, add the onion and cook over a gentle heat for 5 minutes until soft and lightly coloured, then add the potatoes and chillies and fry until golden brown, turning frequently. Add the garam masala, and coconut, and season with salt. Stir well to mix and leave to cool.
3. On a lightly floured board or work surface roll 20 balls of dough the size of a shelled walnut into thin circles, 15cm (6 inches) in diameter. Cut each circle in half. Shape each semi-circle into a cone and fill with the potato mixture. Dampen the top edges with water and press together firmly to seal.
4. Heat oil in a deep-fryer to 180°C (350°F) or until a cube of bread browns in 30 seconds. Deep-fry the samosas, a few at a time, until golden brown all over.

Opposite, clockwise from the top: *Nan; Potato samosas; Lobster tandoori*

LAMB KORMA

150ml (¼pint) plain unsweetened yogurt
1 tablespoon coconut cream
3 garlic cloves, peeled and crushed
2.5cm (1 inch) piece fresh ginger root, grated
1 tablespoon poppy seeds, crushed
2 tablespoons coriander seeds, crushed
2.5 (1 inch) piece cinnamon stick, crushed
6 cloves, crushed
100g (4oz) ghee or butter
3 onions, peeled and thinly sliced
450g (1lb) lean lamb, trimmed and cut into 2.5cm (1 inch) cubes
salt, to taste
¼-1 fresh green chilli, seeded and finely sliced
juice of half a lemon
fresh coriander leaves or parsley, to garnish

Preparation time: 25 minutes
Cooking time: 1 hour

A classic Indian curry, creamy and mild. The korma method can be applied to beef, chicken, even fish. Serve with a selection of chutneys on a bed of rice.

1. Put the yogurt in a small mixing bowl and whisk with a fork until smooth.
2. Pound together the coconut cream, garlic and ginger with a pestle and mortar or process in a food processor for 30 seconds. Add the poppy seeds, coriander seeds, cinnamon and cloves.
3. Melt the ghee or butter in a large, heavy-based saucepan and stir-fry the onions until crisp and brown. Remove the onions and purée in a food processor or pass through a fine food mill.
4. Add the spice mixture to the same saucepan and cook gently for 5 minutes. Add the cubed meat, yogurt and salt, bring to the boil and simmer over a low heat for 45 minutes until the meat is tender and the sauce is brown.
5. Add the finely sliced chilli and lemon juice, stir well and simmer for another 5 minutes.
6. Transfer to a heated serving dish and serve with rice, garnished with fresh coriander.

SPICY CHICK PEAS

4 tablespoons vegetable oil
1 large onion, peeled and coarsely chopped
6 garlic cloves, peeled and finely chopped
1 tablespoon ground coriander seeds
2 teaspoons ground cumin seeds
½ teaspoon cayenne pepper
1 teaspoon ground turmeric
1×225g (8oz) can tomatoes, chopped
675g (1½lb) canned chick peas, drained
300ml (½pint) water
1 teaspoon Garam masala (p 26)
2 teaspoons cumin seeds, roasted then ground
1 tablespoon amchur, ground (p 12)
2 teaspoons paprika
salt
2 tablespoons lemon juice
1 fresh green chilli, finely chopped
1 teaspoon finely grated fresh ginger root
fresh green chilli to garnish (optional)

Preparation time: 10 minutes
Cooking time: 25 minutes
Serves 6

1. Heat the oil in a large frying pan with a lid, add the onion and garlic and fry over a gentle heat for 10 minutes until brown. Lower the heat and stir in the coriander, cumin, cayenne and turmeric. Add the tomatoes with their juice, stir and cook until the sauce is reduced slightly.
2. Add the chick peas and water and stir well to mix. Stir in the garam masala, roast cumin, amchur, paprika, salt and lemon juice. Cover the pan and cook over a gentle heat for 10 minutes. Add the chilli and ginger and cook uncovered for 30 seconds. Garnish with sliced chilli, if liked, and serve with curry and plain boiled rice.

From the left: *Lamb korma; Spicy chick peas; Spinach and moong dhal kahri*

SPINACH AND MOONG DHAL KAHRI

85g (3oz) plain or chick pea flour (besan)
½ teaspoon turmeric
250ml (8oz) plain unsweetened yogurt
1.25 litres (2 ¼ pints) water
2 tablespoons moong dhal (hulled split yellow mung beans)
675g (1 ½lb) fresh spinach, washed, shaken dry and roughly chopped
2 ½ teaspoons salt
2 tablespoons lemon juice
½ teaspoon cayenne pepper
freshly ground black pepper
2 tablespoons vegetable oil
½ teaspoon asafoetida powder (p 13) (optional)
1 teaspoon cumin seeds
2 dried red chillies, seeded and crushed

Preparation time: 20 minutes
Cooking time: 2 hours

This is a spicy and nutritious Indian version of a thick warming winter soup. Serve it with warm chapattis or pitta bread. Moong dhal is available in Indian stores.

1. Sift the flour and turmeric into a bowl. Gradually stir in 4 tablespoons of the water to give a smooth paste.
2. In another bowl, whisk the yogurt until smooth, then gradually stir in the remaining water.
3. Beat the flour mixture together with the yogurt mixture. Pour into a 4½ litre (7½ pint) saucepan and bring to boil over gentle heat. Add the moong dhal, spinach, salt, lemon juice, and cayenne. Bring back to the boil, reduce the heat and simmer very gently for 1½ hours, stirring every 10 minutes. If the kahri gets too thick, thin with a little hot water, to the thickness of pea soup.
4. Taste for seasoning and add salt and pepper to taste, then cover and keep warm.
5. Heat the oil in small frying pan. Add the asafoetida, then two seconds later the cumin, then two seconds later, the chillies. As soon as the chillies darken, stir the mixture once; wait a moment later and stir the mixture once again. Pour the sizzling hot spices over the kahri in the saucepan. Cover the pan and leave until the sizzling stops. Serve at once.

STUFFED SPICED CHICKEN

50g (2oz) butter
1 onion, peeled and finely chopped
2 apples, peeled, cored and finely chopped
100g (4oz) dried prunes, stoned and chopped
50g (2oz) raisins
100g (4oz) dried apricots, chopped
½ teaspoon cinnamon, ground
½ teaspoon black peppercorns, ground
½ teaspoon salt
3 tablespoons cooked rice
1 tablespoon lemon juice
1.5kg (3 ½lb) oven-ready chicken
SPICE PASTE
2 tablespoons coriander seeds, crushed
½ teaspoon black peppercorns, crushed
3 cloves, crushed
2 cardamon pods, seeds extracted
½ teaspoon salt
50g (2oz) butter, softened

Preparation time: 30 minutes
Cooking time: 1 hour 45 minutes
Oven: 190°C, 375°F, Gas Mark 5

1. Melt the butter in a pan, and fry the onion over a gentle heat for 4 minutes until soft and translucent. Add the apples, dried fruit, cinnamon, pepper and salt and cook gently for a further 10 minutes, or until softened. Mix in the rice and lemon juice.
2. Make the spice paste. Mix the spices with the salt then blend with the softened butter. With the fingers or a spoon handle, gently loosen the chicken skin around the breast and push in small amounts of the spice butter paste, spreading it out where possible to coat the flesh. Cut small slashes on the legs and wings and fill with the spice paste.
3. Stuff the chicken cavity with prepared fruit stuffing, and skewer or truss the bird. Lay the bird on one side on a baking dish.
4. Roast in a preheated oven for 45 minutes, then turn the bird on to the other side, and roast for a further 45 minutes, basting from time to time.
5. Transfer to a serving platter. Leave for a few minutes to settle then carve and serve.

AUBERGINE WITH SPICED YOGURT

1 ½ tablespoons black mustard seeds
½ teaspoon cayenne pepper
600ml (1 pint) hot water
7 tablespoons vegetable oil
1 tablespoon panchphoran (p 27)
675g (1 ½lb) aubergines, cut into 2.5cm (1 inch) cubes
1 teaspoon salt
225g (8oz) plain unsweetened yogurt
½ teaspoon freshly ground black pepper
½ teaspoon garam masala (p 26), to sprinkle

Preparation time: 5 minutes
Cooking time: 20 seconds

1. Grind or pound the mustard seeds with the cayenne, add half the water and stir well to mix.
2. Heat the oil in a frying pan with a lid, add the panchphoran, stir once, then add the mustard seed mixture, aubergine and salt. Stir over a moderate heat for 5 minutes or until the liquid is absorbed.
3. Add the remaining water, cover the pan and simmer over a gentle heat for 15 minutes, until the aubergine is tender. Increase the heat and cook briskly until the liquid is reduced by half.
4. Beat the yogurt with the pepper then stir in. Heat gently, sprinkle with garam masala and serve.

INDIAN VEGETABLE FRITTERS

175g (6oz) plain or chick pea flour (besan)
½ teaspoon salt
½ teaspoon bicarbonate of soda
½ teaspoon ground coriander seeds
½ teaspoon ground turmeric
½ teaspoon ground cumin
¾ teaspoon whole ajowan seeds (optional)
teaspoon freshly ground black pepper
300ml (½pint) water
vegetable oil, for deep frying
1 medium potato, peeled and sliced
1 small cauliflower, broken into separate florets

Preparation time: 20 minutes
Cooking time: 40 minutes
Serves 6-8

1. Sift the flour with the salt and bicarbonate of soda into a mixing bowl. Add the spices, then slowly whisk in the water, to make a smooth batter.
2. Heat the oil in a deep-fryer to 180°-190°C/350°-375°F or until a cube of bread browns in 30 seconds.
3. Dip the potato slices into the batter to coat thoroughly. Shake off any excess and fry until golden-brown and crisp. Remove with a slotted spoon.
4. Coat and fry the cauliflower in the same way.
5. Serve the fritters hot, with tomato chutney.

WHOLE SPICE, WHOLE RICE

50g (2oz) ghee or butter
2 onions, peeled and finely chopped
2 teaspoons turmeric, ground
2 teaspoons cinnamon, ground
1 teaspoon whole allspice
½ teaspoon whole coriander seeds
½ teaspoon black peppercorns
1 teaspoon salt
225g (8oz) basmati or long-grain rice
600ml (1pint) chicken stock, boiling

Preparation time: 5 minutes
Cooking time: 20 minutes

1. Melt the ghee in a large heavy-based saucepan.
2. Fry the onion gently for 5 minutes until transparent, then add the spices and salt and cook for a further 2 minutes. Add the rice and stir in to the hot spice mixture for 2-3 minutes until the grains are transparent, then pour in the boiling stock.
3. Stir once then cover the pan with tin foil and place the lid on top. Cook over the lowest possible heat for 15 minutes by which time all of the liquid will be absorbed and the rice will be tender.
4. Remove the tin foil. Lay a clean teatowel over the pan and place the lid on top. Stand in a warm place for 5-10 minutes to fluff up the rice. Fork up the rice and serve, garnished with sliced bananas, chopped coriander or chopped coriander and garlic, moistened with a little lemon juice.

From the bottom, clockwise:
Indian vegetable fritters;
Stuffed spiced chicken;
Aubergine with spiced yogurt

SOUR AUBERGINES

2 tablespoons salt
450g (1lb) aubergines or courgettes, halved lengthways and cut into ¾cm (⅓inch) slices
4 tablespoons vegetable oil
2 teaspoons ground fennel seeds
½ teaspoon ground ginger
1 teaspoon ground cumin seeds
½ teaspoon ground turmeric
½ teaspoon cayenne pepper
½ teaspoon asafoetida powder (p 13) (optional)
350ml (12fl oz) water
1 tablespoon tamarind paste
½ teaspoon salt

Preparation time: 5 minutes, plus draining
Cooking time: 15 minutes

Tamarind paste is often used as a souring agent in Kashmiri and other Indian dishes. For instructions on preparing tamarind paste see p 86. If unavailable lime juice will make an adequate but inferior substitute. Asafoetida, like tamarind, can be found in Asian groceries in powder or lump form.

1. Sprinkle the aubergine slices with salt and leave to drain in a colander for 30 minutes. Rinse the aubergine slices and pat dry with absorbent paper.
2. Heat the oil in a large frying pan, add half the aubergine slices in a single layer and fry until reddish brown. Turn and fry on the other side. Remove the aubergine with a slotted spoon and drain on absorbent paper. Fry the remaining aubergine slices in the same way, then drain.
3. Combine the fennel seeds with the ginger, cumin, turmeric and cayenne. Add the asafoetida to the pan, then the spice mixture and 2 tablespoons of the water. Stir for 30 seconds over a gentle heat, then add a further 2 tablespoons water and stir for a further 10 seconds. Add the tamarind, salt and the remaining water.
4. Return the aubergines to the pan, and bring to the boil. Turn the aubergines in the sauce, cover the pan, lower the heat and cook gently for 5 minutes. Transfer to a warmed serving dish and serve with curried lamb and a rice dish.

LAMB MADRAS

1 tablespoon mustard oil or butter
1 onion, peeled and finely chopped
2 garlic cloves, peeled and crushed
2 fresh green chillies, seeded and sliced
2 teaspoons chilli powder
2 teaspoons Garam masala (p 26)
450g (1lb) lean lamb, cut into 4cm (1½ inch) cubes
1 tablespoon vinegar
salt
2 tomatoes, skinned, seeded and chopped
1 tablespoon desiccated coconut flakes

Preparation time: 10 minutes
Cooking time: 35 minutes

This is an extremely hot dry lamb curry from southern India. The 'heat' can be adjusted by reducing the amount of chilli used - fresh and powdered. Serves 2-3 as with boiled rice, mango chutney, and a refreshing cucumber and yogurt salad. To serve 4, you will need another curried dish. Used boned leg of lamb or shoulder for this curry.

1. Heat the oil or butter in a heavy-based frying pan, and stir fry the onion, garlic, fresh chillies and chilli powder for 2 minutes. Add the garam masala, then the lamb, vinegar, salt and tomatoes. Stir thoroughly.
2. Cover the pan, and cook for 30 minutes over a moderate heat, adding a little water or lemon juice if it looks like drying out and sticking.
3. Transfer to a heated serving dish, scatter with coconut and serve.

FISH VINDALOO WITH COCONUT MILK

3 tablespoons desiccated coconut
300ml (½ pint) boiling water
4 cod cutlets or steaks, about 3cm (1 ¼ inches) thick
3 tablespoons vegetable oil
1 teaspoon mustard seeds
2 onions, peeled and finely sliced
1 green pepper, cored, seeded and thinly sliced
1 tablespoon cornflour
½ teaspoon salt
½-1 teaspoon vindaloo paste (p 26)
1 tablespoon desiccated coconut, lightly toasted
2 tablespoons lemon juice
fresh coriander, to garnish

Preparation time: 25 minutes
Cooking time: 30 minutes

Vindaloo paste is very fiery and should be used with discretion.

1. Put the coconut in a sieve set over a bowl, pour over the boiling water and leave to infuse for 20 minutes, pressing the coconut with the back of a wooden spoon to extract as much liquid as possible.
2. Pat the cod steaks dry with absorbent paper. Heat the oil in a large frying pan. Add the mustard seeds, and as soon as they jump, add the onion and green pepper and fry over a gentle heat for 3-4 minutes, until beginning to soften. Add the cornflour and stir until thoroughly combined.
3. Add the coconut liquid, salt and vindaloo paste to taste. Stir and bring slowly to boil over a low heat.
4. Add the cod to the pan. Spoon over the sauce, cover and simmer very gently for 25 minutes, or until the fish is firm and flakes easily.
5. Sprinkle the toasted coconut and lemon juice over the fish, garnish with coriander and serve with plain boiled rice, and a cucumber and yogurt salad.

From the left, clockwise: *Lamb Madras; Whole spice, whole rice (recipe p 62); Fish vindaloo with coconut milk; Sour aubergines*

SPICY PRAWN RICE

225g (8oz) basmati or long-grain rice
salt
1cm (½ inch) piece fresh ginger root, very finely chopped
1 garlic clove, peeled and crushed
175g (6oz) peeled prawns, defrosted if frozen
1 teaspoon garam masala (p 26)
½ teaspoon chilli powder
2 tablespoons lemon juice
50g (2 oz) butter or ghee
TO GARNISH
finely chopped fresh red chilli (optional)
unpeeled prawns

Preparation time: 15 minutes, plus 1 hour marinating
Cooking time: 10 minutes

A tasty, rapidly cooked dish of rice with prawns which could accompany fish sambal, or a vegetable or egg curry.

1. Cook the rice in a large saucepan of boiling salted water for 12 minutes, then drain.
2. Combine the ginger and garlic. Put the prawns in a bowl, add the ginger, garlic, garam masala, ½ teaspoon salt, the chilli powder and lemon juice. Stir well to mix and leave for 1 hour in a cool place.
3. Melt the butter in a large frying pan with a lid, add the rice, and fork through over a gentle heat for 3-4 minutes. Add the prawns with the marinating liquid and fork through. Cover the pan and simmer over the lowest possible heat for 5 minutes.
4. Taste and adjust the seasoning, transfer to a warmed serving dish and garnish with chilli and unpeeled prawns. Serve at once.

MALAYSIAN VEGETABLE CURRY

1 large potato, peeled and cut into small dice
225g (8oz) stringless beans, topped and tailed
2 carrots, scraped and finely sliced
1 small cauliflower, stalk removed and divided into florets
3 fresh green chillies, seeded and finely chopped
1 teaspoon ground turmeric
½ teaspoon Seven Seas spice (p 25)
salt
8 tablespoons plain yogurt
½ fresh coconut, finely grated or 4 tablespoons desiccated coconut soaked overnight in hot water
toasted coconut, to garnish

Preparation time: 15 minutes
Cooking time: 15 minutes

This hot vegetable curry has plenty of sauce and is good served with boiled rice as a vegetarian meal.

1. Put all the vegetables into a large saucepan and stir in the chillies and turmeric. Pour in boiling water to a depth of about 2.5cm (1 inch). Cover, bring to the boil and boil for 10-15 minutes until the vegetables

From the left: *Spicy prawn rice; Malaysian vegetable curry*

are just tender, adding a little extra boiling water if necessary. Add the spice and season to taste with salt.
2. Remove from the heat and stir in the yoghurt and coconut. Return to the heat, bring to just below boiling point, stir well and serve at once, garnished with toasted coconut.

RED PEPPERS WITH PORK AND PRAWN STUFFING

large red peppers, halved and seeded
350g (12 oz) lean pork, minced
100g (4oz) peeled prawns, finely chopped
1 onion, peeled and finely chopped
2 garlic cloves, peeled and crushed
1 tablespoon light soy sauce
2 teaspoons cornflour
½ teaspoon galangal (p 18) (optional)
1 fresh green or red chilli, seeded and finely chopped
4 tablespoons vegetable oil

Preparation time: 20 minutes
Cooking time: 40 minutes
Oven: 180°C, 350°F, Gas Mark 4
Serves 6-8

1. Arrange the pepper halves on separate trays in a bamboo steamer and steam for 10-12 minutes, or until just tender.
2. In a bowl mix all the remaining ingredients together, using the hands. (Avoid touching face or eyes with hands that have been handling raw or dried chilli as this will burn.)
3. Spoon the stuffing mixture into the pepper halves, rounding and smoothing the tops. Arrange the pepper halves close together in a baking dish. Pour in water to a depth of about 1cm (½ inch) around the stuffed peppers. Cover with foil and bake in a preheated moderate oven for 40 minutes or until the stuffing is light browned on top.
4. Serve with plain boiled rice and soy sauce.

PEACH PICKLE

450g (1lb) soft light brown sugar
600ml (1 pint) distilled malt vinegar
1kg (2lb) firm peaches, blanched for 1 minute in boiling water, then skinned, halved and stoned
225g (8 oz) sultanas
25g (1oz) chilli powder
1 teaspoon ground ginger

Preparation time: 10 minutes
Cooking time: 1-1½ hours

This sweet peach pickle is very hot, for eating with curries. Those who dislike the fiery taste can reduce the quantity of chilli, or leave it out altogether.
1. Put the sugar and vinegar into an enamelled or stainless steel saucepan. Stir over a gentle heat until the sugar dissolves, then increase the heat and bring to the boil.
2. Slice the peach halves into the mixture and simmer until tender. Add all the remaining ingredients, stir, then simmer until the liquid has reduced and thickened and the sultanas are soft and swollen.
3. Remove from the heat, stir well to mix, then leave to cool. Pour into hot sterilized jars, seal and store for up to 2 weeks.

From the top: *Peach pickle; Red peppers with pork and prawn stuffing*

From the left: *Courgette chutney; Melon rind pickle*

COURGETTE CHUTNEY

2½kg (5lb) courgettes, topped and tailed
1kg (2lb) ripe, fresh tomatoes, peeled and roughly chopped
450g (1lb) onions, peeled and sliced
6-8 cloves garlic, peeled and chopped
1½kg (3lb) soft, pale brown sugar
175g (6oz) sultanas
4 tablespoons salt
1 tablespoon black peppercorns
1 tablespoon whole allspice
1 tablespoon ground ginger or 2.5cm (1 inch) fresh ginger root, peeled and finely chopped
1 litre (1¾ pints) malt or white vinegar

Preparation time: 10 minutes
Cooking time: 1½ hours

If courgettes are out of season, marrow may be used instead.

1. Cut the courgettes into 2 cm (1 inch) chunks.
2. Put all the ingredients into a large stainless steel or aluminium pan. Bring slowly to the boil, stirring with a wooden spoon until the sugar is dissolved.
3. Simmer the mixture very gently for at least 1½ hours until the mixture is thick and well blended.
4. Ladle into warm sterilized jars while still hot. Cover with waxed paper and non-metallic lids and store in a dry cupboard. Will keep for up to 6 months.

MELON RIND PICKLE

1kg (2lb) melon rind, cut into thin strips
1 litre (1¾ pints) cold water
3 tablespoons salt
500ml (18fl oz) white wine or cider vinegar
1.5kg (3lb) sugar
1 teaspoon ground cinnamon
1 teaspoon ground cloves
2 tablespoons whole cloves
2 tablespoons whole allspice
5×7.5cm (3 inch) cinnamon sticks

Preparation time: 10 minutes, plus soaking overnight
Cooking time: 1 hour

1. Put the melon rind into a large bowl. Mix the water with the salt and pour over the rind. Cover and leave to stand overnight.
2. Drain the rind and place in a large saucepan. Cover with 1 litre (1¾ pints) fresh cold water, bring to the boil and cook for 10 minutes. Drain.
3. Bring 1 litre (1¾ pints) water to the boil in a separate saucepan and add the vinegar, sugar, ground spices and the whole spices tied in a piece of muslin. Bring to the boil and boil for 5 minutes.
4. Add the melon rind to the pan, lower the heat and simmer for 45 minutes.
5. Spoon the rind and liquid into hot, sterilized jars and seal. Leave to mature for at least 4 weeks.

DILL PICKLES

2 medium ridge cucumbers
300ml (½ pint) cider vinegar
75g (3oz) caster sugar
½ teaspoon salt
½ teaspoon ground black pepper
3 cloves
½ teaspoon mustard seed
½ teaspoon dill seed
2 sprigs fresh dill

Preparation time: 10 minutes, plus cooling
Cooking time: 2 minutes

Crisp slices of sweet'n'sour cucumber are invariably served in America with hamburgers or toasted sandwiches. They should not be too thinly sliced, or the hot vinegar will wilt them.

1. Slice both cucumbers into 3mm (1/8 inch) slices, discarding the ends and place in a cooled, sterilized, dry jar.
2. Put all the remaining ingredients into an enamel saucepan, bring to the boil and boil gently for 2 minutes. Pour the mixture into a glass bowl and leave to stand for 2 hours.
3. Strain the mixture into the pan, return to the boil and pour over the cucumber slices in the jar. Stand the jar in running cold water to help cool quickly and make the cucumber crisper.
4. Seal tightly and store in a cool dark place. The pickles are ready to eat after 3-4 days.

PICKLED APRICOTS

1 tablespoon whole allspice
1 tablespoon cloves
2.5cm (1 inch) blade of mace
2.5cm (1 inch) piece of cinnamon stick
500g (1lb 2oz) sugar
350ml (12fl oz) white wine or cider vinegar
1 tablespoon freshly grated nutmeg
1kg (2lb) apricots

Preparation time: 10 minutes
Cooking time: 15 minutes

1. Tie the allspice, cloves, mace and cinnamon stick in a piece of muslin and place in a saucepan with the sugar, vinegar and nutmeg. Stir over a gentle heat until the sugar is dissolved. Add the apricots and simmer for 10 minutes.
2. Using a slotted spoon, transfer the apricots to warm, dry sterilized jars with wide necks and non-metal lids, leaving at least 1cm (½ inch) headroom.
3. Boil the liquid in the pan until reduced to a thick syrup and pour over the apricots just to cover.
4. Seal and store for at least 1 month. (The pickled apricots will keep for 2 years.) Serve with any kind of cold meat.

SAVOURY SPICED PEARS

25g (1oz) whole cloves
25g (1oz) cinnamon sticks
1 teaspoon grated fresh ginger root
1kg (2lb) brown sugar
600ml (1 pint) cider vinegar
2kg (4lb) firm pears

Preparation time: 10 minutes, plus standing overnight
Cooking time: about 25 minutes

1. Put the spices tied in a piece of muslin, the sugar and the vinegar into a saucepan, bring to the boil and boil for 10 minutes.
2. Peel and core the pears, cutting off any soft or brown parts. Put the pears into a large bowl. Pour over the syrup and leave to stand overnight.
3. Drain off the syrup and boil it for 10 minutes in a large saucepan. Add the pears and cook over a very gentle heat for about 15 minutes, until just tender.
4. Spoon the pears into hot, sterilized jars and seal.

From the top, clockwise: *Dill pickles; Savoury spiced pears; Pickled apricots*

BRANDIED PEACHES

4 peaches
4 tablespoons lemon juice
150g (5oz) sugar
8 cloves
2.5cm (1 inch) piece cinnamon stick
250ml (8fl oz) water
2 tablespoons brandy

Preparation time: 5 minutes
Cooking time: 35 minutes, plus chilling
Oven: 160°C, 325°F, Gas Mark 3

1. Put the peaches in a large bowl, pour over boiling water to cover and leave to stand for 1 minute. Drain and skin the peaches, then brush with lemon juice.
2. Put the sugar with the cloves, cinnamon and water in a saucepan and stir over a very low heat until the sugar is dissolved. Boil for about 5 minutes until syrupy, then stir in the brandy.
3. Place the peaches in a casserole and pour over the syrup. Cover and bake in a preheated medium-low oven until the peaches are tender.
4. Remove the cloves and cinnamon stick. Leave to cool, then chill in the refrigerator for 2-3 hours.

RED FRUIT COMPOTE WITH RASPBERRY SAUCE

grated rind of 1 lemon
2.5cm (1 inch) piece cinnamon stick
2 cloves
275g (10oz) sugar
600ml / 4(1 pint) water
450g (1lb) redcurrants and / or blackcurrants, stringed
450g (1lb) strawberries, hulled and sliced
225g (8oz) raspberries
1 teaspoon lemon juice
icing sugar, sifted, to taste
1 tablespoon Cassis or Framboişe liqueur

Preparation time: 25 minutes
Cooking time: 15 minutes
Serves 6-8

1. Put the lemon rind, cinnamon stick, cloves and sugar in a saucepan with the water and stir over a very gentle heat until the sugar is dissolved. Bring to the boil and boil for about 5 minutes until syrupy.
2. Add the redcurrants and strawberries to the pan and poach gently for about 10 minutes. Strain, reserving the liquid, and allow to cool.
3. Meanwhile, sieve the raspberries into a bowl and stir in the lemon juice and icing sugar to taste. Stir in the liqueur and add poaching liquid as necessary to achieve a smooth pouring consistency.
4. Pour the sauce over the compote in a glass serving bowl and chill for 2-3 hours before serving.

Opposite, clockwise from the top: *Cinnamon and orange buttered bananas with rum; Red fruit compote with raspberry sauce; Brandied peaches*

CINNAMON AND ORANGE BUTTERED BANANAS WITH RUM

50g (2oz) butter
1 teaspoon ground cinnamon
1 tablespoon finely grated orange zest
2 tablespoons fresh orange juice
4 bananas, peeled and cut diagonally into 5cm (2 inch) slices
2 tablespoons dark rum or Cointreau
single cream, to serve

Preparation time: 5 minutes
Cooking time: 5-10 minutes

This delicious dessert is very quick to prepare. An excellent way of using up slightly over-ripe bananas.
1. Melt the butter in a large frying-pan over a gentle heat and stir in the cinnamon, orange zest and juice.
2. Add the bananas to the pan and cook gently, turning carefully with a fish slice, until warmed through and softened.
3. Add the rum to the pan and set alight with a match. Serve straight from the pan with single cream handed separately in a jug.

CURATE'S PUDDING

1kg (2lb) cooking apples, peeled, cored and sliced
6 tablespoons water
1 tablespoon sugar
75g (3oz) butter
½ teaspoon cinnamon
225g (8oz) fresh white breadcrumbs
TO FINISH
1 teaspoon sugar
1 teaspoon ground cinnamon

Preparation time: 20 minutes
Cooking time: 50 minutes
Oven: 190°C, 375°F, Gas Mark 5

This is a light and crunchy variation of apple crumble. It is a very economical dish, ideally suited to the modest lifestyle of a country curate.
1. Put the apples into a large, heavy-based saucepan with the water and sugar. Cook over a gentle heat, stirring from time to time, until soft and pulpy.
2. Remove the apples from the heat and beat in a third of the butter and cinnamon. Taste and add a little extra sugar if necessary. Pass through a sieve or work in a food processor until fairly smooth. Transfer to a buttered shallow ovenproof dish.
3. Melt the remaining butter in a frying pan, add the crumbs and stir until golden. Sprinkle the apple purée evenly with the crumbs and sprinkle with the sugar and cinnamon.
4. Bake in a preheated medium-hot oven for 40 minutes or until the top is crisp and brown. Serve with single cream or custard.

UNCLE TOM'S PUDDING

225g (8oz) golden syrup
15g (½oz) butter
2 tablespoons fresh soft white breadcrumbs
225g (8oz) self-raising flour, sifted
100g (4oz) shredded suet
50g (2oz) soft light brown sugar
1 teaspoon ground ginger
1 teaspoon ground cinnamon
1 teaspoon ground allspice
2 eggs, beaten
120ml (4fl oz) milk

Preparation time: 10 minutes
Cooking time: 2 hours 5 minutes
Serves 4-6

1. Bring a large saucepan of water to the boil. Put the golden syrup in a flameproof bowl and set over the boiling water until melted.
2. Grease a 1.25 litre (2 pint) pudding basin with the butter and put in the breadcrumbs and 2 tablespoons of the golden syrup.
3. Cut a double thickness of greaseproof paper and a piece of kitchen foil 10cm (4 inches) wider than the basin. Make a pleat in the centre of the paper.
4. Stir the flour, suet, sugar, spices and eggs quickly into the remaining golden syrup and add sufficient milk to give the mixture a soft dropping consistency.
5. Spoon the mixture into the prepared pudding basin, cover first with the greaseproof, then with the foil and tie securely with string. Place in a large saucepan and pour in boiling water to come halfway up the sides of the basin. Boil gently for 2 hours, topping up with more boiling water if necessary.
6. Remove the greaseproof and foil covering and gently run a palette knife around the edge of the pudding. Turn the pudding out on to a serving plate. Serve hot with a jug of custard.

From the left: *Uncle Tom's pudding; Curate's pudding (recipe p 70)*

CHEESE MUFFINS

350g (12oz) plain flour
1 teaspoon cayenne pepper
1 teaspoon English mustard powder
4 teaspoons baking powder
1 tablespoon chopped fresh parsley or chives
salt
freshly ground black pepper
2 eggs
175ml (6fl oz) milk
100g (4oz) mature cheddar cheese, grated

Preparation time: 15 minutes
Cooking time: 15 minutes
Oven: 200°C, 400°F, Gas Mark 6
Makes 20-25

1. Sift the flour into a mixing bowl with the cayenne, mustard powder, baking powder, parsley and salt and pepper.
2. Make a well in the centre and break in the eggs. Using a wooden spoon, gradually draw the flour into the eggs, beating all the time. Gradually add the milk, beating well between each addition. Stir in the cheese, to form a soft, sticky dough.
3. Turn the dough on to a lightly floured board or surface and with floured hands shape into 5cm (2 inch) rounds about 1cm (½ inch) thick.
4. Place on a lightly greased baking sheet and bake in a preheated hot oven for 10-15 minutes. Serve immediately, split and buttered.

SAFFRON CAKE

½ teaspoon saffron strands
150ml (¼ pint) boiling water
15g (½oz) dried yeast
150ml (¼ pint) tepid milk
25g (1oz) caster sugar
450g (1lb) strong plain flour
1 teaspoon salt
100g (4oz) butter
175g (6oz) currants
grated rind of ½ lemon

Preparation time: 20 minutes, plus soaking overnight, proving and cooling
Cooking time: 1 hour
Oven: 200°C, 400°F, Gas Mark 6
then: 180°C, 350°F, Gas Mark 4
Makes 1 round loaf

One of the oldest traditional English cake recipes, to which the saffron gives warm flavour as well as a distinctive yellow colour.
1. Put the saffron into a small bowl with the boiling water and leave to soak overnight.
2. Sprinkle the yeast over the milk and ½ teaspoon sugar in a separate bowl and leave in a warm place for 10 minutes, till frothy.
3. Sift the flour with the salt into a mixing bowl, add the butter and rub in with the fingertips until the mixture resembles coarse breadcrumbs. Stir in the currants, lemon rind and the remaining sugar.
4. Add the yeast mixture to the flour and beat well to mix. Strain in the saffron liquid and beat again.
5. Grease a 20cm (8 inch) round cake tin and pour in the mixture. Cover with a clean cloth and leave in a warm place to rise almost to the top of the tin.
6. Bake in a preheated hot oven for 30 minutes, then reduce the oven temperature and bake for a further 30 minutes, without opening the oven door. Turn the cake on to a wire rack to cool completely. Serve cut into slices, plain, or buttered.

From the left: *Saffron cake; Cheese muffins*

CARAWAY TEA BREAD

350g (12oz) plain flour
3 teaspoons baking powder
175g (6oz) caster sugar
75g (3oz) butter, diced
150ml (¼pint) milk
1 egg
3 teaspoons caraway seeds, lightly toasted, then ground

Preparation time: 20 minutes
Cooking time: 1 hour
Oven: 190°C, 375°F, Gas Mark 5
Makes 1 large loaf

One of the nicest uses for caraway seeds, and an excellent tea loaf to be eaten either plain, warm, or cold with butter. A classic from the old fashioned nursery tea table.

1. Sift flour with baking powder into a warmed mixing bowl. Add the sugar.
2. Add the butter to the bowl and rub in lightly but quickly with the fingertips until the mixture resembles coarse breadcrumbs.
3. Scald the milk and allow to cool slightly. Mix with the egg and ground caraway seeds.
4. Add milk and egg mixture to the dry ingredients and beat to a smooth dough. Turn the mixture on to a floured board and knead lightly.
5. Turn into a greased 18 cm (7 inch) round cake tin and bake in the middle of the preheated oven until the top feels firm and springy to the touch.
6. Cool a few minutes in the tin then turn out on to a wire tray to cool. Serve warm or cold.

POPPYSEED LOAF

40g (1½oz) poppyseeds
200ml (⅓pint) milk
2 eggs
100g (4oz) soft light brown sugar
150ml (¼pint) corn oil
1 teaspoon almond essence
225g (8oz) self-raising flour
½ teaspoon baking powder
1 teaspoon ground cinnamon
1 tablespoon skimmed milk powder

Preparation time: 20 minutes, plus soaking and cooling
Cooking time: 25-30 minutes
Oven: 190°C, 375°F, Gas Mark 5
Makes 1 large loaf

Usually used to decorate fancy breads, poppyseeds become the main flavouring ingredient in this subtly flavoured loaf.

1. Grease a 23×13 cm (9×5 inch) loaf tin and line with greased greaseproof paper.
2. Put half the poppyseeds into a small bowl. Add the milk and leave to soak for 1 hour.
3. Whisk the eggs with the sugar in a bowl until light and pale, then gradually add the oil and almond essence, whisking until smooth.
4. Sift the flour with the baking powder, cinnamon and skimmed milk powder. Fold into the egg and sugar mixture. Stir in milk and poppyseeds.
5. Pour the mixture into the prepared tin, smooth the top and sprinkle with the remaining poppyseeds.
6. Bake in a preheated moderately hot oven until just firm to the touch, then turn out on to a wire rack. Leave to cool completely and serve cut into slices.

MARY BALL WASHINGTON'S GINGERBREAD

100g (4oz) butter
100g (4oz) soft dark brown sugar
350g (12oz) plain flour
1 teaspoon cream of tartar

150g (5oz) sultanas
150ml (5fl oz) warm milk
3 tablespoons sherry
2 tablespoons ground ginger
2 teaspoons ground cinnamon
3 teaspoons freshly grated nutmeg
225g (8oz) golden syrup
100g (4oz) treacle
3 eggs
finely grated rind of 1 large orange
1 teaspoon bicarbonate of soda, dissolved in
2 tablespoons warm water

Preparation time: 20 minutes
Cooking time: about 1 hour
Oven: 160°C, 325°F, Gas Mark 3
then: 150°C, 300°F, Gas Mark 2
Makes 2 gingerbreads, 18cm (7 inches) square

A 200 year old American recipe, attributed to the mother of the famous president of the U.S.A.

1. Grease two square 18 cm (7 inch) baking tins and line them with greased greaseproof paper or non-stick silicone paper.
2. In a bowl, cream the butter with the sugar until light and fluffy.
3. Sift the flour with the cream of tartar into a separate bowl and add the sultanas.
4. In a third bowl combine the milk, sherry, spices, syrup, treacle and eggs.
5. Fold the flour mixture alternately with the milk and spice mixture into the creamed butter and sugar. Beat well until thoroughly combined. Finally beat in the orange rind, and the dissolved bicarbonate of soda.
6. Pour the mixture into the prepared tins and bake in a preheated moderately slow oven for 30 minutes, then reduce the oven temperature and bake for a further 30-40 minutes. Allow to cool in the tins, then turn out on to a wire rack and leave to cool.
7. To serve, cut into small squares, which can be buttered if liked.

From the left: *Mary Ball Washington's gingerbread; Caraway tea bread; Poppyseed loaf*

to its requisite
flavor and
subtle
aroma
the culinary
art and
excites the
appetite.
Brillat-Savarin
called it the mustard
for gourmets, and said:
NET Wt 500g

FLAVOURINGS

RECIPES

BLACHAN, BLACHEN OR BALACHONG

Easily recognizable to anyone familiar with the cuisine of Indonesia and Malaysia, blachan is claimed by the Siamese as their invention. It is made from shrimps or prawns which are salted, dried, pounded and left to ferment in the humid heat to develop a full earthy flavour and very pungent aroma. It can vary in colour from the palest pink to a deep umbrish red and is usually sold in block form, although a pinkish paste or powder are sometimes available. Blachan is never eaten raw, as the aroma of uncooked blachan, politely described as gamey, is off-putting in the extreme. Once cooked, however, it blends with and enhances other foods and becomes almost indistinguishable. Blachan is normally used in peanut-sized chunks or smaller; it can be dry fried, ground and added to a recipe, or included with other spices in any initial frying. If dry frying blachan alone, it should be wrapped in foil, fried for 3-4 minutes, then unwrapped and used according to the recipe; the foil will contain the all-pervasive smell. Store unused blachan in an airtight jar in the refrigerator, where it can be kept almost indefinitely. Blachan can be bought in Chinese, Malay and Indian supermarkets.

Uses: Blachan is an essential ingredient in Indonesian and Malaysian cooking. It features in innumerable spicy rice, vegetable, meat, poultry and fish dishes – as well as in spicy peanut sauces for satés (p 98) – barbecued skewers of marinated meat or prawns – and for Gado-gado salad (p 118). The native cuisine of Thailand and Java also use blachan – partnered with fresh coriander and fiery chillies. Blachan may also be roasted and used as a condiment.

Capers

Blachen

CAPERS
Capparis spinosa

Capers are the tiny unopened green flower buds of a bramble-like spiny shrub, native to the drier regions of southern Europe and North Africa. The buds are hand-picked and packed into jars of strongly salted wine vinegar. The finest capers, known as *non-pareilles*, measure 3 mm (⅛ inch) and are round and hard. Larger capers are more bud shaped and less expensive. Capers have an aromatic pungency, somewhat acidic due to the capric acid which develops when they are pickled. They are often described as having a 'goaty' taste. Capers are widely available. They store well if kept immersed in their pickling liquid.

Uses: Not surprisingly, capers feature strongly in Mediterranean cooking, especially in dishes from Provence, where *non-pareilles* are produced. They are of value in reducing oiliness, and have an affinity with garlic and lemon: the term *à la grenobloise* refers to fish with a caper, lemon and anchovy sauce. Capers are used to great effect in the classic French mayonnaise-based sauces such as *rémoulade, tartare* and *tapenade.* The French also include capers in savoury butters to serve with fish: *beurre noir,* for turbot or skate and *beurre de capres* which is served with many different fish dishes. In Italy, capers are irreplaceable in *vitello tonnato, salsa verde* and as part of pizza toppings. In northern Europe, capers are used in German and Scandinavian savoury sauces and caper sauce is a traditional British sauce for mutton and lamb.

CAROB
Ceratonia siliqua

Carob pods, or locust beans, are the dried seed pod of a leguminous tree that grows in the Mediterranean, Middle East and India. The pods have a shiny leathery appearance and are 13-30 cm (5-12 inches) long and 6 mm (¼ inch) thick. They contain a number of oval reddish-brown seeds. In the autumn, when the pods turn brown, they are harvested and the seeds are removed. The pods are then cooked, roasted and ground to make carob powder. Carob pods have a rather unpleasant odour, but the powder has a warm chocolate-like aroma and sweet flavour. Both carob pods and powder may be found in health food shops.

Uses: Carob is mainly used as a subsitute for cocoa and chocolate; carob 'chocolate' bars, carob coated biscuits, carob chip cookies and carob milk drinks are all available at health food shops. Carob is naturally sweet and, unlike chocolate, does not contain caffeine, so is especially useful in cooking for anyone trying to reduce sugar intake or for those allergic to chocolate. In cooking, two dessertspoonfuls of carob powder are roughly equivalent to one square of chocolate, although remember that because carob is sweet it cannot replace plain or dark chocolate. Carob is used in some Middle Eastern sweetmeats: it blends especially well with honey, vanilla and cinnamon.

Carob

Chestnut

CHESTNUT OR SWEET CHESTNUT

Castanea sativa

Chestnuts are the fruit of a tree which has been cultivated in southern Europe for thousands of years; nowadays France, Italy, Spain and Portugal are all important producers. The chestnuts are contained within prickly capsules: when these ripen they split, releasing the nut. The most expensive variety is the marron which is specially cultivated for its large square size and ease of peeling. Chestnuts have more starch and less oil than any other nut and are easily digested.

Shelled fresh chestnuts may be bought from good greengrocers; the brown inner skin will need to be removed before cooking. Whole skinned chestnuts are available in tins from specialist shops and dried chestnuts can be bought in Italian grocers and health food shops. Chestnut purée – plain and vanilla-sweetened – can be found in supermarkets and delicatessens. Chestnut 'flour' is an important ingredient/flavouring in Italy: it can be bought in Italian stores and health food shops. Fresh chestnuts should be kept in a warm room for a week or so to allow them to dry and shrink slightly, making peeling easier. Dried chestnuts will keep for up to 18 months in a cool dry place. Soak in warm water until soft enough to cut before use.

Uses: Fresh chestnuts are seldom eaten raw but can be roasted, steamed, boiled – or laboriously preserved in sugar, glazed with syrup and sold at great expense as *marrons glacés*. In Britain chestnuts are almost exclusively included in savoury dishes: partnered with apples in light soups, combined with onions and bacon in pigeon stews, used as a stuffing for Christmas turkeys or combined with Brussels sprouts. In the rest of Europe chestnuts have both sweet and savoury uses. France uses chestnuts in robust main meal soups, elegant soufflés and in purées to serve with boar, hare and venison. Sweetened chestnut purées are the basis of many French gâteaux and crêmes. In Italy dried chestnuts are added to stews, fresh ones are made into soups and chestnut flour is used for cakes and desserts.

CITRUS FRUITS

gen. Citrus

For many reasons, not least their aromatic pungency, the family of citrus fruits holds a unique place among flavourings, as subtly different aromas and tastes can be drawn from the fruits, juice, rind, flowers and leaves. The fruits are produced by shrubs or small trees which flourish in tropical and warm temperate regions. The most often seen members of the family are oranges, lemons, limes, grapefruit and clementines. Kumquats belong to a related genus, *fortunella*. All citrus fruit are rich in Vitamin C, their sweetness depending on the amount of sugar contained in each species. Buy fruit that feel relatively heavy for their size, indicating juiciness, and store in a cool airy place. 'Cut mixed peel' is a mixture of candied orange, lemon and citron peel. Uncut candied peel, which can be found in specialist grocers, is prepared from better quality fruit and has had less chance to lose its aroma and flavour; it should be used where possible in preference to the cut sort. Store all candied peel in an airtight container. The essential oils from several citrus fruits are sold as essences (p 81) and the flowers of the orange tree are used to make orange flower water (p 81).

Uses: The culinary uses of citrus fruits are innumerable; citrus fruits appear in all manner of dishes for breakfast, lunch, tea and dinner. The orange has perhaps the most varied use. It has a classic savoury affinity with duck and game (*caneton à l'orange* and Cumberland sauce) and is also found in many desserts and sweet sauces. Segments of fresh orange make a refreshing addition to summer salads. For a less prominent flavour, grated orange rind may be included in game, poultry and fish stuffings and sauces; in southern France a sliver of thinly pared orange rind is included in *bouquet garnis* and *court bouillons*. Orange rind is also the base of liqueurs such as Cointreau, Triple Sec and Grand Marnier.

Orange juice provides a base for many cocktails and punches and candied peel is included in many European cakes and pastries to give tang and bite. Orange flower water is popular as a flavouring for the syrupy pastries and sweetmeats eaten throughout the Middle East. The rind of the tangerine or mandarin orange has a more distinct scent than the orange; its classic use is in *crêpes suzette*.

Lemon is the most popular souring agent in European cooking. Its fresh natural sharpness is useful in fish and poultry dishes, salad dressings and mayonnaises – and it is invaluable in desserts to counteract excessive sweetness. It has a particular affinity with egg – for example in Greek *Avgolemono* soup (p 88) and in British lemon meringue pie. Lemon rind provides a refreshing pungency in savoury stuffing mixtures and in all types of baked goods, while slices or wedges of lemon can be used as a garnish and flavour enhancer in many drinks from tea to gin and tonic. The pared rind's zest also adds that final touch of distinction both to the martini and genuine Italian espresso coffee. Perhaps its greatest contribution to beverages, however, has been that to which it has given its name: lemonade.

Lime flesh, juice and rind are used in place of lemon in many instances where a more acid or pungently refreshing quality is required. It is used to 'cook' fish flesh in the South American *ceviche* and it features in many mixed pickles. It is found in many Caribbean dishes and also in most of their mixed drinks, such as the daiquiri.

Grapefruit flesh and juice can be used in many of the same ways as orange in sweet dishes such as mousses, sorbets and creams, with slightly more bitter and less aromatic results.

Citrus fruits

COCOA AND CHOCOLATE
Theobroma cacao

Cocoa beans are borne inside the spindle-shaped fruit of a tree which flourishes in the moist tropical climates of Central and South America and West Africa. The ribbed, pointed, melon-shaped fruit hang directly off the trunk and larger branches amidst glossy dark green leaves. The pods contain a pinkish pulp which surrounds the pinkish coloured cocoa beans. The beans are allowed to ferment, and dried in the sun where they turn a dark chocolate brown. They are then roasted, shelled and ground to a powder. This is the basis from which all chocolate products are made. To make drinking chocolate, some of the fat (cocoa butter) is removed (and nowadays dried milk is added). When drinking chocolate is treated with an alkali to reduce its acidity, it darkens, loses some of its flavour and sweetness, and cocoa is produced. Plain chocolate is made by adding sugar and extra cocoa butter to the ground cocoa beans; bitter cooking chocolate is made by adding less sugar. Milk chocolate is produced when condensed milk is added to plain chocolate.

Nearly all types of chocolate are easily available, in many different forms and combined with a huge number of other flavourings – the exception is plain unsweetened chocolate or baker's chocolate, which can only occasionally be found at some specialist foodstores. For flavouring good quality bitter chocolate or cocoa should be used. Store blocks of chocolate wrapped in foil in a cool place for 1-2 months.

Uses: Chocolate is best known as a flavour for sweet dishes. Countless cakes, notably Black Forest gâteau, Devil's food cake (p 130) and sachetorte are based on it, and it can be the basis of soufflés, mousses, ice-creams, sweet sauces and biscuits. Chocolate combines with vanilla, cinnamon, coffee, rum, brandy and rose-water. In Australasia it is combined with orange to make a flavour known as jaffa. Cocoa and drinking chocolate are soothing bedtime drinks and can be included in many milk-based puddings and cakes. Cocoa beans are used in the manufacture of several alcoholic beverages: notably *crême de cacao*. Less universal are chocolate's savoury uses. In Mexico, Spain, Italy and southern France the alluring bitterness of unsweetened chocolate is used to great effect with robustly flavoured and densely textured savoury foods such as hare, pigeon, venison – even octopus.

Cocoa and chocolate

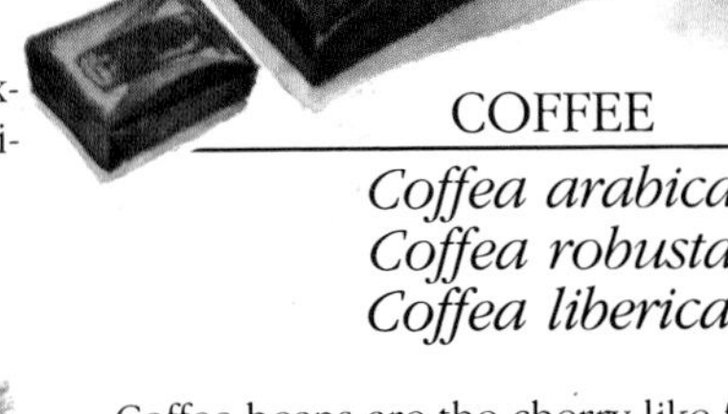

Coconut

COCONUT
Cocos nucifera

The coconut palm, native to Malaysia, is cultivated on tropical coasts throughout the world. From the coconut are derived many different flavouring products. Coconut juice, which makes a refreshing tropical drink, is contained within unripe green coconuts. It should not be confused with coconut milk or cream, which is a thick sweet liquid contained in ripe coconuts. If the latter is unavailable, a good substitute can be made by soaking desiccated coconut in boiling water, then squeezing out the liquid. Commercially-produced cream of coconut is coconut milk that has been formed into solid blocks – it can be reconstituted in boiling water. Coconut meat can be eaten fresh or dried. Desiccated coconut is vacuum-dried coconut flesh, sold in varying sized flakes. Imported ripe coconuts are often seen in markets and greengrocers. Cream of coconut can be found on the shelves of quality grocers, Indian and Oriental food shops and speciality delicatessens.

Uses: Like ginger and cinnamon, in the West coconut is used almost exclusively as a flavouring for sweet dishes: cakes, biscuits (such as macaroons) and confectionery (such as coconut ice). Desiccated coconut is nearly always used – it combines especially well with chocolate and 'tropical' fruits such as orange or lime and pineapple, and makes an attractive garnish when lightly toasted. Coconut milk and cream are less commonly used but can make a delicious change in sweet dishes, adding an exquisite subtlety to custards, creams and fruit sauces. They are also indispensable as a base for *piña coladas* and other delicious coconut cocktails. In South-East Asia coconut milk is an important savoury cooking ingredient. Savoury rice dishes, spicy peanut sauces for meat *satés* (p. 98), salads and deceptively hot noodle dishes all include coconut milk, and it is included in many southern Indian dishes, for example in *molé* (a spicy sauce to accompany fish, eggs or chicken).

COFFEE
Coffea arabica
Coffea robusta
Coffea liberica

Coffee beans are the cherry-like fruit of a small evergreen tree cultivated in bush form throughout the tropics, although most of the coffee beans available in the UK come from Africa and Latin America. Each ripe 'cherry' generally contains two coffee beans. There are some 25 different species of coffee, each with a highly distinctive flavour, although most coffee for sale is blended. Coffee is sold as green (or unroasted) beans, roast beans, ready-ground, or in various forms of 'instant'. Most are available from supermarkets, delicatessens and coffee merchants. Coffee for use as a flavouring should be made very strong and concentrated – alternatively a strong black instant coffee or coffee essence may be used, although for cold desserts the superior flavour of 'real' coffee is preferable. Store all coffee in airtight jars in cool dry places.

Uses: Coffee blends well with vanilla, spirits, spices (notably nutmeg and cinnamon), nuts (especially walnuts), and of course cocoa – a combination better known as mocha. It can be included in chocolate or spice cake mixtures, made into a syrup to serve with fruit dishes or even used in savoury marinades for lamb or beef. But coffee's inimitable flavour is best used in cold sweet dishes: mousses, jellies, granitas, ice creams and custards – coffee-cream filled eclairs are especially delicious. Coffee can be used in creams and icings for sophisticated meringues, gâteaux, tortes, malakoffs and charlottes. Coffee-based alcoholic drinks such as Tia Maria and Crême de Café are popular as is Irish coffee; coffee flavoured with whisky and sugar and topped with a layer of cream.

DRIED MUSHROOMS

Dried edible fungi are an important flavouring in many parts of the world, including China, Japan, central and southern Europe. There are many different types – which can be loosely divided into those which are cultivated (Shiitake, Matsutake, Padi-straw and Cloud Ear) and those which grow wild. Dried mushrooms have a highly concentrated flavour which, combined with the fact that they will keep for over a year, makes them useful in the kitchen. They can be found in Continental delicatessens, and in specialist and Oriental food shops. Before being used, they usually need to be soaked for 30 minutes in warm water, stock or wine; the soaking liquid can then also be added to the dish. The main types of dried mushroom are described below.

Shiitake *(Lentinus edodes)* and **Matsutake**, also known as Japanese tree mushrooms, are cultivated in China and Japan on logs from deciduous trees, then dried in the sun or over charcoal fires. They have a delicate fine flavour and are the most widely used mushroom in Oriental cooking, featuring in dishes such as steamed chicken and *tori mushiyaki*. **Padi-straw mushrooms** *(Volvanella volvacea)* are small conical Chinese mushrooms which are cultivated on wet rice straw and dried over charcoal. They should be stored in an airtight jar as they begin to smell if allowed to get damp. Straw mushrooms are used in China with steamed or fried chicken and to give flavour to vegetarian dishes. **Wood or Cloud Ear** *(Auricularia polytricha)* is a Chinese mushroom which is cultivated on wood or gathered wild. It contributes a fine earthy flavour to Chinese soups, chicken and fish dishes. **Morels** *(Morchella esculenta)* are small, wrinkled, wild mushrooms with a very savoury flavour that grow throughout the world – although several varieties are now cultivated. The finest morels, *Morchella deliciosa,* are said to come from the Jura region of France. Morels have a delicate flavour that blends with the classic simple flavours of French cooking; like Chantarelles they are delicious with eggs.

Chantarelles *(Cantharellus cibarius)* or **Girolles** are elegant, golden, spindly mushrooms which have a delicious flavour and can be found in the Alps and southern Germany.

Boletus mushrooms *(Boletus edulis)* are popular in Europe. They have large brown caps and honeycombed undersides – sliced and dried they are known as *cèpes* in France and *funghi porchini* in Italy. They have a strong, meaty taste.

Dried mushrooms

Coffee

ESSENCES

Essences are highly concentrated flavourings which can be extracted from flowers (such as roses and orange blossom), nuts (such as almonds), fruits (such as citrus fruits), spices (such as cinnamon and cloves) and herbs (such as peppermint). They can be produced in three different ways: by steeping the ingredient in a solvent such as water or alchohol to extract the flavour; by distillation (the method favoured to extract the volatile flavoured oils from aromatic herbs and spices); or by creating them artificially from synthetic chemical compounds.

A profuse selection of essences can be found in grocers, delicatessens and herbalists, and some (peppermint and rosewater for example) can be bought from chemists. Rosewater and orange flower water are widely available in Asian, Middle Eastern and Greek stores. Good quality non-synthetic essences are expensive, but far superior to the cheaper artificial ones. All essences should be stored in tightly-stoppered bottles in a cool, dark place and should not be kept for more than 3 months.

Uses: Although they are used extensively by the food industry, essences are not widely used in Western home cooking, apart from in a few specific cases. A few drops of peppermint essence are compulsory in peppermint creams and vanilla essence is often an ingredient of mixtures for cakes and biscuits (although a vanilla pod will give a far superior flavour). Rosewater and orange flower water are crucial ingredients for anyone attempting to prepare authentic Middle Eastern puddings, desserts and savouries. They are traditional flavourings for the honeyed syrups that drench sweet nut pastries such as *baklava* and *konafa*, and rosewater flavours the sophisticated ground rice puddings and fruit salads that are popular throughout the Arab world. Rosewater is believed to have been introduced to India by the Moguls. Nowadays it is an everyday ingredient in Indian puddings and drinks. It is found in *gulab jaman* (small milk powder balls steeped in a cardamom and rosewater flavoured syrup), *kulfi* (cone-shaped ice cream), and used to flavour sweet *lassi* (a refreshing yogurt drink) and sherbets. Both rosewater and orange flower water were staple ingredients of the English kitchen until Victorian times.

Essences

LIQUORICE

Glycyrrhiza glabra

The liquorice plant is a perennial legume which is native to south-eastern Europe and the Middle East. Its root descends vertically for about 1 m (3 feet) and sends out horizontal rhizomes; it is the root and rhizome which are harvested, dried and used as a flavouring. The dried root has a brown, woody exterior and yellowy, fibrous interior. It is normally sold in 10 cm (4 inch) lengths and is about 1 cm (½ inch) thick. Liquorice root is also available as a ground spice and as black cylindrical sticks 8 mm (⅓ inch) in diameter and 12 cm (5 inches) long – these are produced from a boiled, solidified root extract. Natural liquorice has a slightly aromatic fragrance and a sweet-sour flavour. It has been cultivated in Europe since the Middle Ages, and was once grown in Yorkshire near Pontefract. Liquorice root, powders and sticks are available from good health food shops and herb shops. The dried roots should be sliced, crushed or ground before use, and all liquorice products should be stored in a cool, dark, dry place.

Uses: The bitter-sweet liquorice root has been enjoyed as a natural confection for thousands of years. In the Middle Ages it was used as a cough remedy and in the sixteenth and seventeenth centuries it was used to darken gingerbread. In Britain it is best known as a flavouring for confectionery – Pontefract Cakes and liquorice allsorts probably being the best known examples. It is an essential part of the taste of traditional malt beers such as stout, and in southern Turkey, Syria and the Lebanon, liquorice is boiled with water to make *sous,* a popular refreshing drink which is served ice-cold.

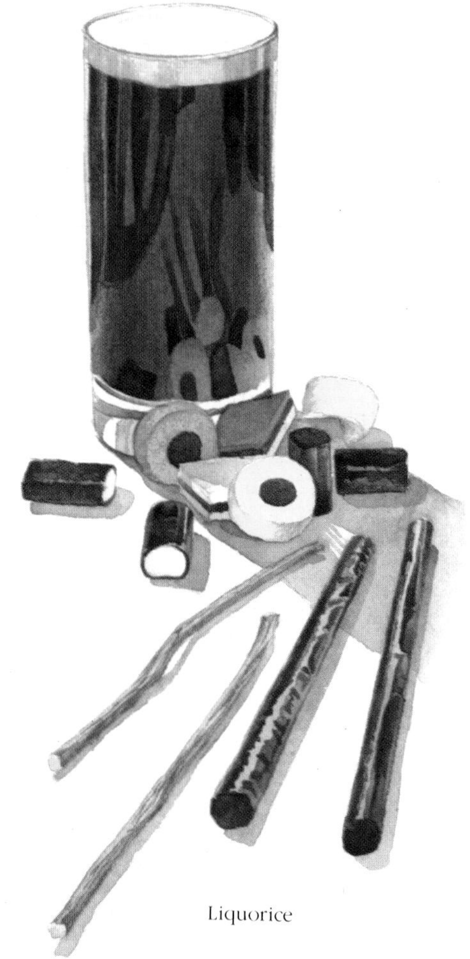

Liquorice

Monosodium glutamate

MONOSODIUM GLUTAMATE

Variously referred to as Taste Powder, Ve-tsin, Gourmet Powder and MSG, monosodium glutamate is a white crystalline salt of glutamic acid – glutamic acid being a component of gluten, the mixture of proteins that occurs naturally in wheat and other cereals. MSG is widely used as a seasoning for foods, especially by the food industry: it has little taste of its own but possesses the remarkable ability of emphasizing other flavours, especially those of meat and vegetables.

MSG is sold in small tins in Chinese supermarkets, specialist grocers and at some chemists. It should be used very sparingly, if at all. MSG occurs naturally in soy sauce.

Uses: Monosodium glutamate is used in vast quantities by the food industry and catering trade, usually to mask blandness and boost weak flavours. It is included in many savoury products including canned goods, bottled sauces and stock cubes. The Chinese often include a pinch of Ve-tsin in stir fries and sauces for pork or beef; in its natural form, as soy sauce, it is used to add sparkle to innumerable Chinese and Japanese dishes. See also: SOYA (p 85).

MUSTARD

fam. Cruciferae

Mustard is a condiment prepared from the seeds of three plants of the cabbage family. There are three types of seeds: white, brown and black, and the huge number of different mustards available are based on combinations of these three seed types, blended with other flavouring ingredients such as wine, vinegar, allspice, peppercorns, tarragon, chillies and garlic. Most supermarkets sell a basic range of mustards, but for a more exotic range look in delicatessens and quality grocery shops where a vast number of mustards containing innumerable different flavourings can be found. Mustard powder in its familiar yellow tin can be easily found in grocers and supermarkets.

Prepared mustards will keep for about 6 months in airtight jars. Powders will keep for 3-4 months in tins. Remember that mustard's pungency is destroyed by heat, so for a fiery result it should be added to sauces or stews after the cooking is finished.

All mustards are highly effective in bringing out the flavour of most meats, particularly beef, pork and game. Many cheese, egg and vegetable dishes can also benefit from the use of mustard.

English mustard is a combination of white and black mustard seeds, wheat flour and turmeric – which gives it its familiar yellow colour. Mustard powder should be mixed with cold water and left for 15 minutes to develop its fiery flavour, a milder flavour can be achieved by mixing the powder with milk or cream and a drop of sugar. Ready mixed English mustard is not as strong as the freshly prepared kind. The hot sharpness of English mustard combines as a condiment with simple strong-tasting fare such as sharp Cheddar cheese, country sausages, roast beef, pork and gammon. It is traditionally included in Welsh rarebit, and in mustard sauce to serve with oily fish such as mackerel and herrings. It is essential in piccalilli.

Bordeaux mustard consists of black mustard seeds blended with unfermented claret, often

flavoured with herbs, especially tarragon. Dark brown and aromatic, it has a mild sweet/sour taste and is the connoisseur's choice to accompany grilled steaks and cold meats. It is traditionally used to spread on the bread that tops *carbonnade de boeuf*, a traditional French beef and ale stew.

Dijon mustard from Burgundy is made from husked black seeds blended with salt, spices and white wine or verjuice – an acid juice made from unripe green grapes. Many varieties are available, but all are a palish grey-yellow colour with a subtle flavour which varies in pungency from mild to very hot. Dijon mustards are used in preference to any other type in delicate classic sauces such as Cumberland, devil and *rémoulade*, and in vinaigrette dressings.

Meaux mustard is a mixture of crushed and ground black seeds mixed with vinegar and spices. Many varieties are available but the most popular is sold in wide-mouthed stoneware jars, the cork secured with red sealing wax. Meaux mustards have an unusual crunchy texture and a fairly hot flavour. They can be employed relish-fashion with cold meats and hams and included in mayonnaises, vinaigrettes and cheese sauces and used to give texture to vegetable purées, supplying a contrasting crunchy texture and slightly spicy flavour.

German mustard is a combination of strong black mustard flour and vinegar. Smooth, slightly sweet and aromatic, it is less pungent than English mustard but more so than Bordeaux. German mustard is often flavoured with herbs, especially tarragon, and is best partnered with the various types of sausage popular in that country – *knackwurst, bockwurst* and so on, or with cold cuts.

American mustard is made from white mustard seeds, white wine, sugar and vinegar. It is pale yellow, mild and sweet and has a smooth sauce-like consistency. It makes an excellent accompaniment for hot dogs and hamburgers and can be spread lightly over chops and sausages before grilling.

Mustard

Nuts

NUTS

Nuts are the edible kernels of hard-shelled fruits and seeds, and are one of the most ancient foods known to man.

For flavouring purposes buy whole nuts in their shells in small quantities from grocers and supermarkets. They will keep well in a cool place for about two months. Shelled nuts deteriorate far more readily and should be covered and stored in a dark place for short periods only.

Almonds *(Prunus dulcis)* have perhaps the most versatile flavouring properties. They can be bought shelled, unshelled, blanched, slivered, flaked, diced and ground. For thousands of years ground sweet almonds have been used for baking and thickening sauces. They still feature prominently in the cooking of Iran and are a crucial ingredient in the delicate Mogul cuisine of north India and Kashmir where they are included in numerous savoury dishes such as *kormas* and *pilaus* and also in sweet dishes such as *kulfi* (Indian ice cream). In the Middle East almonds can be included in *mezzes* (a selection of hors d'oeuvres), in stuffings and sauces for meat and poultry and in all types of pastries and sweetmeats. In the West almonds are fried with trout, made into a traditional English soup and included in numerous rich cakes and light biscuits. Almonds can be candied and made into praline, itself an essential flavouring in many sweet dishes and in confectionery.

Bitter almonds *(Prunus amara)* are less available and should only be used cooked, as they are poisonous in their raw state. They can be used to great effect with sweet almonds in cakes and biscuits and also in pork and chicken dishes.

Cashew nuts *(Anacardium occidentale)* have a particularly fine, sweet taste and texture and are popular in South America, India and Asia. In China they feature in spicy Szechuan dishes and are widely used in southern India.

Ginkgo nuts *(Ginko biloba)* are also a favourite ingredient in Oriental cuisines, notably that of Japan. The plum-like fruits' kernels impart sweetness and a flowery aroma.

Hazelnuts (*gen. Corylus*) are almost as versatile as almonds. Ground hazelnut 'flour' is a baking standby and features a great deal in confectionery cake and biscuit-making as well as to a lesser degree in savoury cooking. Popular in the regional dishes of the Middle East hazelnuts have an affinity with fish and liver. The French use them in their compound butter, *beurre noisette*, to garnish cold hors d'oeuvres and to enrich white sauces.

Macadamia nuts *(Macadamia ternifolia),* native to Australia, are also grown in California, Hawaii and Florida. They have a rich, full buttery texture and sweet taste, similar to the candle nut so popular in Oriental cooking. Being more readily available in the West, they can be used as a substitute. Most frequently eaten on their own, with drinks, they can also be ground, imparting a rich sweetness to soups, and *saté*-like sauces.

Peanuts *(Arachis hypongaea)* are highly nutritious nuts. They are widely used in the Middle East to garnish rice and couscous dishes and in Africa to add substance to spicy chicken stews. Ground peanuts give body to much South-East Asian cooking and are one of the characteristic flavourings of Indonesian *saté* sauces. Peanut butter, smooth or crunchy, makes an ever-popular spread and can be made into cookies and sauces.

Pine nuts *(Pinus pinea)* were a favourite of the Ancient Romans and today are still an indispensable ingredient in the Mediterranean area. They are very popular in sweet and sour dishes, and in stuffings for vegetables. In the Middle East they are often combined with dried fruit in stuffings for poultry, vegetables and vine leaves.

Pistachio nuts *(Pistacia vera)* are also much-loved nuts in the Middle East and Mediterranean areas, appearing in Lebanese savoury dishes, syrupy *filo* pastries and in Turkish Delight. They are popular in Europe and India as a flavouring for ice-cream, and can also be found decorating cakes and in nougat.

Walnuts *(Juglans regia)*, can be used as a sweet or a savoury flavouring, or eaten on their own. They can feature in cheese soufflés, soups, stuffings for poultry, pasta sauces and in innumerable biscuits and pastries. See also: CHESTNUT (p 79), COCONUT (p 80).

OILS

The oils used in cooking are generally extracted by the pressing of various nuts, seeds, vegetables and plants. Apart from considerations such as the temperatures to which they may be heated and their relative content of unhealthy saturated fats, they are usually chosen for their flavour. They may also be selected for their lack of it, for instance in the frying of subtly flavoured foods. In fact, oils are normally tasteless, no matter what their source, and derive any flavour they do have from traces of the other elements present in their origins. Commercial refined oils, therefore, which have been specially treated to stabilize them for longer shelf-life, have more muted flavours. Unrefined oils, normally made by straightforward cold pressing techniques, have true full flavours, but do tend to go cloudy and rancid more rapidly.

Buy oils from supermarkets, good grocers and health food shops. The more esoteric nut oils are available from some delicatessens and Continental food shops. Store all oils in cool dry places away from the light, which otherwise encourages decomposition.

Olive oil is undoubtedly the foremost flavourer. The most sought-after and expensive olive oils are 'virgin', that is, produced by the first pressings. They can vary in colour from a rich yellow to deep green and those of Tuscany, which have a sweet taste with a hint of nuttiness, and of Provence, which have an aromatic floweriness, are especially prized. Good quality olive oil is a crucial ingredient in authentic Mediterranean cooking, giving a wonderfully rich flavour to food that is fried or sautéed in it. It is the only correct oil for a real French dressing. Drizzled over freshly cooked pasta it acts as a sauce, and is used in the same way in the Middle East on hummus and yogurt to serve with kebabs.

Peanut oil, also known as arachide oil, is generally popular as a substitute for, or alternative to, olive oil, having a good but mild smell and no flavour. Because of its lack of flavour it is preferred by many in the cooking of fish and poultry, and for dressings and mayonnaises.

Almond oil and walnut oil have very distinctive flavours that limit their range of use. They usually feature in salad dressings and mayonnaise, but are seldom used in baking and confectionery.

Sesame oil, sunflower oil and safflower oil are most prized for their light, neutral tastes, which can be put to subtle use in light dressings for green leaves. The Chinese often include small amounts of sesame oil in stir-fries to add an extra nutty flavour.

Soya oil is widely used throughout the world as a cooking oil. Its flavour is less attractive than other vegetable oils but it is inexpensive and keeps well, making it an excellent all-purpose oil, especially useful as a base for a blend of oils.

Mustard seed oil, surprisingly, has a fairly bland flavour when heated. It is used throughout Southern India, where it is cheaper than *ghee*, adding a subtle but identifiable flavour to the local spicy dishes.

Palm oil is the distinctive flavour base of most West African cooking. It has a high fat content but is an excellent oil for frying.

Corn, vegetable and wheatgerm oils are almost entirely tasteless. If they impart any flavour in cooking it is normally an unpleasant one and a sign that the food has been badly cooked or that the oil is stale. Corn oil is traditionally used in some American dishes such as corn fritters. See also SOYA (p 85).

Oils

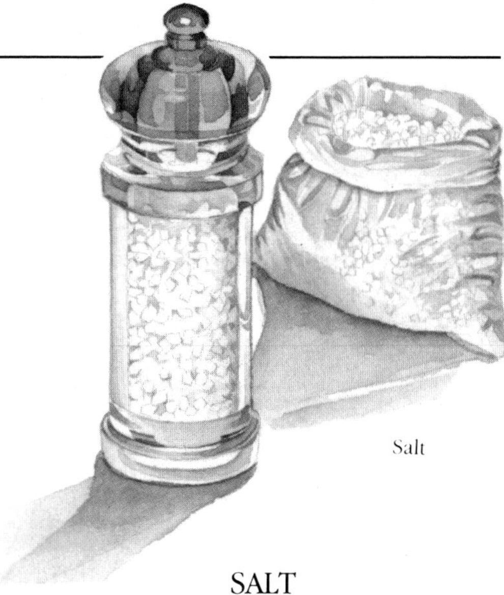
Salt

SALT

Sodium chloride

Most 'table' and 'cooking' salt is chemically manufactured and contains additives to make it free-flowing. More nutritious and tastier varieties, such as bay salt (or *gros-sel*), Maldon salt and sea salt are made by the evaporation of estuary or bay water, and along with mined rock salt are gaining in popularity and availability.

Store all forms of salt in a tightly sealed containers in a cool dry place, as it absorbs atmospheric moisture very readily.

Uses: As well as being a ubiquitous condiment and seasoning for savoury and sweet dishes, salt contributes greatly to the flavour of many preserved foods such as hams, bacon, salt beef, kippers, smoked salmon and salt cod. It is used to draw out the bitter juices in aubergines and courgettes before cooking. The taste of many nuts, too, would be unrecognizable if they were unsalted. In the Mediterranean fish and poultry are buried and cooked in a crust of salt which is then chipped off at the table (see p 100).

SAUCES

A few commercially made sauces, usually with a vinegar base, have won well-deserved status as flavouring agents.

Worcestershire sauce, a British adaption of an Indian recipe, is an inheritance from the British raj in India. The thin dark sauce is made to a secret recipe, but it almost certainly contains vinegar, soy, molasses, tamarinds (p 86), ginger, anchovies, garlic, limes, chillies and sugar. Used sparingly, it acts as a taste catalyst and is the surprise ingredient in many a chef's special *tour de force*.

Tabasco is a thin fierce red pepper sauce, made from a small red Mexican variety of chilli. It was introduced to the southern states of the USA from Mexico in the nineteenth century and has since become indispensable in the more strongly flavoured dishes of American regional cuisines such as Tex-Mex and Creole.

Anchovy essence is made from the pounded flesh of the fish and is a relic of a favoured condiment of the Ancient Romans and similar to the blachan (p 78) of Indonesia. As well as adding strength to fish dishes, especially pies, it can be included in traditional English meat pies.
Mushroom ketchup is made from the liquor of cooked mushrooms and adds earthiness to many full flavoured meat and fish dishes.
Walnut ketchup is a product of pickled green walnuts and goes very well with a variety of cheese and green vegetable dishes.
Tomato ketchup is one of the vast array of sauces and ketchups, popular as everyday table condiments. Top grade tomato ketchup is bright red and contains no artificial flavourings. It can be included in barbecue sauce.
Bean sauces are important ingredients in Chinese cooking. Black bean sauce (or brown bean sauce) is a thick dark paste and is often used instead of soy when a thicker sauce is required in stir-fry cooking. Yellow bean sauce is salty and pungent. It can be used in stir-fries and stews, especially in recipes from northern China. Bean sauces can be bought in cans and bottles from Chinese supermarkets.
Hoisin sauce is a thick soya based sauce much used in Chinese recipes for shellfish, spare ribs and duck. It has a sweet slightly hot flavour.
Oyster sauce is based on a blend of soy sauce and oysters. Used in the same way as soy sauce, it adds a rich strong flavour to Chinese beef, pork and poultry dishes. See also: SOYA, TOMATO PURÉE (p 86).

Sauces

Soya

SOYA

Glycine max

The beans of a bushy leguminous plant which is native to eastern Asia, soya is among mankind's oldest cultivated crops, and has been grown in China for thousands of years. The plant is a member of the bean and pea family and grows from 30cm-2m (1-6½ feet) high. The pods, 2.5-7.5cm (1-3 inches) long, contain the seeds or beans which are possibly the richest source of vegetable protein. Highly nutritious, the beans are eaten fresh and dried, and are used to make several products essential to the cooking of the Orient and of increasing popularity in the West. Flour and oil are made from the beans themselves. A milk produced from soya bean flour is used to make *tofu* or bean curd, a nutritious cheese-like vegetable jelly. By fermenting the beans in a brine containing various cereal flours, soy sauce and *miso* (a thick red, white or brown paste) are produced. *Tamari* is a naturally (as opposed to chemically) fermented soy sauce which is a by-product from the manufacture of *miso* . *Miso* and *tofu* can be found in Japanese food stores. Bean curd, dried bean curd skins and soy sauce can all be found in Chinese shops.
Uses: Soya bean flour is much used in commercial cake manufacture and confectionery as well as in vegetarian cooking. Soya bean oil is favoured by vegetarians and is used as a common base for margarines. Bean curd is a staple ingredient in Far Eastern cooking.

Good soy sauces can be recognized by their pungent aroma and 'meaty' taste. They also hold a foamy head if shaken vigorously. Soy sauce comes in a variety of colours and strengths (light to dark), the potency generally being indicated by the richness of brown. Soy sauce has been used as a condiment in the same way as salt is used in the West, in the East for thousands of years. It is the only natural foodstuff to contain monosodium glutamate (p 82) and brings out the flavour of all manner of fish, meat, poultry and vegetable dishes – particularly rice. *Miso* is characteristically used in Japan to thicken and enrich soups and sauces. See also: OILS (p 84).

SUGAR

A sweet tasting substance that exists naturally in plants and animals. There are many different sugars, the most common source being the sap of the sugar-cane, a perennial sub-tropical grass native to Asia but now grown throughout the tropics. A sugar syrup, when cooked to evaporate the natural moisture will burn slightly, or caramelize, and develop a pleasant, slightly smoky flavour. Caramel is much used in confectionery and in the making of many sweet dishes, such as oranges in caramel and crème caramel.

Sugars of all sorts also find use in savoury cooking, often as caramelized glazes – particularly for hams and vegetables.
Natural brown sugars like demerara and muscovado come from raw sugar cane. They vary in colour from deep brown to golden and are moist and full in flavour. They can be used in spiced fruit cakes and gingerbreads.
Light brown or soft dark brown sugars are refined white sugars that have been coated in molasses. They are just as sweet as natural brown sugar but have less flavour.
White refined sugars such as granulated, castor, icing and preserving sugar are very refined, retaining little flavour other than intense sweetness and really only varying in texture.
Molasses is the natural syrup extracted from the cane which as well as being intensely sweet has a distinct rich, warm flavour of its own. The cooking of the USA makes much use of molasses, notably in Boston baked beans (p 106).
Maple syrup is a deliciously aromatic, clear, thin syrup that is extracted from the sap of a variety of the North American maple tree. Graded according to quality, the best and most expensive maple syrup is light and clear. Its traditional use is as an accompaniment to waffles and pancakes on the American breakfast table.
Treacle is produced by refining molasses and has a slightly sweeter taste.
Golden syrup is a pale thick treacle, produced by the further refining of an uncrystallizable syrup produced by sugar refining. It is less sweet than sugar and like treacle is used in cakes and puddings, notably as a topping for steamed puddings and as an ingredient of brandy snaps.

Sugar

TAMARIND

Tamarindus indica

The giant leguminous tamarind tree is native to tropical east Africa, but has been cultivated in the Indian subcontinent for centuries and is now grown in many parts of the tropics, notably the Caribbean area. A sour brown juice is produced from the dried pods and this gives an essential acidity to many savoury dishes from South-East Asia, India and the Caribbean. The tree can grow up to 2.5 m (8 feet) high and bears curved pods about 23 cm (9 inches) long which are dark brown when ripe. The pods contain up to ten dark brown seeds, most of which are removed before they are processed. Tamarind is available in Indian and West Indian shops as a fibrous, sticky pulp of dark brown, partly dried pods and seeds, which has been compressed into rectangular cakes. To prepare it, steep the pulp in boiling water, allow the water to cool, then gently rub it to a purée with the fingers. Sieve the purée and discard the seeds and fibre. Excess tamarind purée will keep for up to a week in the refrigerator, but should not be kept in a metal container. If tamarind is unavailable, lemon or lime juice will make a poor but usable substitute. The high acid content of tamarind ensures a long life and it can safely be stored in a cool place for many months, if kept in an airtight container.

Uses: Tamarind is used in Indian, South-East Asian and Caribbean cooking in much the same way as vinegars and lemon juice are in European cuisines. It is included in all types of savoury stews and spicy sauces and as an effective preservative it is a basic flavouring for a variety of chutneys; tamarind fish, for instance, is a common relish made from several types of Indian fish. Because of its high pectin content, tamarind is often included in sweet jams and jellies, for example in guava jelly. Tamarind also features in Arab cookery: in the Middle East tamarind teas and waters have long been favoured as refreshing drinks and it is used as a flavouring for stews and vegetable dishes. In the West tamarind is commonly used in the manufacture of soft fruit drinks and Worcestershire sauce. See also SAUCES (p 84).

Tamarind

Tomato purée

TOMATO PURÉE

Tomato purée, paste or concentrate is a reduction of cooked tomatoes, usually the flavourful and aromatic plum tomatoes of the Mediterranean region. The intensity of flavour produced by the repeated process of rendering down develops a quality entirely of its own – quite different to that of tomatoes themselves. Highly acid yet very sweet, tomato purée has an almost meaty taste. The full flavour develops during prolonged cooking. Sold in cans or tubes in most supermarkets and delicatessens, it keeps very well when sealed in its container. Once opened it should be used as soon as possible or the flavour will degenerate.

Uses: Tomato purée is often diluted for use as a substitute for fresh tomatoes in cooking or as a quick tomato sauce. However, it is at its best when used to give zest and strength to meat and fish casseroles and sauces for pasta. Used sparingly it can give a little of the same subtle force, and a delicate colour, to soups, lighter stews and egg dishes. Mixed with olive oil, garlic, herbs and other flavourings it makes a gloriously rich dressing for salads containing tomatoes or any of the other vegetable fruits, such as sweet peppers or avocados. Mixed with mayonnaise, it makes a traditional prawn cocktail sauce, and tomato purée is also indispensable in sauces for barbecued meats and poultry. A drop or two can give a hint of richness to any savoury dough or batter mixture.

TRUFFLES

Truffles are highly aromatic edible fungi which usually grow about 30 cm (1 foot) underground in the vicinity of certain trees and herbs. Unlike other fungi they cannot be cultivated and can only be detected by specially trained dogs and pigs, factors which contribute to their legendary scarcity and resulting in fabulous prices – they are man's most expensive foodstuff. The aroma of fresh truffles is virtually indescribable, even by the most descriptive gourmets. It is slightly reminiscent of garlic but that is the nearest comparison that can be made. Truffles can be found in the best gourmet shops in season – November to December for white truffles and a few months later for the black. Fresh truffles will keep for several days in the refrigerator, wrapped in tissue paper in an airtight jar, otherwise their pervasive aroma will penetrate anything they are stored with. Canned truffles, truffle peelings and truffle essence, equally exorbitantly priced, are available in high quality delicatessens. They keep well but are vastly inferior alternatives to the fresh fungi. There are a number of species of truffle, but the best known and most prized are:

The Black or Perigord truffle *(Tuber melanosporum)* which is coal black and, usually, walnut sized. It is found in the Perigord region of south-west France and has a rich aroma and almost no flavour. It is most often eaten cooked, included in minute quantities in pâtés, terrines and in stuffings for poultry and game birds. More extravagantly black truffles are sometimes fried and dressed in a champagne sauce, or wrapped in pastry, baked and served *en croûte*. Their jet black colour is used to great effect in garnishing, particularly of pale-coloured meats and aspics. The French are also fond of including minute quantities of truffle when wrapping small game birds in bacon before roasting.

The Italian white truffle is found throughout the Piedmont region. It is normally larger than the black truffle, creamy coloured and almost potato-like in appearance. It has a very strong perfume but little flavour, and is consequently usually eaten raw; shaved finely over *risottos*, plain pastas and egg dishes. White truffle is also sometimes used in the vegetable fondue *bagna cauda*. Truffle lovers also include either variety of truffles in simple salads, dressed lightly in best quality olive oil and lemon juice.

Truffles

Vanilla

VANILLA
Vanilla planifolia

Made from the pod of a climbing member of the orchid family, vanilla is native to the rain forests of Central America but is now cultivated throughout the tropics. The black or greenish-yellow pods are harvested while still unripe and flavourless, dipped briefly in boiling water and put to 'sweat' in airtight containers. This promotes an enzyme reaction which causes the flavour to develop. The essential oil 'vanillin' is exuded and forms a crystalline frosting around the pods as they dry. Dried pods are available from quality food shops, better confectioners and some delicatessens. The black variety have the best flavour, evidenced by their headily pungent floral aroma. They will keep in airtight containers for some months and can be used many times – provided they are washed and dried after each use. As vanilla is almost entirely destined for sweet dishes, the pods are commonly stored in containers filled with sugar. They will continue to impart a fine full flavour to several changes of contents for 1-2 years. Using the sugar also makes it easier to regulate the amount of flavour, as vanilla can easily be overpowering. If required to flavour custards or syrups directly, the pods can be removed after use, washed, dried and returned to the sugar jar.

Vanilla essence, made by steeping the pods in alcohol, is also available (although the pods provide a far superior means of flavouring). All too often, however, vanilla essence is made synthetically from clove oil, and has only a shadow of the real flavour.

Uses: Vanilla was being used to flavour the Aztecs' beloved chocolate when the Spaniards first came upon both products and brought them back to Europe, and the combination has continued ever since – particularly in confectionery. Vanilla has become such a standard ingredient in sweet foods that it is often barely thought of as a flavouring in its own right and is regarded as more of a neutral base, such as in vanilla ice cream. Its flowery, spicy sweetness is popular as a flavouring for cakes and biscuits and is also included in icings, frostings, butter creams and in crème pâtissière.

VINEGAR

The word vinegar is derived from the French *vin aigre* or 'sour wine'. Vinegars are produced when bacteria attack the alcohol contained in alcoholic liquids such as wine or ale, and oxidize it into acetic acid – the resulting sour liquid being known as vinegar. The most common vinegars are made from red or white wines and beers (malt vinegar) although vinegars made from cider, sherry and white currant juice are increasingly available. In the Orient, vinegars are commonly made from fermented *sake* (rice wine). Strong distilled or white vinegar is made by distilling natural vinegar in a vacuum.

A huge variety of different ingredients can be steeped in wine vinegar to produce flavoured vinegars. These include herbs – such as tarragon, mint, basil and thyme – garlic, chillies, flowers and fruits, such as raspberries and gooseberries.

Uses: Apart from their common use in preserving, vinegars are an indispensable flavouring for many different foods. Malt and distilled vinegars add their own distinctive flavours to traditional pickles and relishes, as well as to classic piquant sauces such as mint and horseradish. The flavoured vinegars come into their own in vinaigrettes and sauces, giving an instant herbal subtlety or spicy tang; for instance, shallot vinegar makes excellent *béarnaise* sauce and chilli flavoured vinegar is a superb dressing for simple seafood dishes. A little wine vinegar included in a marinade will have a tenderizing effect on meat and poultry and a dash of wine vinegar will add piquancy to stews, sauces and Welsh rarebit. Cider vinegars can be used in fruit pickles and relishes, but have a sharp flavour which suits little else. Sherry vinegars are rather sweet and make unusual salad dressings, particularly where some acid constituent like citrus fruit needs balancing. The rather honeyed refinement of rice wine vinegars is ideal in authentic Chinese sweet and sour sauces and is an essential flavouring for the rice in Japanese *sushi* dishes. Raspberry vinegars and other fruit and flower vinegars were traditionally used diluted, as refreshing cold drinks.

Vinegar

Wines, spirits and liqueurs

WINES, SPIRITS AND LIQUEURS

Almost all alcoholic beverages find use in the flavouring of food. In most cases, unless the liquor is added just before serving, the cooking process drives off all the alcohol itself and the flavour is provided by the elements which go to make up the taste of the drink.

Uses: Red wine lends particular enhancement to dishes subjected to long, slow cooking, such as casseroles and stews – like *coq au vin* or *boeuf bourguignon* - and meat pâtés and terrines. White wine has a particular role in delicate *court bouillons* for the poaching and baking of whole fish, such as salmon, and for cooking shellfish, such as mussels and clams. It is also used in the accompanying sauces. Vermouths are also effective in conjunction with robustly flavoured fish. Champagne lends a particular luxurious subtlety to fine seafood, such as langoustine. Sherry finds its way into soups and fish sauces, and into trifles and fruit salads. Port is classic in many English game dishes such as jugged hare and Cumberland sauce, as well as providing a rich finish to game soups and fragrant fruit such as melon. Madeira is used in much the same way as sherry, but is more common with ham dishes and *de rigueur* in aspics and jellies.

Brandy is used whenever a stronger 'meatier' taste is required. The essential flavour of brandy is somewhat akin to vanilla, and it is therefore used in similar dishes such as chocolate mousse.

Rum is very widely used. It features occasionally in Creole and Caribbean savoury dishes, but is more well known as a flavouring for cakes, pastries and sweet dishes, especially in sophisticated chocolate desserts.

The applications of eaux-de-vie and liqueurs are innumerable even for the scope of an entire book. Perhaps best known and most reliable are the uses of orange flavoured liqueurs in sweet dishes such as soufflés and *crêpes suzette*, Kirsch in *clafoutis* and Pernod in fish dishes.

Beer is commonly used to give robustness to meat stews, and some fine hams are cured in it. It is also highly effective as a *court bouillon* for strong flavoured fish, such as pike.

JAPANESE PORK AND WATERCRESS SOUP

450g (1lb) lean pork, cut into 1cm (½ inch) dice
1.5 litres (2½ pints) water
1 teaspoon salt
pinch of MSG (optional)
6 tablespoons aka-miso or salted red bean paste (p 85)
1 large bunch watercress, coarsely chopped
2 spring onions, finely chopped
2.5cm (1 inch) piece fresh ginger root, grated

Preparation time: 10 minutes
Cooking time: 15 minutes
Serves 4-6

1. Put the pork with the water into a large saucepan and add the salt and MSG. Bring to the boil, then lower heat and simmer for 5 minutes or until the pork is tender.
2. Mix a little of the cooking liquid with the miso, then stir into the pan. Add the watercress and bring to the boil, then lower the heat and simmer for 2 minutes. Stir in the spring onions and ginger.
3. Serve immediately in warmed soup bowls, ideally drink with china spoons.

AVGOLEMONO (CHICKEN SOUP WITH EGG AND LEMON)

1 litre (1¾ pints) homemade chicken stock
2 egg yolks
5 tablespoons lemon juice
1 tablespoon water
finely pared rind of 1 lemon, to garnish (optional)

Preparation time: 3-5 minutes
Cooking time: 2 minutes

Avgolemono is a characteristically Greek egg and lemon juice mixture which is added to sauces and soups just before serving to give a distinctive sharp, refreshing taste. Once the egg and lemon is added, the soup must not be allowed to boil or the egg will 'scramble'. The richer the chicken stock, the better the soup will taste.
1. Bring the stock to the boil in a covered saucepan, then remove from the heat.
2. Using a fork, beat the egg yolks in a bowl with the lemon juice and water for about 1 minute, until light and frothy.
3. Gradually add 5 tablespoons of the stock, one at a time, to the egg and lemon mixture, beating constantly.
4. Tip the egg and lemon mixture into the remaining stock and stir over the lowest possible heat for 1 minute, without letting it boil. Serve at once in warmed soup bowls, garnished with lemon rind and accompanied by warm wholemeal pitta bread.

Opposite, clockwise from the top: *Chestnut Soup; Turkish borscht; Avgolemono (chicken soup with egg and lemon); Japanese pork and watercress soup*

CHESTNUT SOUP

450g (1lb) peeled fresh chestnuts, chopped, or canned unsweetened chestnut purée
1 celery stick, chopped
1 onion, peeled and chopped
1.25 litres (2¼ pints) hot chicken stock
½ teaspoon sugar
salt
freshly ground black pepper
1 teaspoon grated lemon rind
warm croûtons, to garnish

Preparation time: 5 minutes
Cooking time: 30 minutes

1. Put the chestnuts, celery and onion into a large saucepan with the stock, sugar and salt and pepper. Bring to the boil, then lower the heat and simmer, half-covered for 20 minutes. Sieve.
2. Stir in the lemon rind, simmer for a further 5 minutes and serve in warmed individual soup bowls, sprinkled with warm croûtons.

TURKISH BORSCHT

4 tablespoons vegetable oil
2 large onions, peeled and chopped
2 celery sticks, chopped
3 potatoes, about 350g (12oz), peeled and diced
1 large green pepper, cored, seeded and diced
1×225g (8oz) can tomatoes
3 garlic cloves, peeled and crushed
3 large raw beetroot, about 450g (1lb), grated
1.25 litres (2¼ pints) beef or chicken stock
1 bay leaf
1 teaspoon dill seeds, crushed
2 sprigs parsley
salt
freshly ground black pepper
2 tablespoons wine vinegar
150ml (¼ pint) soured cream or plain unsweetened yogurt (optional)

Preparation time: 25 minutes
Cooking time: 45 minutes
Serves 6-7

1. Heat the oil in a large saucepan, add the onions, celery, potatoes and green pepper and fry over a gentle heat for about 5 minutes, stirring occasionally, until the onion is soft and lightly coloured.
2. Add the tomatoes, garlic, grated beetroot, stock and herbs. Bring to the boil, then lower the heat and simmer very gently for about 35 minutes, until the vegetables are tender. Taste and adjust the seasoning, add the vinegar and simmer for a further 5 minutes.
3. Remove the bay leaf and serve the soup, with soured cream swirled over each bowl, if liked.

From the right, clockwise: *Gravad lax; Prawn, mangetout and hazelnut salad; Potato salad with lobster, ham and truffle*

GRAVAD LAX

2 tablespoons sea salt
1½ tablespoons soft light brown sugar
1 teaspoon crushed black peppercorns
1 tablespoon gin or brandy
2 tablespoons finely chopped fresh dill or
2 teaspoons dried dill
750g (1½lb) fresh salmon, middle cut or tailpiece, cut into 2 fillets but unskinned
fresh dill or fennel leaves, to garnish

DRESSING

4 tablespoons olive oil
1 tablespoon white wine vinegar
1 tablespoon German mustard
salt
freshly ground black pepper

Preparation time: 10 minutes, plus marinating
Serves 6

This method of preparing salmon is popular in Scandinavian countries, where it is often preferred to smoked salmon. The raw fish is marinated in a light, spicy pickle and then served finely sliced, with a dressing passed separately. It makes an attractive summer starter.

1. Combine the salt, sugar, peppercorns, gin and dill in a bowl and stir well to mix. Spread a quarter of the mixture over a large plate and lay one fillet on top, skin side down. Spread half the remaining mixture over the cut side. Place the other salmon fillet, skin side up, on top and spread with the remaining mixture, rubbing it in well. Cover the salmon with tin foil, then lay a board or plate on top and weight down with a couple of cans.

2. Chill the salmon in the bottom of the refrigerator for between 36 hours and 5 days, turning it once a day.

3. Slice the salmon thinly and arrange the slices overlapping on a board or serving dish. Garnish with fresh dill.

4. Combine all the dressing ingredients in a jug, whisk with a fork to blend thoroughly, then leave to stand for 10 minutes. Whisk again and hand separately with the Gravad Lax.

POTATO SALAD WITH LOBSTER, HAM AND TRUFFLE

450g (1lb) waxy potatoes, cooked in their skins, peeled and sliced
1 lobster tail, peeled and thinly sliced
1 thick slice cooked ham, about 75g (3oz), diced
2 canned pimientos, drained and diced
1×25g (1oz) jar chopped truffles or 1×15g (½oz) can whole truffles
DRESSING
6 tablespoons olive oil
3 tablespoons lemon juice
salt
freshly ground black pepper

Preparation time: 10 minutes, plus standing

This elegant and luxurious salad should be eaten as a course on its own, either as a dinner-party starter or the main dish for a summer lunch.

1. Combine the potatoes, lobster, ham, pimiento and truffle in a large salad bowl, mixing lightly with two forks.
2. Thoroughly combine the dressing ingredients and pour over the salad. Toss lightly to coat all the ingredients in dressing. Leave to stand at room temperature for 30 minutes before serving, to allow the truffle aroma to penetrate the other ingredients.

PRAWN, MANGETOUT AND HAZELNUT SALAD

225g (8oz) mangetout or stringless French beans, topped and tailed
100g (4oz) peeled prawns, defrosted if frozen
DRESSING
3 tablespoons olive oil or 2 tablespoons olive and 1 tablespoon walnut oil
2 tablespoons lemon juice
salt
freshly ground black pepper
50g (2oz) hazelnuts, whole or halved, skins removed and lightly toasted, to garnish

Preparation time: 5 minutes, plus cooling
Cooking time: about 8 minutes

1. Put the mangetout or beans in a double boiler or steamer, cover and steam for about 6 minutes. Add the prawns and steam for a further 2-3 minutes, until the prawns are heated through and the mangetout barely tender.
2. Turn the mangetout and prawns into a dish.
3. Thoroughly combine the ingredients for the dressing and spoon over the salad, tossing gently to mix.
4. Leave to cool for at least 2 hours. Just before serving, sprinkle with the hazelnuts and a grinding of black pepper. Serve at room temperature, with brown bread and butter.

SAVOURY CHOUX BUNS

85g (3¼oz) butter
225ml (8fl oz) water
100g (4oz) plain flour, sifted 3 times
pinch of salt
3 eggs, beaten
75g (3oz) jar red or black lumpfish roe
few drops of Tabasco sauce
1 tablespoon lemon juice
150ml (5fl oz) double cream, whipped
TO GARNISH
lemon wedges
fresh dill

Preparation time: 15 minutes, plus cooling
Cooking time: 15 minutes
Oven: 220°C, 425°F, Gas Mark 7

1. Put the butter in a small saucepan with the water and heat gently until the butter is melted.
2. Bring just to the boil, then add the flour. Remove from the heat and beat the mixture with a wooden spoon until it leaves the sides of the pan clean. Beat in the salt. Leave the mixture to cool for 5 minutes.
3. Gradually add the beaten eggs to the mixture, little by little, until the mixture is glossy but not stiff and holds its shape.
4. Drop small dessertspoonfuls of the mixture on to a lightly greased, dampened baking sheet and bake in the centre of a preheated hot oven for about 15 minutes until the buns are well risen and crisp.
5. Meanwhile combine the lumpfish roe, Tabasco, lemon juice and whipped cream in a bowl. Stir well.
6. Remove the buns from the oven and immediately split them to allow the steam to escape. Allow to cool completely then, using a teaspoon, fill them with the lumpfish roe mixture. Garnish with lemon wedges and a sprig of dill and serve immediately.

Below: *Savoury choux buns*

SAVOURY SOFT ROES

100g (4oz) butter
2 teaspoons made English mustard
2 teaspoons Worcestershire sauce
salt
freshly ground black pepper
450g (1lb) soft herring roes
4 slices hot buttered toast

Preparation time: 5 minutes
Cooking time: 5 minutes

1. Put the butter in a saucepan with the mustard, Worcestershire sauce, salt and pepper. Heat gently until the butter is melted, then add the roes and cook over a gentle heat for about 5 minutes.
2. Pile the buttered roes on to the hot buttered toast and serve immediately.

GAME TERRINE WITH TRUFFLES

1 × 1kg (2lb) pheasant with its liver, skinned and boned
50g (2oz) streaky bacon rashers, rinded
75g (3oz) veal escalope, beaten out thinly
2 tablespoons Cognac
125g (4oz) streaky bacon rashers, beaten flat
2 bay leaves
FORCEMEAT
100g (4oz) lean pork
100g (4oz) pork fat
100g (4oz) lean veal
2 shallots or 1 onion, peeled and finely chopped
1 canned truffle, with liquid, coarsely chopped
½ teaspoon ground allspice or Quatre epices (p 24)
pinch of ground cloves
salt
freshly ground black pepper

Preparation time: 45 minutes, plus marinading overnight
Cooking time: about 1½ hours
Oven: 180°C, 350°F, Gas Mark 4

The Périgord region in central south-west France is rich in game, and this classic terrine – in which wild duck, rabbit or partridge may be substituted for pheasant – is a handsome way of serving it. The subtle, dense flavour and aroma of truffles are brought out to the full in a terrine which should be chilled for 3 days or more in the refrigerator to allow the flavour to develop.

1. Using a very sharp small knife cut the pheasant breast and leg meat into 1×3.5cm (½×1½ inch) thin strips, reserving any odd bits. Cut the rinded bacon rashers and veal escalope into thin strips of equal size. Place the pheasant, bacon and veal strips in a large bowl and pour over the Cognac. Cover and leave to marinate overnight in the refrigerator.
2. Line a 1.25 litre (2¼ pint) terrine with the flattened bacon rashers, saving enough to cover the top.
3. Grind the pork, pork fat and veal for the forcemeat with any reserved pheasant bits, twice in the mincer, using the finest blade, or process in a food processor.
4. Add the shallots, truffle, allspice or Quatre epices, salt and pepper.
5. Put the minced meat mixture in a large bowl and stir well to mix. Lift the pheasant, veal and bacon strips from the marinade with a slotted spoon.
6. Spread a third of the forcemeat mixture over the base of the terrine, and cover with a layer of the drained meat strips, pressing them into the forcemeat and making sure they do not touch the bacon-lined walls of the terrine. Make alternating layers of forcemeat and meat strips, ending with a layer of forcemeat. Press down well.
7. Cover the terrine with the reserved streaky bacon rashers and arrange the bay leaves crossed on top.
8. Cover the top of the terrine with foil, then with a lid, pressing it down firmly. Insert a fine skewer through the hole in the terrine lid to pierce the foil.
9. Stand the terrine in a baking tin and pour in boiling water to a depth of 3.5cm (1½ inches). Bring to the boil on top of the stove. Transfer to a preheated moderate oven and cook for 1½ hours, or until a fine skewer inserted for 30 seconds through the hole in the lid is hot when withdrawn. Remove the terrine from the oven and allow to cool, then

weight down the foil and chill in the refrigerator.
10. To unmould, dip the terrine into hot water, then turn out on to a serving platter. Serve cut into thick slices with a lightly dressed, crisp, green salad and a potato salad if liked. The terrine will keep well in the refrigerator for up to a week.

BRIE TART

225g (8oz) Brie cheese, rinded and diced
150ml (5fl oz) double cream
½ teaspoon powdered saffron
375g (13oz) flaky pastry, defrosted if frozen
1 egg beaten, to glaze
1 teaspoon herb mustard
1 teaspoon fresh ginger root, finely chopped
2 teaspoons finely chopped fresh parsley
2 tablespoons top of the milk
3 eggs, beaten
salt
freshly ground black pepper

Oven: 140°C, 275°F, Gas Mark 1
then: 220°C, 425°F, Gas Mark 7
then: 180°C, 350°F, Gas Mark 4
Serves 6-8

This delicious tart is best served alone as an hors d'oeuvre to preceed a light main course.

1. Put the Brie in a flameproof dish, add the cream and saffron and place in a preheated oven for 10-15 minutes (depending on how ripe the brie is) to melt.
2. Increase the oven temperature. Roll out the pastry to a 35×25cm (14×10 inch) rectangle. Cut 2×2.5cm (1 inch) strips from each side of the rectangle. Roll out the rectangle again to measure 33×23cm (13×9 inches).
3. Brush the edges of the rectangle with water and place a pastry strip along each edge, dovetailing the edges. Brush the edging strips with water then place the remaining strips on top of the first set. Press down lightly on the border to seal. Prick the pastry base with a fork and knock up the outside edges with a sharp knife. If liked, score the edges with a sharp knife. Brush the edges with beaten egg to glaze.
4. Place crumpled greaseproof paper in the case, gently fitting it into the corners. Fill with dried beans or baking beans and bake blind for 15 minutes.
5. Remove the weighting paper, lightly press down the base if necessary and return to the oven for 5 minutes.
6. Meanwhile make the filling: beat the melted Brie and the cream with the mustard, ginger and parsley until smooth. Stir in the milk and eggs, and season with salt and pepper. Spoon into the flan case.
7. Reduce the oven temperature and bake the flan in the oven for about 40 minutes until the filling is firm and lightly browned and the pastry crisp and golden. Serve hot or cold, cut into quarters.

From the left: *Savoury soft roes; Game terrine with truffles; Brie tart*

Above: *Tempura with dipping sauce*

TEMPURA

12-16 jumbo prawns, peeled but with the tails left on
450g (1lb) white fish fillets, skinned and cut into 2 × 3.5cm (¾ × 1½inch) pieces
8 whole mushrooms, stalks removed
1 small bunch spring onions, cut into 3.5cm (1½ inch) lengths
2 green peppers, cored, seeded and cut into rings
1 small aubergine, thinly sliced into rounds
12 cauliflower florets
1 onion, peeled and cut into wedges
1 canned bamboo shoot, drained and cut into thin rounds (optional)
salt
3 tablespoons saké or dry sherry
900ml (1½pints) vegetable oil
4 tablespoons sesame oil

BATTER

1 egg
150ml (¼pint) water
100g (4oz) plain flour
50g (2oz) cornflour

Preparation time: 30 minutes
Cooking time: 20-30 minutes
Serves 4-6

One of the most celebrated Japanese dishes, tempura consists of small pieces of fish or vegetables dipped in a light batter and fried until crisp and golden brown. The addition of sesame oil to the frying oil gives a distinctive, nutty flavour. Tempura should be eaten immediately it is ready, so the cook must be prepared to stand over the stove until the last pieces of food have been fried.

1. Arrange all the ingredients in neat heaps on a large serving platter. Sprinkle lightly with salt and saké.
2. Prepare the batter just before cooking the tempura. Put the egg in a large bowl and beat in the water until light and frothy. Combine the flour and cornflour and sift into the bowl, whisking lightly to mix with chopsticks or a fork. Do not overmix or the batter will be heavy. The batter should be fluid, about the consistency of single cream: add a little extra water if necessary.
3. Heat the vegetable oil with the sesame oil in a deep-fryer or wok until just smoking (about 170°C, 340°F, or until a stale bread cube browns in 40 seconds). Pat the tempura ingredients dry with absorbent paper. Using chopsticks, dip each piece quickly into the batter then lower into the hot oil and fry until light golden brown. Several pieces may be fried at once, but do not overcrowd the pan or the oil will cool down and the tempura will be greasy. Keep the oil clear by removing any loose bits of batter with a slotted spoon.
4. As soon as each piece is cooked, remove with chopsticks or a slotted spoon and drain quickly on crumpled absorbent paper. When a plateful of pieces are ready serve immediately, with the dipping sauce or sprinkled with salt or a little soy sauce.

DIPPING SAUCE

250ml (½ pint) chicken stock
4 tablespoons sweet vermouth, sweet sherry or mirin (Japanese rice wine)
4 tablespoons light soy sauce
1 pinch MSG (optional)
1 medium turnip, peeled and grated

1. Combine the stock, vermouth, soy and MSG in a small pan and bring to the boil. Pour the sauce into individual bowls, one for each diner, and place a little grated turnip in each.

CHINESE SAVOURY BUNS

15g (½oz) dried yeast
1 cup tepid water
pinch of salt
pinch of sugar
225g (8oz) plain flour
2 tablespoons vegetable oil
225g (8oz) lean pork, minced
6 spring onions, finely chopped
6 dried Chinese mushrooms, soaked for 20 minutes in cold water, then finely chopped (p 81)
1 tablespoon black bean sauce (p 85)
pinch of sugar

Preparation time: 30 minutes, plus proving
Cooking time: 30 minutes
Oven 120°C, 250°F, Gas Mark ½
Makes 10-12

1. Make the dough. Put the yeast with the water, salt and sugar in a bowl and leave until frothy. Sift the flour into a large mixing bowl and leave to warm in a preheated low oven for 2-3 minutes. Make a well in the centre of the flour and pour in the yeast liquid, gradually work the liquid into the flour, and stir well to mix. Knead the sticky dough in the bowl until it becomes smooth and elastic. Cover the bowl with cling film and leave in a warm place for about 2 hours until doubled in size.
2. Meanwhile, make the filling: heat the oil in a frying pan over a moderate heat. Add the pork, and spring onions and fry for 3-4 minutes.
3. Mix the pork mixture with the mushrooms, bean paste and sugar.
4. Roll the raised dough into a thick sausage shape on a floured board and cut into 2cm (¾ inch) rounds.
5. Lightly flatten out each round and spoon 1 tablespoon filling into the centre. Moisten the edge with water, pull up the sides. and pinch the top together to make a flower shape. Repeat until all the dough is used up.
6. Arrange the buns in bamboo or metal steamers, cover, and steam over a pan of boiling water for 30 minutes, or until risen, white and firm. Check the pan from time to time and add a little boiling water if it shows signs of drying out. Serve the buns hot.

PERSIAN STUFFED APPLES

8 medium cooking apples, cored
175g (6oz) cooked chicken, skin removed, finely chopped
3 tablespoons fresh soft breadcrumbs
2 tablespoons chopped walnuts or pine nut kernels
2 tablespoons seedless raisins
salt
freshly ground black pepper
2.5cm (1 inch) stick cinnamon
¼ teaspoon ground cloves
½ teaspoon ground ginger
1 teaspoon ground turmeric
50g (2oz) butter
2 tablespoons sugar

Preparation time: 20 minutes
Cooking time: 45 minutes
Oven: 180°C, 350°F, Gas Mark 4

The combination of meat and fruit is typical of Middle Eastern cooking.
1. Carefully scoop out a hole about 3.5cm (1½ inches) wide at the end of each apple.
2. In a bowl combine the chicken, breadcrumbs, nuts and raisins and season with salt and pepper.
3. Grind the cinnamon stick and add to the mixture with the cloves, ginger and turmeric. Stir well.
4. Score the apples around the centre with a sharp knife and loosely stuff with the chicken mixture.
5. Place the apples in a single layer in a baking dish. Top each one with a knob of butter and sprinkle with the sugar. Pour in enough water to come halfway up the apples.
6. Bake in a preheated oven for 45 minutes or until the apples are tender. Serve hot.

Below: *Chinese savoury buns*

WHITING WITH ORANGE CREAM SAUCE

4 whiting, filleted and skinned
4 tablespoons orange juice
2 tablespoons lemon juice
3 egg yolks
150ml (5fl oz) dry white wine
150ml (¼pint) double cream
½ teaspoon cayenne pepper
salt
white pepper
100 g (4 oz) butter
3 tablespoons plain flour
TO GARNISH
orange segments
matchstick strips of orange rind

Preparation time: 5 minutes
Cooking time: 35-40 minutes

1. Arrange the whiting fillets in a deep dish and pour over half the orange and half the lemon juice.
2. In the top half of a double boiler or heatproof bowl combine the egg yolks, wine, cream and the remaining orange and lemon juice. Stir over a pan of simmering water until the sauce thickens to a creamy consistency. Add the cayenne and salt and pepper to taste. Gradually add 40g (1½oz) of the butter, whisking between each addition. Keep the sauce warm over the lowest possible heat.
3. Spread the flour out on a plate and season with salt and pepper. Lift the whiting fillets from the marinade and dip in seasoned flour to coat on all sides.
4. Heat the remaining butter in a large frying pan, add the whiting fillets and fry for 5-6 minutes, turning once, until golden brown.
5. Arrange the fried whiting fillets on a warmed serving dish and garnish with orange segments and orange rind, accompanied by the sauce.

FRIED TROUT WITH MUSHROOMS, CREAM AND RICARD

3 tablespoons plain flour
salt
white pepper
4 trout, about 300-350g (10-12oz) each, cleaned
75g (3oz) butter
1 tablespoon vegetable oil
225g (8oz) mushrooms, sliced
2 garlic cloves, peeled and crushed
3 tablespoons Ricard
8 tablespoons double cream
sprigs of watercress to garnish

Preparation time: 4 minutes
Cooking time: 15 minutes

Below, from the left: *Whiting with orange cream sauce; Fried trout with mushrooms, cream and Ricard*

This is an ideal way of cooking farmed trout, which need a boost in flavouring.
1. Spread the flour out on a plate and season with salt and pepper. Dip the trout in the seasoned flour, turning to coat on all sides.
2. Heat the butter with the oil in a large frying pan. Add the trout and fry over a moderate heat for 5 minutes on each side, until cooked through and browned. Transfer the trout to a warmed serving dish and keep warm.
3. Add the mushrooms and garlic to the pan and fry over a moderate heat for 5 minutes or until softened, stirring from time to time. Add the Ricard and cream and allow to bubble for 1-2 minutes, stirring. Taste and adjust the seasoning.
4. Pour the sauce over the fish and serve at once, garnished with watercress sprigs.

Above, from the bottom: *Stewed scallops; Squid Greek style*

SQUID GREEK STYLE

500g (1 ¼lb) cleaned squid, cut into rings
100ml (3 ½fl oz) olive oil
4 garlic cloves, peeled and finely chopped
1 × 400g (14oz) can tomatoes
3 tablespoons red wine vinegar
2 bay leaves
1 sprig fresh rosemary
225g (8oz) small pickling onions, peeled
300ml (½pint) water
½ teaspoon salt

Preparation time: 10 minutes
Cooking time: 30-40 minutes
Serves 2 as a main course, 4 as a starter

1. Pat the squid dry with absorbent paper. Heat the oil in a large frying pan, add the squid with the garlic and fry for 2-3 minutes until the garlic begins to colour. Add all the remaining ingredients and simmer, covered, for 30 minutes, or until the squid is white and tender and the onions are soft.
2. Serve with buttered rice as a main course, or with hot crusty bread as a starter.

STEWED SCALLOPS

150ml (¼pint) dry white wine
150ml (¼pint) water
1 tablespoon white wine vinegar
½ teaspoon ground mace
1 clove
12 scallops, shells removed and halved crossways
75g (3oz) peeled prawns, defrosted if frozen
1 tablespoon butter
1 tablespoon plain flour
6 tablespoons fresh orange juice
1 tablespoon chopped fresh dill
salt
freshly ground black pepper

Preparation time: 5 minutes
Cooking time: 25 minutes
Serves 2 as a light main course, 4 as a starter

This is an adaptation of an eighteenth century recipe for cooking scallops, taken from a famous cookbook of that time.
1. Combine the wine, water, vinegar, mace and clove in a small saucepan. Bring to the boil, then lower the heat and simmer, covered, for 10 minutes.
2. Pour the wine mixture into a wide saucepan and add the scallops and prawns. Simmer over a gentle heat for 5 minutes.
3. Remove the scallops and prawns with a slotted spoon and keep warm. Strain the liquid, return to the pan and measure, adding white wine if necessary to achieve 300ml (½ pint).
4. Work butter with the flour to a paste and add it in small pieces to the hot liquid, whisking between each addition. Simmer for 2-3 minutes until thickened, then add the orange juice, dill and salt and pepper to taste. Return scallops to the pan for 1-2 minutes just to heat through.
4. Serve immediately on hot plates.

FISH SAMBAL

3 tablespoons desiccated coconut
300ml (½pint) boiling water
1 whole grey or red mullet or bream, about 750g-1kg (1½-2lb), gutted and cleaned but unskinned
1 tablespoon cornflour
salt
300ml (½pint) vegetable oil
1½ teaspoons ground turmeric
1 tablespoon coriander seeds, ground
1 teaspoon fennel seeds, ground
1 teaspoon mustard seeds, ground
2 small onions, peeled and chopped
2-5 fresh green chillies, seeded and finely sliced
lime wedges, to garnish

Preparation time: 10 minutes
Cooking time: 20 minutes

1. Put the coconut in a sieve set over a bowl, pour over the boiling water and leave to infuse for 20 minutes, pressing the coconut with the back of a wooden spoon to extract as much liquid as possible.
2. Pat the fish dry with absorbent paper. Mix the cornflour with half a teaspoon salt and coat the fish.
3. Heat the oil in a large frying pan, add the fish and fry on both sides over a moderate heat, until the skin is crisp and golden. Drain on absorbent paper.
4. Drain off all but 2 tablespoons oil from the pan. Add the ground spices and fry, stirring, until lightly browned. Add the onion and chillies and fry over a moderate heat, stirring, for 3 minutes.
5. Add the coconut liquid and salt to taste and bring to the boil. Return the fish to the pan and spoon over the sauce. Cook over a gentle heat for 20 minutes or until the liquid has evaporated. Transfer to a serving plate, garnish with lime wedges and serve.

NASI GORENG

6 tablespoons vegetable oil
2 eggs, lightly beaten
225g (½lb) lean beef, trimmed of fat and cut into matchstick pieces
50g (2oz) peeled prawns
2 fresh green chillies, seeded and finely chopped
1 onion, peeled and finely chopped
1 garlic clove, peeled and crushed
350g (12oz) cold cooked rice
1 peanut sized piece of blachan, crushed (p 78)
1 tablespoon dark soy sauce
salt
TO GARNISH
7.5cm (3 inch) piece cucumber, diced
2 tomatoes, quartered

Preparation time: 10 minutes
Cooking time: 12 minutes

1. Heat 1 tablespoon of the oil in a frying pan, add the eggs and cook over a moderate heat for 2-3 minutes to make a thin, flat omelette. Remove from the pan, cut into thin strips and reserve.
2. Heat the remaining oil in the pan, add the beef, prawns, chillies, onion and garlic and fry over a moderate heat for about 5 minutes, stirring all the time with a wooden spoon.
3. Add the rice, and stir until well mixed and warmed through. Add the blachan and soy sauce, and turn until the rice is evenly browned. Add salt to taste.
4. Pile on to a warmed serving dish, arrange the sliced omelette on top and garnish with diced cucumber and tomato wedges. Serve at once.

BEEF AND PORK SATÉ

450g (1lb) rump steak, cut into thin strips
450g (1lb) pork fillet, cut into thin strips
MARINADE
3 garlic cloves, peeled and crushed
1 small onion, peeled and finely chopped
2 teaspoons soft dark brown sugar
1 tablespoon lemon juice
2 tablespoons dark soy sauce
SATÉ SAUCE
150g (5oz) creamed coconut
450ml (¾pint) hot water
1 teaspoon coriander seeds, crushed
1 teaspoon cumin seeds, crushed
1 teaspoon fennel seeds, crushed
2 garlic cloves, peeled and crushed
1cm (½inch) cube blachan, crushed (p 78)
100g (4oz) crunchy peanut butter
1 teaspoon soft dark brown sugar
2 fresh green chillies, seeded and finely chopped
3-4 tablespoons lemon juice

Preparation time: 30 minutes, plus marinading
Cooking time: about 15 minutes

1. Combine all the marinade ingredients in a large bowl. Add the beef and pork strips and turn to coat in the marinade. Cover and leave for 30 minutes.
2. Meanwhile, make the sauce: dissolve the coconut cream in the hot water and leave to stand for 20 minutes, stirring from time to time.
3. Put the coriander, cumin and fennel in a frying pan and set over a moderate heat until the spicy aroma comes out. Add the garlic, blachan, peanut butter, sugar, chillies and coconut milk and stir over a gentle heat until smooth. Simmer very gently, uncovered, for 10 minutes.
4. Lift the beef and pork strips from the marinade and drain, reserving the marinade. Thread on to small wooden skewers and place under a hot grill for 5 minutes, basting occasionally with the marinade.
5. Add the lemon juice to the hot saté sauce and serve in a warmed bowl sprinkled with chopped chilli with the saté skewers. Serve with plain boiled rice.

From top left, clockwise:
Nasi goreng; Fish sambal; Malaysian devilled potatoes; Beef and pork saté

MALAYSIAN DEVILLED POTATOES

350g (12oz) cold cooked potatoes, diced
1cm (½ inch) piece blachan (p 78) dissolved in
1 teaspoon hot water
½ teaspoon red chilli powder, dissolved in
1 tablespoon cold water
4 tablespoons vegetable oil
2 medium onions, peeled and chopped
1 garlic clove, peeled and crushed
2 fresh green chillies, seeded and finely chopped
½ teaspoon cumin or celery seeds, crushed
1 stalk lemon grass or 1 small piece lemon rind

Preparation time: 10 minutes
Cooking time: 10-12 minutes

This hot, spicy potato dish goes well with curried eggs or may be included as part of a selection of Indonesian dishes.

1. Put the potato in a bowl, add the blachan and chilli powder and stir lightly to mix.
2. Heat the oil in a large saucepan, add the onions, garlic and chillies (reserving ½ teaspoon for decoration) and fry over a gentle heat for 5 minutes, until the onion is soft and lightly coloured. Add the cumin seeds and lemon grass and fry for a further 2 minutes, stirring.
3. Add the potato mixture to the pan and fry for a further 5 minutes, turning from time to time and scraping the bottom of the pan to prevent it catching, until the potatoes are well browned.
4. Remove from the heat and allow to stand for 2 minutes. Transfer to a warmed serving dish, sprinkle with the reserved chillies and serve at once.

Above: *Chicken in salt*

CHICKEN IN SALT

1.25kg (2¾lb) oven-ready chicken
1.5kg (3lb) coarse salt
1 egg white, lightly beaten

Preparation time: 5 minutes
Cooking time: 1½ hours
Oven: 200°C, 400°F, Gas Mark 6

This intriguingly simple method of cooking chicken seals in all the flavour but does not make it taste salty. The salt can be saved and used again. A large, dish or chicken brick, deep enough to contain the chicken is essential.

1. Pat the chicken dry with absorbent paper.
2. Line the base and sides of the casserole with tin foil, leaving an overlap long enough to pull up over the chicken and cover it entirely.
3. Spoon a layer of salt about 2cm (¾ inch) deep into the foil-lined casserole. Place the chicken on top and pack more salt round the sides, then cover generously with salt. Pull up the foil overlap and tuck it around the bird, making sure it is completely covered with foil.
4. Bake in a pre-heated hot oven for 1½ hours. Remove the foil and salt casing and place the chicken on a warmed carving dish. Serve with new potatoes.

VARIATION

A 1.25kg (2¾lb) fish such as bream may be cooked in the same way, but will only need to be baked for half the time.

HONEYED CHICKEN WITH MEAUX MUSTARD

15g (½oz) butter
1 chicken jointed into 4
salt
3 tablespoons Meaux mustard
1½ tablespoons soft light brown sugar
2 tablespoons thick honey
2 tablespoons fresh orange juice
1 tablespoon dry sherry
1 orange, peeled and segmented (optional)

Preparation time: 15 minutes
Cooking time: about 1 hour
Oven: 190°C, 375°F, Gas Mark 5
then: 140°C, 275°F, Gas Mark 1

1. Melt the butter in a roasting tin in a preheated oven, add the chicken pieces, skin side up, sprinkle with salt and roast for 10 minutes.
2. In a small bowl, combine the mustard, sugar and honey, beating with a wooden spoon until smooth.
3. Spread the mixture over the chicken pieces and roast for a further 30-40 minutes, basting occasionally, until cooked through and the juices run clear when the thickest part is pierced with a skewer.
4. Reduce the oven temperature. Transfer the chicken pieces to a warmed serving dish and keep warm.
5. Pour the tin juices into a saucepan, discarding any blackened sediment. Add the orange juice and sherry and stir over a gentle heat until warmed through. Taste and adjust the seasoning.
6. Garnish the chicken with orange segments and serve with the sauce and Périgord salad (p 122).

POACHED LEMON CHICKEN

1.5kg (3¼lb) fresh chicken with giblets
300ml (½pint) white wine
thinly pared rind and segmented flesh of 2 lemons
1 onion, chopped
1 carrot, chopped
1 celery stick, chopped
1 bay leaf
6 whole black peppercorns
pinch of dried thyme
pinch of salt
1 tablespoon sugar
20g (¾oz) plain flour
20g (¾oz) butter
3 egg yolks
1 tablespoon double cream
fresh coriander, to garnish

Preparation time: 10 minutes
Cooking time: about 1 hour
Oven: 140°C, 275°F, Gas Mark 1

This chicken recipe is a good choice for a summer lunch or dinner party. It is light yet substantial and requires very little advance preparation. It would look pretty served on a bed of fresh green tagliatelle.
1. Put the chicken in a large saucepan with half the wine, the lemon rind, onion, carrots, celery stick, bay leaf, peppercorns, thyme and flavourings and the chicken giblets except for the liver.
2. Pour in enough water to come to the top of the legs and bring to simmering point. Poach the chicken with the water barely moving for about 50 minutes or until the juices run clear when the thickest part of the leg is pierced with a skewer.
3. Meanwhile, liquidize the lemon segments with the remaining wine in a food processor or electric blender.
4. Make a *beurre manié* by working together the flour and butter with a fork in a bowl to achieve a smooth, fairly stiff paste.
5. Lift the cooked chicken from the pan, remove the skin and slice the flesh from the bones. Cover and keep the chicken meat warm in a preheated oven.
6. Boil the cooking liquid briskly to reduce to about 300ml (½ pint). Strain and return to the rinsed out pan with the lemon and wine mixture. Add the sugar and stir over a low heat. Taste and adjust the seasoning. You may need to add a little more sugar, depending on the acidity of the lemons used.
7. Bring to the boil, then gradually whisk in half-teaspoons of the *beurre manié*, to achieve a pouring consistency. Simmer gently for 2 minutes, stirring occasionally with a wooden spoon.
8. Remove from the heat and allow to cool for 1 minute. Whisk in the egg yolks and cream. Pour the lemon sauce over the chicken, garnish with coriander and serve at once with a crisp green salad.

IRANIAN CHICKEN WITH SAFFRON

1.5kf (3 ½lb) fresh chicken, joined into 8
salt
freshly ground black pepper
3 tablespoons vegetable oil
25g (1oz) butter
1 large onion, peeled and thinly sliced
2 garlic cloves, peeled and crushed
600ml (1 pint) water
1 teaspoon saffron strands
juice of 1 large lemon
peel of 1 tangerine, blanched and finely shredded
4 carrots, peeled and cut into matchstick lengths
1 tablespoon demerara sugar
5 tangerines, peeled and segmented

Preparation time: 20 minutes
Cooking time: 1 hour 20 minutes

1. Pat the chicken pieces dry with absorbent paper and season with salt and pepper.
2. Heat the oil and butter in a flameproof casserole, add the chicken pieces and fry over moderate heat for 5-6 minutes, turning once. Remove the chicken.
3. Add the onion and garlic to the casserole and fry over a gentle heat for 5 minutes until soft and lightly coloured. Return the chicken to the pan and add the water, saffron, lemon juice and salt and pepper. Bring to the boil, then simmer for 30 minutes.
4. Add the tangerine peel, carrots and sugar to the casserole. Cover and simmer for a further 30 minutes, or until the chicken and carrots are tender.
5. Add the tangerine segments to the stew and simmer, uncovered, for a further 10 minutes.
6. Transfer the chicken to a heated platter and serve.

From the left: *Poached lemon chicken; Iranian chicken with saffron*

SADDLE OF HARE WITH CHESTNUT SAUCE

2 large saddles of hare, plus legs and trimmings
225g (8oz) streaky bacon rashers
1 carrot, chopped
1 celery stalk, chopped
1 onion, chopped
1 sprig thyme
600ml (1 pint) water
24 cooked peeled chestnuts or 1 large can unsweetened whole chestnuts
150ml (5fl oz) single cream
4 tablespoons Drambuie
salt
freshly ground black pepper

Preparation time: 40 minutes
Cooking time: 1 hour
Oven: 190°C, 375°F, Gas Mark 5

1. Using a small, sharp knife, carefully cut away the thin, shiny membrane covering the saddles. Wrap the bacon rashers round the saddles and place in a roasting tin. Cover and roast for 30-40 minutes.
2. Meanwhile put the hare trimmings in a saucepan with the chopped vegetables, thyme and water. Bring to the boil, then lower the heat and simmer, uncovered, for 30 minutes. Strain the stock and measure out 150ml (5fl oz).
3. Put the chestnuts into a food processor or electric blender with the measured stock and half the cream. Process until smooth, then pour into a small saucepan and heat through gently.
4. Add the Drambuie and the remaining cream and extra stock, if necessary, to give a pouring consistency. Season to taste with salt and pepper.
5. Remove the bacon rashers from the saddles of hare. Carve the hares into small pieces and roll up the bacon rashers. Serve the meat and bacon with the chestnut sauce handed separately in a warmed sauceboat. Buttered noodles would make a good accompaniment to this dish.

DUCK WITH POMEGRANATE AND WALNUT SAUCE

6 tablespoons vegetable oil
1 large onion, peeled and coarsely chopped
½ teaspoon ground turmeric
250g (9oz) shelled walnuts, ground
900ml (1½ pints) chicken stock
salt
freshly ground black pepper
2.5kg (5½lb) duck, jointed into 4
150ml (5fl oz) fresh or concentrated pomegranate juice or passion fruit juice
8 tablespoons fresh lemon juice
50g (2oz) sugar
fresh coriander, to garnish

Preparation time: 25 minutes
Cooking time: 1¾ hours

An Iranian feast dish which is traditionally served to honour a special guest.
1. Heat 4 tablespoons of the oil in a heavy-based pan. Add the onion and turmeric and fry over a gentle heat for 5 minutes, until the onion is soft and lightly coloured. Transfer the onion to a flameproof casserole, add the walnuts, stock and salt and pepper and bring to the boil. Lower the heat and simmer for 30 minutes.
2. Heat the remaining oil in the frying pan, add the duck pieces and fry over a moderate heat for 5-6 minutes, turning once, until browned.
3. Transfer the duck pieces to the casserole. Turn to coat with sauce and simmer, covered, over a very low heat for 1 hour, stirring occasionally and skimming off the fat that rises to the surface.
4. Combine the pomegranate juice with the lemon juice and sugar and add to the casserole, stirring gently to mix. Simmer for a further 20 minutes or until the duck is tender and cooked through.
5. Serve the duck pieces on a bed of rice, garnished with coriander. Pour some of the sauce over and hand the remainder separately.

From the left: *Saddle of hare with chestnut sauce; Duck with pomegranate and walnut sauce; Roast duck with green peppercorn and orange sauce*

ROAST DUCK WITH GREEN PEPPERCORN AND ORANGE SAUCE

2 ¼kg (5lb) fresh roasting duck, with giblets
1 onion, peeled and chopped
1 celery stick, sliced
600ml (1 pint) water
3-4 tablespoons dry Cinzano
juice of 3 oranges
1 tablespoon green peppercorns
salt
orange slices, to garnish

Preparation time: 30 minutes
Cooking time: about 2 hours
Oven: 220°C, 425°F, Gas Mark 7
then: 200°C, 400°F, Gas Mark 6

Fatty birds like duck are much enhanced by a fresh-tasting, slightly astringent sauce. This is a variation on the orange sauce which traditionally accompanies roast duck: green peppercorns give it a slight bite. Cinzano is useful in the kitchen, as are most herby vermouths, because it subtly brings out existing flavours without overpowering them. If unavailable dry white wine may be substituted.

1. Put the duck giblets in a large saucepan with the onion, celery, water and 1 tablespoon of the Cinzano. Bring to the boil, lower the heat and simmer for 30 minutes. Strain the stock.
2. Pat the duck dry with absorbent paper. Lay the duck on its side on a wire rack in a roasting tin. Roast in a preheated oven for 10 minutes.
3. Reduce the oven temperature and roast for a further 30 minutes. Turn the duck on its other side and roast for a further 1 hour, basting from time to time with the stock combined with the juice of 1 orange.
4. Turn the duck on its back and roast for a further 15 minutes. Transfer the duck to a warmed serving dish and keep warm while making the sauce.
5. Drain off the fat in the roasting tin. Set the tin over moderate heat, pour in the remaining Cinzano, 4 tablespoons of stock, the juice of the 2 remaining oranges, and add the peppercorns. Bring to the boil, stirring and scraping the base and sides of the tin to dislodge any sediment.
6. Simmer for a few minutes to allow the flavours to blend, adding a little more Cinzano and stock if necessary. Taste and adjust the seasoning.
7. Pour a little sauce over the duck to moisten and garnish with orange slices. Carve the duck and serve with the green peppercorn sauce handed separately in a warmed sauceboat.

SZECHUAN FRIED CHICKEN

4 chicken breasts, skinned and cut into large dice
1 teaspoon salt
1 tablespoon cornflour
225g (8oz) bamboo shoots, cut into large dice
3 tablespoons Hoisin sauce (p 85)
4 tablespoons brown bean sauce
1 teaspoon light soy sauce
2 teaspoons white wine vinegar
4 tablespoons vegetable oil
6 garlic cloves, peeled and sliced
½ teaspoon Szechuan (anise) peppercorns, crushed
2 tablespoons sherry
cucumber fans, to garnish

Preparation time: 8 minutes, plus soaking
Cooking time: 10-12 minutes

Pungent, sweetish, and hot, this excellent way of cooking chicken breasts is typical of dishes from the Szechuan region, renowned for their peppery taste.
1. Place the chicken pieces in a bowl, add the salt and pour over fresh cold water to cover. Leave to soak for 20 minutes. Drain the chicken, pat dry with absorbent paper and toss in the cornflour to coat thoroughly.
2. In a bowl, mix the bamboo shoots with the sauces and vinegar.
3. Heat the oil in a wok, add the chicken, garlic and pepper and fry for 2-3 minutes, stirring constantly. Add the bamboo shoot mixture, stir well and cook for 1 further minute. Add the sherry, stir, and simmer until the sauce thickens.
4. Transfer to a heated serving platter, garnish with cucumber fans and serve immediately.

CHINESE BRAISED BEEF

2 tablespoons vegetable oil
1kg (2lb) topside of beef, tied
2 tablespoons dark soy sauce
2 tablespoons dry sherry
2 garlic cloves, peeled
1 star anise flower
1 tablespoon sugar
freshly ground black pepper
TO GARNISH
radish roses
spring onions

Preparation time: 5 minutes
Cooking time: about 2 hours 10 minutes

Unlike most Chinese final assembly dishes, this one can be left quietly cooking on top of the stove.
1. Heat the oil in a small deep flameproof casserole, add the beef and fry over a brisk heat, turning often, to brown on all sides.
2. Add the soy sauce, sherry and garlic and bring to the boil. Add the anise, cover and cook over a very gentle heat for 1 hour or until cooked through.
3. Turn the beef, add the sugar, sprinkle with pepper, cover again and cook for 1 further hour, adding extra stock if necessary.
4. Remove the string, slice the beef thickly, and arrange on a serving dish. Pour over the juices and garnish with radish roses and spring onions.

PORK AND PRAWN BALLS WITH RED-COOKED CABBAGE

225g (8oz) lean pork belly, rinded, boned and diced
100g (4oz) peeled prawns
4 spring onions, finely chopped
1 egg
2 tablespoons cornflour
½ teaspoon salt
1 teaspoon finely grated fresh ginger root
½ teaspoon Chinese five spice (p 25)
vegetable oil, for deep frying
1 Chinese or savoy cabbage, about 500g (1lb), stalk removed and shredded
4 tablespoons vegetable oil
1 garlic clove, peeled and finely chopped
½ teaspoon grated fresh ginger root
3 tablespoons light soy sauce
6 tablespoons chicken stock
3 teaspoons sugar
spring onions, to garnish

Preparation time: 30 minutes
Cooking time: 20 minutes

This Chinese dish has more of the style of home cooking than standard restaurant food. The pork balls are first deep-fried, then steam-cooked with the cabbage for extra flavour.
1. Chop the pork very finely with the prawns. Add the spring onions and continue chopping to make a fine paste.
2. Transfer the mixture to a large bowl, add the egg, cornflour, salt, ginger and spice and mix very thoroughly. Shape into walnut-sized balls.
3. Heat the oil in deep-fryer to 180°C (350°F) or until a cube of bread browns in 30 seconds. Fry the pork and prawn balls in batches of 6.
4. Cook the cabbage: heat the oil in a wok with a lid, add the cabbage and stir-fry over a high heat until coated in oil. Add the garlic and ginger and stir-fry for a further 2-3 minutes. Add the soy sauce, stock and sugar, stir for 30 seconds, then cover and simmer gently for 3-4 minutes.
5. Place the pork and prawn balls in a single layer on top of the cabbage, cover and cook over the lowest possible heat for 10-15 minutes, shaking the wok from time to time.
6. Lay the cabbage on a heated serving plate and arrange the pork and prawn balls on top. Garnish with spring onions and serve at once.

STIR-FRIED BEANSPROUTS, WATER CHESTNUTS AND MUSHROOMS

4 tablespoons vegetable oil
1 garlic clove, peeled and crushed
1 teaspoon grated fresh ginger root
4-5 spring onions, trimmed and sliced diagonally into 2.5cm (1 inch) pieces
6 Chinese dried mushrooms, soaked in warm water, for several hours, stemmed and sliced, soaking liquid reserved
6 canned water chestnuts, drained and sliced
450g (1lb) beansprouts
½ tablespoon cornflour
2 tablespoons light soy sauce
salt

Preparation time: 5 minutes
Cooking time: 6 minutes

A fresh-tasting, quickly cooked Chinese vegetable stir-fry, with an exciting combination of flavours and textures. Beansprouts should never be over-cooked or they lose their delicate crispness.

1. Heat the oil in a wok over a moderate heat, lower the heat slightly, then add the garlic, ginger and spring onion, and fry, stirring constantly, for a few seconds. Add the mushrooms and water chestnuts and fry just long enough to heat through.
2. Add the beansprouts, stirring thoroughly. In a cup, mix the cornflour to a smooth paste with the soy sauce and 4 tablespoons of the reserved mushroom soaking liquid. Stir into the wok as soon as the beansprouts become transparent. Turn the heat to low and simmer for 1-2 minutes until the liquid thickens.
3. Serve at once with plain boiled rice and a chicken or meat dish, preferrably one that can be left cooking on the stove while you are stir frying, such as Chinese braised beef (opposite).

From the left, clockwise: *Chinese braised beef: Stir-fried beansprouts, water chestnuts and mushrooms; Pork and prawn balls with red-cooked cabbage; Szechuan fried chicken*

CRACKLING CORN BREAD WITH BACON BITS

275g (10oz) coarse yellow cornmeal
1 teaspoon salt
½ teaspoon bicarbonate of soda
1 teaspoon baking powder
175g (6oz) cooked streaky bacon rashers, rinded and crumbled
65g (2½oz) flour
2 tablespoons molasses
1 egg
450ml (15fl oz) buttermilk

Preparation time: 10 minutes
Cooking time: 30 minutes
Oven: 200°C, 425°F, Gas Mark 7
Serves 6-8

1. Butter a 25cm (10 inch) roasting tin or square baking tin 20cm x 2.5cm (8×1 inch). Sieve together the cornmeal, salt, bicarbonate of soda, baking powder and flour and add the bacon bits.
2. Combine the molasses, egg and buttermilk and add to the dry ingredients. Mix until smooth.
3. Warm the prepared tin for 3 minutes in a preheated oven and then pour in the mixture. Bake for about 25 minutes until well-risen and brown. Cut into squares or slices to serve.

BOSTON BAKED BEANS

450g (1lb) dried haricot beans, soaked overnight, drained
350g (12oz) salted pork belly, rinded, cut into 2.5cm (1 inch) cubes
1 large onion, peeled and coarsely chopped
2 tablespoons molasses or black treacle
2 teaspoons soft dark brown sugar
2 teaspoons English mustard powder
2 teaspoons Worcestershire sauce
½ teaspoon salt
freshly ground black pepper

Preparation time: 10 minutes
Cooking time: about 3 hours
Oven: 180°C, 350°F, Gas Mark 4

A classic American dish, warming and filling, which can be eaten as soon as the pork is tender, or left safely in the oven for up to 1 hour longer without spoiling, though you may need to add more water if the dish shows signs of drying out.
1. Put the haricot beans in a large saucepan, cover with fresh cold unsalted water and bring to the boil. Simmer for about 1½ hours until the beans are tender.
2. Drain the beans, reserving the cooking water. Put the beans into a deep casserole with a lid. Reheat the bean cooking water.
3. Add the pork and onion to the beans, stirring well to mix.
4. Combine 300ml (½ pint) of the bean water with the molasses, sugar, mustard and Worcester sauce and pour over the beans. Pour in more bean water, to come just above the beans. Season with the salt and plenty of pepper.
5. Cover and cook in a preheated moderate oven for 1½ hours, or until the pork is tender.

Opposite, from the top:
Sausages in barbecue sauce; Crackling corn bread with bacon bits; Hot Creole mustard; Boston baked beans

SAUSAGES IN BARBECUE SAUCE

1 tablespoon dripping
450g (1lb) large pork sausages
2 onions, peeled and coarsely chopped
4 tablespoons oyster sauce (p 85)
1 tablespoon tomato purée or tomato ketchup
1 tablespoon mild French or German mustard
4 tablespoons white wine or water

Preparation time: 5 minutes
Cooking time: 30 minutes
Oven: 180°C, 350°F, Gas Mark 4

1. Melt half the dripping in a large frying pan, add the sausages and fry for 5 minutes over a moderate heat, turning often, until the fat runs.
2. Using a slotted spoon, transfer the sausages to an ovenproof dish. Add the onions to the frying pan, adding the remaining dripping if required, and fry for 2-3 minutes. Add the onions to the sausages.
3. Combine the remaining ingredients in a bowl and spoon over the sausages and onions.
4. Bake in a preheated moderate oven, basting from time to time, until the sausages are well browned. Serve with hot jacket potatoes, Boston baked beans and Hot Creole mustard.

HOT CREOLE MUSTARD

3 teaspoons Dijon mustard
2 teaspoons plain flour
2 teaspoons English mustard powder
1 teaspoon grated horseradish
½ teaspoon white pepper
1 teaspoon caster sugar
¼ teaspoon salt
150ml (5fl oz) hot water

Preparation time: 5 minutes, plus cooling
Cooking time: 5 minutes

1. Combine all the ingredients except the water in a small saucepan.
2. Add the water, stir well to mix and simmer for 2 minutes.
3. Remove from the heat and allow to cool completely. Transfer to an airtight screwtop jar and store in the refrigerator. Serve with hamburgers or steaks.

DEVILLED STEAK

1 tablespoon Dijon mustard
1 teaspoon English mustard powder
cayenne pepper
750g (1 ½lb) thick rump steak, trimmed of fat and cut into 4 equal pieces
1 tablespoon vegetable oil
4 tablespoons red wine
1 teaspoon Worcestershire sauce
salt

Preparation time: 5 minutes, plus marinating
Cooking time: 8-12 minutes

As well as adding flavour, mustard has a tenderizing effect on steak.

1. Combine the Dijon mustard, English mustard and cayenne and spread thinly over the steaks on both sides. Set aside for at least 30 minutes.
2. Heat the oil in a large frying pan. Add the steaks and fry rapidly for 2-3 minutes over a high heat, turning once, to seal on both sides. Lower the heat to moderate and cook for a further 4-8 minutes (depending on how you like steak cooked), turning from time to time, until the steaks are done to your liking. Transfer the steaks to warmed individual dinner plates.
3. Add the wine and Worcestershire sauce to the pan juices and season with salt. Stir well, allow to bubble for a few seconds, then pour over the steaks and serve at once with a green salad.

BARBECUED BEEF

1kg (2 ¼lb) lean rump steak, trimmed of fat, sliced into strips, about 2×7.5cm (¾×3 inches)

MARINADE

4 tablespoons light soy suace
1 tablespoon Worcestershire sauce
1 tablespoon clear honey or soft light brown sugar
1 tablespoon lemon juice
1 clove garlic, peeled and crushed

TO SERVE

8 soft baps
1 crisp lettuce or ½ head curly endive

Preparation time: 5 minutes, plus marinating
Cooking time: 5 minutes
Serves 8

1. Combine all the ingredients for the marinade and beat with a fork until thoroughly blended. Put the beef strips in a large bowl and pour over the marinade. Leave for 1 hour, turning and basting the beef once or twice.
2. Lift the beef strips from the marinade, reserving any excess marinade. Thread the beef strips loosely on long kebab skewers with handles and cook over a preheated barbecue for about 5 minutes, turning

frequently and basting with the remaining marinade if any.
3. To serve, split the baps, lay a few lettuce leaves on the bottom, and fill them with the beef strips.

VARIATION
For extra flavour put a pat of herb butter in each bap.

GREEK LAMB KEBABS

750g (1 ½lb) boneless lamb, trimmed and cut into 2.5cm (1 inch) cubes
2 large Spanish onions, peeled, and cut into wedges
3 peppers (red, green and yellow), cored, seeded and cut into 2.5cm (1 inch) pieces
MARINADE
4 tablespoons olive oil
4 tablespoons ouzo or retsina
3 garlic cloves, peeled and crushed
1 tablespoon coriander seeds, roughly crushed
salt
freshly ground black pepper
fresh coriander, to garnish

Preparation time: 20 minutes, plus marinating
Cooking time: about 15 minutes

A heady mixture of Greek ouzo or retsina with garlic and coriander makes these kebabs taste excitingly different.
1. Arrange the lamb cubes in a shallow dish. Combine the marinade ingredients and pour over the lamb, stirring to coat well. Cover and leave to marinate for at least 1 hour.
2. Lift the lamb from the marinade and thread on to long kebab skewers, alternating with pieces of onion and pepper.
3. Grill over a barbecue or under a preheated moderate grill, turning from time to time, and basting frequently with the remaining marinade, for about 15 minutes, until the lamb is cooked but still slightly pink in the centre. Transfer to heated plates, garnish with coriander and serve with a Greek-style salad of tomatoes, onions, olives and crumbled feta cheese and plenty of hot pitta bread to mop up the delicious aromatic juices.

MULLED ALE

4 cloves
½ teaspoon finely chopped fresh ginger root or a good pinch of ground ginger
2.5cm (1 inch) piece cinnamon stick, crushed
15cm (6 inch) strip of thinly pared orange rind, all pith removed
50g (2oz) sugar
150ml (5fl oz) water
1 ½pints beer or brown ale
orange slices, to garnish

Preparation time: 5 minutes
Cooking time: 15 minutes

For smarter occasions, a 70cl bottle of claret may be used instead of ale.
1. Put cloves, ginger, cinnamon and orange rind in a muslin bag and place in a saucepan with the sugar and water. Stir over a gentle heat until the sugar is dissolved. Simmer very gently for 10 minutes.
2. Add the wine to the pan and heat very gently to just below boiling point. Remove the muslin bag and serve at once, garnished with orange slices.

Opposite, from the top: *Devilled steak; Barbecued beef*
Below: *Greek lamb kebabs*

Opposite, clockwise from the bottom: *Tongue in caper sauce; Mulled ale (recipe p 109); Hannah Glasse's stuffed shoulder of lamb; Gammon with spiced peaches*

TONGUE IN CAPER SAUCE

SAUCE

20g (¾oz) butter
2 shallots, peeled and finely chopped
20g (¾oz) plain flour
300ml (½ pint) hot chicken or beef stock
1 tablespoon sherry
4 tablespoons double cream
salt
freshly ground black pepper
2 teaspoons Dijon mustard
1 tablespoon capers
8 large slices tongue

Preparation time: 10 minutes
Cooking time: 30 minutes
Oven: 180°C, 350°F, Gas Mark 4

1. Melt the butter in a saucepan, add the shallots and fry over a gentle heat for 1 minute, then sprinkle over the flour and cook, stirring, for 2 minutes.
2. Remove from the heat and gradually stir in the stock. Stir in the sherry and cream. Season to taste with salt and pepper, then stir in the mustard and capers. Return to the heat and bring slowly to the boil, stirring, then lower the heat and simmer for 1-2 minutes. Allow to cool.
4. Arrange the tongue slices on a platter, pour over the sauce and serve garnished with fresh parsley.

GAMMON WITH SPICED PEACHES

2kg (4½lb) joint smoked gammon, soaked overnight in cold water
1 carrot, chopped
1 onion, peeled and chopped
1 celery stick, chopped
1 bay leaf
3 tablespoons bourbon or Southern Comfort
1 tablespoon demerara sugar
1 tablespoon mild American mustard
24-30 cloves
bottled spiced or brandied peaches, to serve

Preparation time: 20 minutes, plus soaking
Cooking time: 2½ hours
Oven: 200°C, 400°F, Gas Mark 6
Serves 4-6

1. Put the gammon with the carrot, onion, celery and bay leaf in a large saucepan and pour in cold fresh water to cover. Cover the pan, bring slowly to the boil and simmer very gently for 2 hours. Remove from the heat and leave to cool overnight in the cooking liquid.
2. Next day, remove the gammon from the pan and pat dry with absorbent paper. Strip off the rind and score the fat surface into diamonds. Stick a clove in each diamond.
3. Combine the Bourbon, sugar and mustard until smooth then spread the mixture over the scored fat.
4. Wrap the gammon joint loosely in foil, and bake in a preheated oven for 20 minutes. Open up the foil and bake for a further 20 minutes, or until the glaze is brown and shiny.
5. Turn off the oven and leave the joint to stand for 10 minutes, to allow the juices to settle.
6. Carve the gammon into thin slices, garnish with spiced peaches and serve hot.

HANNAH GLASSE'S STUFFED SHOULDER OF LAMB

1 leg of lamb, about 1.5kg (3-3½lb), boned

STUFFING

50g (2oz) breadcrumbs
3 hard-boiled eggs, shelled and chopped
100g (4oz) oysters or peeled prawns
25g (1oz) shredded suet
3 anchovy fillets, finely chopped
1 onion, peeled and finely chopped
1 teaspoon fresh thyme, or a pinch of dried thyme
1 teaspoon finely chopped parsley
1 egg, beaten
1 teaspoon anchovy essence or oyster sauce (p 85)
½ teaspoon freshly grated nutmeg
salt
freshly ground black pepper

SAUCE

20g (¾oz) butter
½ onion, peeled and finely chopped
20g (¾oz) plain flour
150ml (5fl oz) wine
200ml (7fl oz) stock
1 teaspoon anchovy essence or oyster sauce
1-2 anchovy fillets, finely chopped
½ teaspoon freshly grated nutmeg

Preparation time: 20 minutes
Cooking time: 2½ hours
Oven: 230°C, 450°F, Gas Mark 8
then: 200°C, 400°F, Gas Mark 6

1. Mix together all the stuffing ingredients.
2. Stuff the lamb with the mixture and sew it loosely.
3. Place the lamb in a roasting tin in a preheated hot oven for 20 minutes, then reduce the oven temperature and roast for a further 2 hours or until the lamb is cooked through and the juices run clear when it is pierced with a fine skewer. Transfer the lamb to a heated serving dish and keep warm.
4. Make the sauce: melt the butter in a frying pan, add the onion and fry over a gentle heat for 5 minutes, until soft and lightly coloured. Stir in the flour, add the remaining sauce ingredients and simmer for 2 minutes.
5. Pour off the fat from the roasting tin, pour in the sauce and bring to the boil, stirring well. Serve with roast potatoes, accompanied by the sauce.

STEAK AND KIDNEY PUDDING

225g (8 oz) plain flour
salt
100g (4oz) shredded suet
75ml (3fl oz) cold water
2 tablespoons plain flour
½ teaspoon English mustard powder
500g (1lb) stewing steak, trimmed and cut into 2.5cm (1 inch) cubes
2 lamb's kidneys, skinned, cored and chopped
100g (4oz) mushrooms, chopped
1 clove
pinch of powdered mace
freshly ground black pepper

Preparation time: 30 minutes
Cooking time: about 3¼ hours
Oven: 190°C, 375°F, Gas Mark 5

There is no better example of traditional English cooking than homemade steak and kidney pudding.

1. Grease a 1.2 litre (2 pint) pudding basin.
2. Make the pastry. Sift the flour and a pinch of salt into a mixing bowl and rub in the suet. Using the blade of a knife, stir in enough cold water to make a soft, firm dough. Knead the dough lightly, then roll it out into a circle 5mm(¼ inch) thick and 10cm (4 inches) all round larger than the top of the basin. Cut a triangular quarter out of the pastry and reserve. Lift the pastry into the basin, centre it carefully and ease it into the basin so the cut edges overlap slightly.
3. Combine the 2 tablespoons flour with the mustard powder. Dust the beef cubes lightly with the mixture. Mix the beef with the kidneys, mushrooms and spices.
4. Trim excess pastry off around the top edge of the basin and fill the lined basin with the mixture. Season with salt and pepper. Pour in enough cold water to come within 2.5mm (1 inch) of the top of the basin. Fold the pastry edge over the filling and brush the edge with water.
5. On a floured board, roll the remaining dough into a circle and use it to cover the basin. Press the edges together to seal, then trim with a knife.
6. Cover loosely with a pleated and greased circle of foil about 4cm (1½ inches) larger than the top of the basin and tie securely around the edge with string.
7. Stand the basin on a square of cloth and knot the corners over the top to make a handle. Set the basin on an upturned saucer in a large saucepan and pour in boiling water to come halfway up the sides of the basin. Cover, bring to the boil and boil gently for 3 hours, topping up with more boiling water from time to time.
8. Lift the pudding from the saucepan and remove the foil covering. Set the basin on a baking sheet and bake in a preheated oven for 10-15 minutes, until the pastry lid is cooked and crisp.
9. Serve the hot pudding straight from the basin, wrapped in a clean table napkin or tea-towel.

BOEUF EN DAUBE PROVENÇALE

MARINADE
4 tablespoons olive oil
1 onion, peeled and chopped
3 shallots, peeled and chopped
3 garlic cloves, peeled and chopped
150ml (¼ pint) red wine
1 celery stick, chopped
1 carrot, scraped and sliced
1 sprig thyme
1 sprig parsley
1 bay leaf
½ teaspoon salt
10 whole black peppercorns, lightly crushed

DAUBE
31kg (2lb) beef topside in one piece
3 garlic cloves, peeled and chopped
225g (8oz) carrots, scraped and roughly sliced
225g (8oz) onions, peeled and roughly chopped
1 thick slice gammon or bacon, about 175g (6oz)
1×215g (7½oz) can chopped tomatoes
3 tablespoons brandy
1 sprig thyme
1 sprig parsley
1 bay leaf
10 black olives, stoned

Preparation time: 30 minutes, plus marinating overnight
Cooking time: 3½ hours
Oven: 160°C, 325°F, Gas Mark 3

1. Prepare the marinade: gently heat the oil in a small saucepan, add the onion, shallots and garlic and simmer for 1-2 minutes. Add the wine, celery, carrot, herbs, salt and pepper. Simmer gently, partially covered, for 20 minutes. Remove from the heat and allow to cool.
2. Put the beef in a large bowl and pour over the marinade. Cover and leave to marinate, overnight, turning the beef once or twice.
3. Remove the beef from the marinade and place in a deep casserole with a lid. Add the garlic, carrots and onions and place the gammon on top of the beef. Strain the marinade, add the tomatoes with their juice and the brandy and pour over the beef. Lay the herbs on top.
4. Cover the casserole with foil, then with the lid and cook in a preheated low oven for 2½ hours. Taste and adjust the seasoning, add the olives and cook for a further 30 minutes, uncovered, until the beef is cooked through and tender.
5. To serve, carve the beef into thick slices and arrange them overlapping on a bed of hot buttered noodles. Cut the gammon into dice and sprinkle on top. Strain the stock, reserving the olives and vegetables and ladle a little over. Garnish with the reserved olives and serve with the vegetables and a green salad.

FLEMISH BEEF STEW

750g (1 ½lb) lean stewing steak, trimmed and cut into 2.5cm (1 inch) cubes
2 tablespoons plain flour
3 tablespoons vegetable oil
225g (8oz) onions, peeled and sliced
2 garlic cloves, peeled and crushed
1 tablespoon soft dark brown sugar
450ml (¾pint) real ale or Guinness
1 beef stock cube, crumbled
1 tablespoon red wine vinegar
1 tablespoon Dijon mustard
pinch of ground cloves
salt
freshly ground black pepper

Preparation time: 20 minutes
Cooking time: 3¼ hours
Oven: 150°C, 300°F, Gas Mark 2

A classic dish from the Low Countries, with a thick, beery gravy which combines well with buttered noodles or mashed potatoes for a cold weather meal.

1. Sprinkle the beef cubes with the flour to coat thoroughly.
2. Heat the oil in a flameproof casserole, add the beef cubes and fry over a moderate heat for 3-4 minutes, turning once or twice, until browned on all sides. Using a slotted spoon remove the beef from the casserole and set aside.
3. Add the onions and garlic to the casserole and fry over a gentle heat for 5 minutes, until soft and lightly coloured. Add the sugar and fry for 1 further minute.
4. Combine the ale, stock cube, vinegar and mustard, and add to the casserole. Stir and bring to the boil.
5. Return the beef to the casserole, add the cloves and season with salt and pepper. Cover and cook in a preheated oven for about 3 hours, or until the beef is tender.
6. Serve straight from the casserole with hot buttered noodles and broccoli.

From the left, clockwise:
Boeuf en daube provençale;
Steak and kidney pudding;
Flemish beef stew

LAMB COUSCOUS WITH DRIED FRUITS

2 tablespoons vegetable oil
1kg (2lb) boneless lamb, trimmed and cut into 2.5cm (1 inch) cubes
1 large onion, peeled and chopped
600ml (1 pint) water
2.5cm (1 inch) stick cinnamon
1 teaspoon salt
8 dried apricots
8 prunes, stones removed
thinly pared rind and juice of 1 lemon
1 tablespoon clear honey
Chilli sauce, to serve (optional)

Preparation time: 10 minutes
Cooking time: 2 hours
Serves 6

A mildly spiced lamb stew, sweetened with dried fruit, makes an unusual and hearty dish, very popular in the Middle East, where it is traditionally eaten with fluffy grains of couscous and a little fiery Chilli sauce, served separately.

1. Heat the oil in a flameproof casserole, add the lamb and fry over a moderate heat for 5-6 minutes, turning from time to time, until browned on all sides. Using a slotted spoon, remove the lamb from the casserole and set aside.
2. Add the onion to the casserole and fry over a gentle heat for 5 minutes until soft and lightly coloured.
3. Return the lamb to the casserole, add the water, cinnamon and salt. Cover and simmer over a gentle heat for 45 minutes.
4. Add the apricots, prunes, lemon rind, lemon juice and honey and stir well to mix. Cover and simmer for 1 further hour, or until the lamb is very tender and the fruit is soft.
5. Serve straight from the casserole, accompanied by steamed couscous or boiled rice and Chilli sauce.

LAMB STUFFED WITH PINE NUTS AND CORIANDER

2kg (4½lb) leg of lamb, boned and trimmed of fat
3 tablespoons olive oil
1 tablespoon coriander seeds, crushed
4 garlic cloves, peeled and crushed
salt
freshly ground black pepper
STUFFING
65g (2½oz) long-grain rice, cooked and drained
50g (2oz) currants or seedless raisins
50g (2oz) pine nuts
½ teaspoon ground cinnamon
salt
freshly ground black pepper
½ egg, beaten

Preparation time: 10 minutes
Cooking time: 2½-3 hours
Oven: 180°C, 350°F, Gas Mark 4
Serves 6

1. Pat the lamb dry with absorbent paper. Combine the oil with the coriander seeds, garlic and salt and pepper to taste and rub the lamb inside and out with the mixture.
2. In a bowl combine all the stuffing ingredients and stir well to mix. Spoon into the cavity in the lamb. Roll the lamb and tie in several places with fine string, or secure with meat skewers.
3. Place the stuffed lamb in a large roasting tin and roast in a preheated moderate oven for 2½-3 hours, until done to your liking, basting from time to time.
4. Transfer the lamb to a warmed carving dish and serve carved into slices, garnished with Persian stuffed apples (p 95) and with a selection of salads.

SULTAN'S PILAFF

4 tablespoons vegetable oil
2 onions, peeled and chopped
2 garlic cloves, peeled and finely chopped
175g (6oz) long-grain rice
450ml (¾pint) boiling water
1 chicken stock cube, crumbled
2 tablespoons seedless raisins or currants
2 tablespoons blanched almonds or pine nut kernels
½ teaspoon ground cinnamon
salt
freshly ground black pepper
225g (8oz) cooked lamb, trimmed and diced

Preparation time: 30 minutes, plus 'resting'
Cooking time: 20 minutes

1. Heat the oil in a large frying pan. Add the onion and garlic and fry over a gentle heat for 5 minutes, until soft and lightly coloured. Add the rice and fry, stirring all the time, for a further 3 minutes.
2. Gradually pour in half the boiling water, stirring well to mix. Reduce the heat and simmer gently, shaking the pan from time to time, until nearly all the water is absorbed. Add a further 4 tablespoons water, with the stock cube, raisins, almonds and cinnamon. Shake the pan and simmer gently until the water is absorbed.
3. Continue adding the water 4 tablespoons at a time, shaking the pan between each addition and waiting for the water to be absorbed, until the rice is tender. Season to taste with salt and pepper. Add the diced lamb, forking it through the rice, and simmer for 2 minutes.
4. Turn off the heat under the pan. Cover the pan with a clean folded tea-towel and leave to stand for 10 minutes, until the rice is fluffy.
5. Transfer to a heated serving dish and serve at once.

Opposite, clockwise from the left: *Sultan's pilaff; Lamb couscous with dried fruit; Lamb stuffed with pine nuts and coriander served with Persian stuffed apples (recipe p95)*

PORK MEDALLIONS IN VERMOUTH WITH CORIANDER

500g (1 ¼lb) pork fillet, cut into 2.5cm (1 inch) medallions
2 teaspoons ground coriander
1 tablespoon vegetable oil
25g (1oz) butter
1 Spanish onion, peeled and finely chopped
1 Bramley apple, cored and finely diced
salt
freshly ground black pepper
1 teaspoon sugar
150ml (5fl oz) white vermouth
150ml (5fl oz) chicken stock
2 egg yolks
1 tablespoon finely chopped parsley

Preparation time: 15 minutes
Cooking time: 1 hour
Oven: 180°C, 350°F, Gas Mark 4

1. Sprinkle the pork medallions with the coriander.
2. Heat the oil and butter in a frying pan, add the pork and fry over a brisk heat, turning, for 2-3 minutes, to seal and brown. With a slotted spoon, transfer the pork to a casserole.
3. Add the onion to the pan and fry over a gentle heat for 5 minutes, until soft and lightly coloured. Add the apple and fry for a further 2-3 minutes. Season with salt, pepper and sugar, then add to the pork and stir well. Pour in the vermouth and stock and stir well again.
4. Cook in a preheated moderate oven for 45 minutes or until the pork is tender. Remove the pork with a slotted spoon and arrange on a warmed serving dish. Keep warm.
5. Purée the apples and onions with the cooking liquid and stir in the egg yolks. Taste and adjust the seasoning. Heat the sauce over a very gentle heat in a saucepan making sure it does not boil.
6. Pour the sauce over the pork and sprinkle with the parsley. Serve with broccoli and buttered rice.

From the top: *Pork chops with cider; Pork medallions in vermouth with coriander*

PORK CHOPS WITH CIDER

2 tablespoons vegetable oil
4 pork chops, about 175g (6oz) each, trimmed of fat
1 large onion, peeled and finely chopped
1 celery stick, finely chopped
2 teaspoons brandy or Calvados
150ml (5fl oz) cider
salt
white pepper
2 teaspoons sugar
2 eating apples
2 teaspoons lemon juice
25g (1oz) butter
150ml (5fl oz) double cream
1 egg yolk

Preparation time: 20 minutes
Cooking time: 20 minutes
Oven: 180°C, 350°F, Gas Mark 4

1. Heat the oil in a large heavy-based pan. Add the chops and fry over a moderate heat for about 4 minutes on each side, to seal and brown. Transfer the pork chops to a casserole and keep warm in a preheated moderate oven.
2. Add the onion and celery to the pan and fry over a gentle heat for 5 minutes, until soft and lightly coloured. Add the brandy and cider and simmer for 2 minutes. Season with salt and pepper and a pinch of sugar. Pour over the pork chops and cook in the oven for 10 minutes, until the chops are tender and cooked through.
3. Peel and core the apples and slice them into rings, Brush the apple rings with lemon juice and the remaining sugar. Heat the butter in the rinsed out pan, add the apple rings and fry for about 2 minutes on each side. Keep warm.

4. Strain the liquid from the casserole and sieve it, reserving the onion and celery. Transfer the pork chops to a warmed serving dish and keep warm. Combine the egg yolk with the cream. Heat the strained liquid gently in a saucepan. Add 1 tablespoonful of the hot liquid to the egg and cream mixture and stir into the pan. Heat gently without boiling and pour over the chops. Garnish with the apple rings and serve at once, with the reserved vegetables.

MEXICAN ENCHILADAS WITH SALSA CRUDA

4 tablespoons vegetable oil
12 tortillas
500g (1 ¼lb) lean minced beef
2 garlic cloves, peeled and crushed
2 green chillies, seeded and finely chopped
1 tablespoon Worcestershire sauce
225g (8oz) Cheddar cheese, grated
1 onion, peeled and finely chopped
SALSA CRUDA
1 × 400g (14oz) can chopped tomatoes
½-1 tablespoon chilli powder
½ tablespoon sugar
salt
freshly ground black pepper

Preparation time: 40 minutes
Cooking time: 30 minutes
Oven: 180°C, 350°F, Gas Mark 4
Serves 6

Mexicans enjoy hot food and enchiladas consist of tortillas – thin pancakes made of maize flour – wrapped round various highly seasoned, fiery fillings, and baked with an even hotter sauce.

1. Heat the oil in a large frying pan, add the tortillas in batches and fry for 2 minutes, to soften. Drain on absorbent paper.
2. Add the minced beef to the pan with the garlic and chillies and fry for about 5 minutes, turning constantly, until the meat has lost all its pinkness. Remove from the heat, add the Worcestershire sauce, and season to taste with salt. Stir in three-quarters of the cheese and onion.
3. Lay the tortillas on a board or work surface and spoon a portion of filling on to the centre of each. Roll up and arrange close together, in a 30cm (12 inch) square baking dish.
4. Make the sauce: put the tomatoes with their juice, chilli powder to taste, the sugar and salt to taste in a small saucepan. Bring to the boil, then lower the heat, cover and simmer for 10 minutes.
5. Pour the sauce evenly over the tortillas, sprinkle with the reserved grated cheese and bake in a preheated moderate oven for 15-20 minutes, until the cheese has melted.
6. Serve with Salsa di crema agria and Mexican salad.

From the top: *Mexican salad (recipe p 118); Salsa de crema agria; Mexican enchiladas with salsa cruda*

SALSA DE CREMA AGRIA

2 tablespoons sesame seeds
300ml (½ pint) soured cream
25g (1oz) black olives, stoned and chopped
50g (2oz) canned pimiento, drained and finely chopped
¼ teaspoon Tabasco sauce

Preparation time: 5 minutes
Cooking time: 5 minutes

This is a spicy Mexican soured cream sauce, often partnered with enchilladas and tacos.

1. Roast the sesame seeds in a dry pan over a moderate heat until they jump, shaking the pan to prevent the seeds from burning.
2. Combine all the remaining ingredients in a bowl.
3. Sprinkle with the sesame seeds and serve.

MEXICAN SALAD

225g (8oz) green beans, topped and tailed
50g (2oz) blanched almonds, toasted and chopped
1×225g (8oz) can red kidney beans, drained
50g (2oz) cucumber, diced
1×225g (8oz) can butter beans, drained
50g (2oz) red pepper, halved, deseeded and diced
DRESSING
85ml (3fl oz) salad oil
25ml (1fl oz) wine vinegar
½ teaspoon annatto seeds (p 13)
½ teaspoon sugar
½ teaspoon made mustard
1 tablespoon finely chopped mint
salt
freshly ground black pepper

Preparation time: 10 minutes
Cooking time: 10 minutes

1. Cook the green beans in a saucepan of boiling salted water for 5-10 minutes until they are tender but still have some bite, then drain and place in a bowl. Mix the almonds with the green beans.
2. In a second bowl combine the kidney beans with the cucumber. Combine the butter beans with the red pepper in a third bowl.
3. Combine all the dressing ingredients, whisking with a fork to dissolve the sugar and mustard. Divide the dressing between the three bowls and stir well.
4. Arrange the salads in three sections on a large serving dish.

Below: *Gado-gado salad*

GADO-GADO SALAD

225g (8oz) beans, topped, tailed and halved
225g (8oz) white cabbage, shredded
225g (8oz) carrots, scraped and finely sliced
225g (8oz) waxy potatoes, peeled and diced
225g (8oz) beansprouts
1 cucumber, quartered lengthways and sliced
2 hard-boiled eggs, shelled and sliced
225g (8oz) desiccated coconut
450ml (¾ pint) boiling water
2 tablespoons oil
5 fresh chillies, seeded
3 garlic cloves, peeled and crushed
1 teaspoon blachan (p 78)
1×225g (8oz) jar crunchy peanut butter
2.5cm (1 inch) piece fresh root ginger, grated
1 stalk lemon grass or 1 small piece thinly pared lemon rind
2 teaspoons soft light brown sugar
1 teaspoon lemon juice

Preparation time: 30 minutes
Cooking time: 30 minutes

A festive and unusual party salad, with a rich, hot sauce based on peanuts and coconut.
1. Put all the vegetables, except the cucumber, into a steamer and steam for about 15 minutes or until just tender, removing the beansprouts after 5 minutes.
2. Put the coconut into a strainer set over a bowl, pour over the boiling water and leave to stand for 20 minutes, pressing the coconut with the back of a wooden spoon to extract as much liquid as possible.
3. Arrange all the vegetables in bands on a large flat dish and garnish with hard-boiled eggs.
4. Heat the oil in a frying-pan and fry separately first the chillies, then the garlic, then the blachan. Transfer the chillies, garlic and blachan to a blender, add the peanut butter and coconut milk and process until smooth. Return the mixture to the pan, with the ginger, lemon grass, sugar and lemon juice and slowly bring to the boil uncovered. Stir and pour over the salad. Serve at once with prawn crackers.

AUBERGINE TIMBALE WITH PASTA

175g (6oz) aubergines, thinly sliced
salt
250g (8oz) tagliatelle noodles
6 tablespoons olive oil
3 garlic cloves, peeled and crushed
1 large onion, peeled and coarsely chopped
1×400g (14oz) can tomatoes
2 tablespoons finely chopped parsley or basil
2 tablespoons Marsala or sweet vermouth
freshly ground black pepper
4 tablespoons dry breadcrumbs
50g (2oz) Parmesan cheese, grated
50g (2oz) butter, diced

Preparation time: 20 minutes, plus standing
Cooking time: 50-55 minutes
Oven: 190°C, 375°F, Gas Mark 5

Somewhere between a meatless moussaka and lasagne, this pasta, aubergine and tomato pie is unusual in that it is unmoulded before serving. It can be difficult to cut, so have a knife and a spatula ready.

1. Put the aubergine slices in a colander set over a plate, sprinkle with salt and leave for 20 minutes.
2. Meanwhile, cook the noodles in a large saucepan of boiling salted water until they are lightly cooked and still have a bite to them. Drain, rinse in hot water and drain thoroughly again.
3. Rinse the aubergines under cold running water and pat dry with absorbent paper. Heat the oil in a large frying pan with a lid, add the aubergines, and fry over a moderate heat for 2-3 minutes on each side. Remove and drain on absorbent paper.
4. Heat a further 2 tablespoons of oil in the frying pan. Add the garlic and onion and fry over a moderate heat for 2-3 minutes. Add the tomatoes, cover and simmer for 10-15 minutes. Remove from the heat, add the parsley and Marsala and season to taste.
5. Grease a 20cm (8 inch) springform tin and arrange a third of the noodles in the bottom. Lay half the aubergine slices on top and cover with half the tomato mixture. Build another layer of noodles, aubergine and tomato then finish with the remaining noodles.
6. Mix together the breadcrumbs and Parmesan cheese and sprinkle evenly over the top. Dot with the butter, cover with foil and bake in a preheated medium-hot oven for 40-45 minutes, removing the foil 10 minutes before the end of cooking time. Carefully remove the sides of the tin and transfer to a large plate. Serve hot with a green salad.

RISI E BISI

15g (½oz) butter
50g (2oz) streaky bacon rashers, rinded and diced
1 small onion, peeled and finely chopped
350g (12oz) risotto or long-grain rice
1.5 litres (2½ pints) hot chicken stock
1 × 425g (15oz) can petits pois, drained
½ teaspoon freshly grated nutmeg
2 tablespoons grated Parmesan cheese
2 tablespoons vermouth or white wine
fresh basil, to garnish

Preparation time: 5 minutes
Cooking time: 30 minutes

A classic Venetian starter, whose consistency should be a little more liquid than that of a standard risotto.

1. Melt the butter in a large heavy-based pan, add the bacon and onion and fry over a gentle heat for 5 minutes, stirring, until the onion is transparent.
2. Add the rice and stir for 1-2 minutes until all the grains are coated.
3. Stir in about one-third of the stock and allow to bubble briefly. Lower the heat slightly, then cook, uncovered, over a moderate heat until all the liquid is absorbed. Add another cupful of stock and cook until absorbed. Add the petits pois with the nutmeg and another cupful of stock. Lower the heat, stir lightly with a wooden fork and cook until all the liquid is absorbed. Taste and adjust the seasoning. Stir in all the remaining stock, and continue cooking, uncovered, stirring very gently until the rice is just tender, but with a faint bite to it.
4. Fork in the Parmesan cheese with the vermouth, cook for 30 seconds, then remove from the heat. Cover the pan, laying a folded clean tea-towel under the lid, and leave to stand for 5-8 minutes, until the rice is very tender.
5. Transfer to a hot serving dish and serve with extra Parmesan handed separately if liked.

From the top: *Aubergine timbale with pasta; Risi e bisi*

KOREAN RICE WITH MUSHROOMS AND SESAME

3 tablespoons vegetable oil
100g (4oz) dried mushrooms, soaked, stalks removed and thinly sliced
2 onions, peeled and thinly sliced
275g (10oz) long-grain rice
3 tablespoons light soy sauce
1 tablespoon sesame seeds, lightly toasted and crushed to a powder.
425ml (15fl oz) cold water
2 spring onions, trimmed and cut into 5mm (¼ inch) rounds
½ teaspoon salt
spring onions, trimmed, to garnish

Preparation time: 5 minutes
Cooking time: 35 minutes

1. Heat the oil in a large, heavy-based saucepan, add the mushrooms and onions and fry over a gentle heat for about 5 minutes, stirring often, until the onions are soft and lightly coloured.
2. Add the rice, soy, sesame seeds, water and salt and bring rapidly to the boil over a high heat, stirring once or twice. Stir in the spring onions.
3. Cover the pan, turn the heat to the lowest setting and cook without stirring for 30 minutes, until the rice is tender and all the liquid is absorbed.
4. Garnish with spring onions and serve hot.

From the left: *Korean rice with mushrooms and sesame; Risotto alle funghe*
Opposite, from the top: *Chinese, cucumber and radish salad; Avocado salad; Melon salad*

RISOTTO ALLE FUNGHE

25g (1oz) butter
1 onion, peeled and finely chopped
350g (12oz) risotto or long-grain rice
1 small packet Italian dried mushrooms, soaked in warm water, stemmed and sliced
1.2 litres (2 pints) hot chicken stock
½ teaspoon salt
freshly ground black pepper
4 tablespoons Marsala (optional)
TO SERVE
50g (2oz) butter
50g (2oz) Parmesan cheese, grated

Preparation time: 5 minutes
Cooking time: 35 minutes

1. Melt the butter in a large, heavy-based saucepan, add the onion and fry over a moderate heat for 2 minutes, then add the rice and cook for a further 2-3 minutes, stirring constantly with a wooden spoon.
2. Add the mushrooms and their liquid, stir, then stir in one-third of the stock and allow to bubble. Lower the heat and boil steadily until all the liquid is absorbed. Repeat twice until all the stock has been used and the rice is tender, forking the mixture through lightly with a wooden fork.
3. Taste and adjust the seasoning and stir in the Marsala, if using.
4. Remove from the heat and fork up the rice. Cover the pan with a clean tea-towel and the lid and leave to stand in a warm place for at least 5 minutes, to allow the flavours to blend.
5. Garnish with fresh herbs and serve hot with butter and Parmesan cheese handed separately.

MELON SALAD

2 ripe honeydew or ogen melons, halved, seeded and peeled
1 small red pepper, cored, seeded and sliced
2 tablespoons lemon juice
1 tablespoon sunflower oil
1 teaspoon ground ginger
fresh salad vegetables (lettuce, cucumber), to garnish

Preparation time: 5 minutes

A quickly prepared, delicately flavoured salad which makes a refreshing accompaniment to cold chicken, duck or pork.
1. Cut the melon flesh into 2cm (¾ inch) cubes and put them into a mixing bowl with the red pepper.
2. Combine the lemon juice with the oil and pour over the melon.
3. Sprinkle the salad with the ginger and fork through lightly to coat all the melon with dressing. Serve on individual salad plates with a garnish of fresh salad vegetables.

CHINESE CUCUMBER AND RADISH SALAD

1 medium cucumber, peeled, halved lengthways, seeded and thinly sliced
2 teaspoons salt
1 mooli (Japanese radish), peeled, halved lengthways and thinly sliced
2 large spring onions, thinly sliced
DRESSING
2 tablespoons light soy sauce
1 tablespoon vegetable oil
1 teaspoon wine vinegar
1 teaspoon sesame oil
salt
½ teaspoon caster sugar

Preparation time: 25 minutes, plus salting

1. Put the cucumber in a colander, sprinkle with salt, set over a plate and leave for 20 minutes, to extract the juices. Rinse the cucumber under cold running water and pat dry with absorbent paper.
2. Put the cucumber in a salad bowl with the mooli and spring onions.
3. Thoroughly combine all the dressing ingredients in a jug, then pour over the salad and toss lightly with a fork to coat all the vegetables.
4. Serve at once with grilled pork chops or a platter of cold meats.

AVOCADO SALAD

3 ripe, firm avocados
1 large cooked potato, diced
1 pink grapefruit, peeled and separated into segments, all pith and membrane removed
1 teaspoon crushed red peppercorns or sprig of fresh chervil, to garnish
DRESSING
3 tablespoons olive oil
1 tablespoon walnut oil
1 small garlic clove, peeled and crushed
2 tablespoons lemon juice or white wine vinegar
salt
freshly ground black pepper

Preparation time: 8 minutes

This attractive salad, with its unusual combination of flavours and textures, should be prepared just before serving. It goes especially well with spiced beef or ham.
1. Peel the avocados, remove the stones, and cut into small chunks. Place in a salad bowl with the diced potato and grapefruit segments and mix gently.
2. Combine all the dressing ingredients, whisk with a fork to blend thoroughly, and pour over the salad. Fork gently through, sprinkle with the red peppercorns or garnish with chervil and serve at once.

PÉRIGORD SALAD

1 head cos or iceberg lettuce, coarsely shredded
2 tablespoons chopped walnuts
1 tablespoon olive oil
25g (1oz) butter
1 small garlic clove, peeled and crushed
1 thick slice stale white bread, crusts removed, and diced

DRESSING

2 tablespoons cider or white wine vinegar
salt
freshly ground black pepper
1 teaspoon Dijon mustard
6 tablespoons walnut oil

Preparation time: 6 minutes

The walnut flavour predominates in this unusual salad, which is particularly good eaten with a firm goat cheese and lots of crusty bread.

1. Put the lettuce and nuts in a large salad bowl.
2. Heat the oil and butter in a frying pan, add the garlic and bread and fry over a moderate heat, turning, until the bread croûtons are crisp and golden. Remove with a slotted spoon and reserve while making the dressing.
3. Combine all the dressing ingredients and whisk with a fork until thoroughly blended. Pour the dressing over the salad and toss until the lettuce is thoroughly coated. Scatter the croûtons over and serve.

SALADE NIÇOISE WITH AÏOLI

1 large crisp lettuce or ½ head curly endive or 2 heads radicchio, washed
225g (8oz) firm tomatoes, quartered
225g (8oz) new potatoes, steamed and cooled (optional)
175g (6oz) stringless green beans, topped, tailed, steamed and cooled
4 hard-boiled eggs, shelled and quartered
1 × 90g (3 ½oz) can tuna fish, drained and flaked
8 anchovy fillets
50g (2oz) black olives

DRESSING

6 tablespoons olive oil
2 tablespoons red wine vinegar
1 teaspoon Dijon mustard
salt
freshly ground black pepper

AÏOLI

2-3 cloves garlic, peeled and crushed
½ teaspoon Dijon mustard
½ teaspoon salt
2 egg yolks
300ml (½ pint) olive oil

Preparation time: 30 minutes

A speciality of the resort town of Nice on the French Riviera, this is an earthy, strongly flavoured mixed salad whose ingredients can be varied according to vegetables in season: lightly cooked cauliflower florets, raw carrot slivers and mangetout are all possibilities, but olives, anchovies, hard-boiled eggs and tomatoes are essential to give the salad its typically Niçoise flavour.

1. With the hands, break the lettuce, endive or radicchio into even-sized pieces and arrange in a shallow salad bowl or on a large flat serving dish. Arrange the other ingredients attractively on top.
2. Thoroughly combine all the dressing ingredients in a jug.
3. In a bowl combine the garlic, mustard, salt and egg yolks, pounding the mixture with a wooden spoon. Put the olive oil in a small jug and add very gradually to the garlic mixture, drop by drop, beating constantly with a wooden spoon, until about half the oil is used up and the mixture is beginning to thicken and looks glossy. Add the remaining oil a little more quickly in a thin, steady stream, beating constantly. When all the oil is absorbed, taste and adjust the seasoning.
4. Pour a little of the vinaigrette dressing over the salad at the table and hand the remainder separately with the aïoli handed in a small bowl.

PASTA, PEA AND ARTICHOKE SALAD

225g (8oz) coloured pasta bows or shells
1 × 425g (15oz) can artichoke hearts, drained and sliced
425g (15oz) petits pois, defrosted if frozen
1 canned sweet pimiento, drained and diced
½ teaspoon freshly grated nutmeg
salt
freshly ground black pepper

DRESSING

1 tablespoon white vermouth
1 tablespoon lemon juice
3 tablespoons olive oil
4 tablespoons soured cream

Preparation time: 15 minutes

1. Cook the pasta in boiling salted water for about 10 minutes or according to packet instructions until *al dente*. Drain.
2. Turn the pasta into a large salad bowl and add the artichoke hearts, peas and pimiento. Sprinkle with the nutmeg, season with salt and pepper and turn gently with two forks, making sure the pasta does not break up.
3. Combine all the dressing ingredients in a jug, whisking with a fork until smooth, then pour over the salad and fork through lightly to coat all the ingredients with dressing.
4. Serve the salad at room temperature, on its own or as an accompaniment to grilled fish or veal.

Opposite, clockwise from the bottom: *Périgord salad with Honeyed chicken with meaux mustard (recipe p 100); Aioli; Pasta, pea and artichoke salad; Salad niçoise*

PRALINE SOUFFLÉ

100g (4oz) whole blanched almonds
125g (5oz) sugar
6 eggs, separated
100g (4oz) caster sugar
40g (1 ½oz) flour
40g (1 ½oz) cornflour
600ml (1 pint) milk
2 drops vanilla essence
100 ml (3 ½fl oz) kirsch

Preparation time: 30 minutes plus cooling
Cooking time: 15 minutes
Oven: 160°C, 325°F, Gas Mark 3
Serves 4-6

1. To make the praline, place the almonds and the sugar in a saucepan over the lowest possible heat until the sugar caramelizes and turns brown – about 20 minutes. Pour the mixture on to an oiled baking sheet and leave to harden – about 20 minutes. When cold, crush in a food processor, coffee grinder or rotary grinder.
2. Grease a 15cm (6 inch) soufflé dish and sprinkle with sugar. Cut a strip of greaseproof paper long enough to wrap around the dish and overlap by 5cm (2 inches) and deep enough to extend 7.5cm (3 inches) above the rim. Secure with string.
3. Whisk the egg yolks with the sugar until thick and pale and then mix in the flour and cornflour. Heat the milk to just under boiling point and stir into the mixture very slowly.
4. Place the mixture in a saucepan over very gentle heat, stirring. Bring slowly to the boil and simmer for 2 minutes, whisking if any lumps should appear. Take off the heat and allow to cool slightly.
5. Meanwhile, whisk the egg whites in a large bowl until stiff but moist. Stir the vanilla essence into the egg yolk mixture, beat in two-thirds of the praline and 1 tablespoon of egg white and then fold in the remaining egg whites with a metal spoon, using a figure of eight motion.
6. Pour the mixture into the soufflé dish and sprinkle the top with the remaining praline. Bake for 15 minutes until well risen.
7. Sprinkle with kirsch, remove the paper and serve immediately.

CRANACHAN

75g (3oz) coarse oatmeal
1 tablespoon clear honey
2 tablespoons Scotch whisky or Drambuie
300ml (10fl oz) double or whipping cream, whipped
1 piece stem ginger, chopped, to decorate

Preparation time: 5 minutes, plus chilling
Cooking time: 4 minutes
Serves 4-6

1. Toast the oatmeal in a dry frying pan over a medium heat for 4 minutes until golden. Cool.
2. In a mixing bowl combine the honey and whisky with the whipped cream. Chill until very cold.
3. Just before serving fold the toasted oatmeal into the cream and spoon into individual dishes. Sprinkle the chopped stem ginger on top and serve.

BLACKBERRY MERINGUE PUDDING

4 egg whites
225g (8oz) caster sugar
1 teaspoon cornflour
1 teaspoon white wine vinegar
1 teaspoon vanilla essence
450g (1lb) blackberries
120ml (4fl oz) port
extra sugar to taste
300ml (½pint) double or whipping cream

Preparation time: 25 minutes, plus cooling
Cooking time: about 1 hour
Oven: 180°C, 350°F, Gas Mark 4
then: 120°C, 250°F, Gas Mark ½
Serves 4-6

From the left: *Praline soufflé; Cranachan; Blackberry meringue pudding*

This pudding can be made with any soft fruit cooked with an appropriate liqueur as available: raspberries with Framboise, strawberries with Grand Marnier or Cointreau, cherries with kirsch or blackberries with port, as below. The meringue can be bought, made in the normal way or, best of all, made in the Pavlova way with a soft centre, as in this recipe.

1. Line a baking sheet with a piece of non-stick silicone or lightly greased greaseproof paper.
2. Whisk the egg whites until nearly stiff. Add the sugar a dessertspoon at a time, whisking constantly, until all the sugar is incorporated and the mixture is firm and glossy.
3. Using a large metal spoon, fold in the cornflour, vinegar and vanilla essence in rapid figure of eight movements.
4. Spread the meringue over the paper and bake in a preheated moderate oven for 5 minutes. Reduce the oven temperature and bake for 1 hour. Leave to cool for 2-3 hours.
5. Meanwhile reserve a few perfect blackberries for decoration and gently stew the remainder in the port in a saucepan until soft. Sweeten to taste with sugar and set aside to cool completely.
6. Whip the cream until soft peaks form.
7. Break up the cooled meringue. Arrange one-third of the meringue in the base of a glass bowl and top with a layer of blackberries and a layer of cream. Repeat twice, finishing with cream, and decorate with the reserved blackberries.

LANGUES DE CHAT BISCUITS

3 eggs
90g (3 ½oz) vanilla sugar
90g (3 ½oz) plain flour, sieved

Preparation time: 15 minutes, plus cooling
Cooking time: 7 minutes
Oven: 200°C, 400°F, Gas Mark 6
Makes about 30 biscuits

1. Whisk together the eggs and sugar until thick and creamy. Fold the flour into the creamed mixture, using a large metal spoon, lightly but thoroughly.
2. Place the mixture in a piping bag fitted with a plain nozzle and pipe 5cm (2 inch) lengths on to non-stick silicone paper.
3. Bake in a preheated hot oven for 7 minutes, until light golden. Allow to cool for a few minutes, then carefully transfer the biscuits to a wire rack to cool completely. The biscuits will keep well in an airtight tin for up to a fortnight.

From the top: *Orange-flower creams with Langues de chats biscuits (recipe p 125); Thai-fried banas with lime*

THAI FRIED BANANAS WITH LIME

75g (3oz) butter
4 bananas, peeled
3 tablespoons soft light brown sugar
juice of 3 limes or lemons
slices of lemon or lime, to garnish

Cooking time: 10 minutes

1. Melt the butter in a large frying pan, add the bananas and fry over a gentle heat, turning from time to time, until lightly browned. Transfer to a warmed serving dish and keep warm.
2. Add the sugar to the pan and stir over a gentle heat until dissolved. Pour syrup over the bananas.
3. Sprinkle over the lime juice, garnish with lemon or lime slices and serve at once.

ORANGE-FLOWER CREAMS

6 egg yolks
50g (2oz) vanilla sugar
1 teaspoon cornflour
15g (½oz) powdered gelatine
3 tablespoons water
450ml (¾pint) single cream
1 tablespoon orange-flower water
1 orange, thinly sliced, to garnish

Preparation time: 15 minutes, plus setting
Cooking time: 15 minutes
Serves 6

1. Put the egg yolks, sugar and cornflour in a heat-proof bowl. Set over a pan of simmering water (the base of the bowl must not touch the water) and whisk until the mixture is thick and pale.
2. Put the 3 tablespoons water in a small saucepan and sprinkle the gelatine over. Leave for a few minutes until spongy, then melt over a very gentle heat (on no account allow the gelatine to boil) and stir it into the egg yolk mixture.
3. Bring the cream to just below boiling point and whisk into the mixture with the orange-flower water.
4. Pour the mixture into ramekins and chill in the refrigerator for 2-3 hours or until set.
5. Decorate the orange-flower creams with orange slices and serve with Langues de chat (p 125).

CHOCOLATE TOPPED MERINGUES WITH CHESTNUT CREAM FILLING

4 egg whites
225g (8oz) caster sugar
2 teaspoons cornflour
2 teaspoons vanilla essence
1 teaspoon wine vinegar
100 g (4oz) plain chocolate, broken into pieces
1 tablespoon water
1 × 400g (14oz) tin sweetened chestnut purée
300ml (½pint) double cream, whipped

Preparation time: 15 minutes
Cooking time: 1 hour
Oven: 140°C, 275°F, Gas Mark 1
Makes 12-16 meringues

1. Line 2 baking trays with non-stick silicone paper. In a large clean bowl whisk the egg whites until stiff and dry. Add half the sugar, a teaspoon at a time, whisking between each addition.
2. Sift over the remaining sugar and the cornflour and add the vanilla essence and vinegar. Fold lightly into the mixture with a large metal spoon.
3. Using 2 large spoons or a piping bag fitted with a large plain or rose nozzle, shape the mixture into 24 medium-sized meringues on the prepared baking

sheets. Place on a low shelf in a preheated oven and bake for 1 hour or until set. Cool on a wire tray.
4. Combine the chestnut purée with the whipped cream. Sandwich pairs of meringues together with the chestnut cream.
5. When the meringues are cold, melt the chocolate with the water in a small bowl placed over a pan of simmering water. Fill a piping bag with a plain writing nozzle with melted chocolate, drizzle chocolate over the tops of the meringues and leave to set.

CRANBERRY CHOCOLATE ROULADE

5 eggs, separated
150g (5oz) caster sugar
225g (8oz) plain chocolate, broken into pieces
85ml (3fl oz) water

FILLING

100g (4oz) sugar
3 tablespoons fresh orange juice
3 tablespoons water
225g (8oz) cranberries, topped and tailed
2 tablespoons Grand Marnier or Cointreau
300ml (½ pint) whipping cream, whipped
icing sugar, sifted, to finish

Preparation time: 25 minutes, plus cooling
Cooking time: 30 minutes
Oven: 200°C, 400°F, Gas Mark 6
Serves 6

1. Line a large roasting tin with non-stick silicone or greased greaseproof paper.
2. Put the egg yolks with the sugar in a heatproof bowl set over a saucepan of simmering water. Whisk until light and fluffy.
3. Melt the chocolate in a separate ovenproof bowl over a pan of simmering water. Allow to cool slightly, then stir into the egg yolk mixture.
4. Whisk the egg whites until stiff. Using a large metal spoon, fold one spoonful of whisked egg white into the chocolate mixture, then lightly fold in the remainder.
5. Spoon the mixture evenly into the lined tin and bake in a preheated hot oven for about 15 minutes, until cooked. Turn out the sponge on to non-stick silicone paper sprinkled with caster sugar and quickly peel off the lining paper. Trim off the crisp edges and immediately roll up from one short edge. Carefully unroll and leave to cool completely on a wire tray.
6. Meanwhile, put the sugar, orange juice and water into a saucepan. Add the cranberries and cook gently for about 10 minutes, until tender. Remove from the heat and leave to cool completely. Lay the sponge on a board or work surface. Sprinkle with a little of the cranberry cooking liquid. Using a slotted spoon, spoon the cranberries over the surface of the sponge. Sprinkle the Grand Marnier over then spread with whipped cream.
7. Roll up from a short end and dust thickly with icing sugar. Carefully transfer to a serving plate and cut into slices to serve.

From the left: *Cranberry chocolate roulade; Chocolate topped meringues with chestnut cream filling*

ROSE PETAL TART

1 egg white
petals of 1 pink or red rose
caster sugar
225g (8oz) flaky or puff pastry, defrosted if frozen
150ml (¼ pint) plain unsweetened yogurt
1 egg yolk
2 tablespoons caster sugar
300ml (½ pint) double or whipping cream, whipped
2 tablespoons rosewater

Preparation time: 20 minutes, plus cooling
Cooking time: 1 hour 25 minutes
Oven: 110°C, 225°F, Gas Mark ¼
then: 200°C, 400°F, Gas Mark 6
Serves 6

1. Whisk the egg white until stiff peaks form. Brush each rose petal with beaten egg white, then sprinkle with a little sugar and leave in a cool place to dry.
2. Roll out the pastry to about 5mm (¼ inch) thickness and cut out a 25cm (10 inch) circle. Place on a lightly moistened baking sheet. Raise the oven temperature and bake for about 20-25 minutes until the pastry is well risen, brown and dry underneath. Leave for at least 1 hour to cool completely.
3. Fold the yogurt, egg yolk and sugar into the whipped cream. Whisk in the rosewater.
4. Spoon the rosewater cream over the pastry base. Decorate with the frosted rose petals and serve immediately.

TURKISH PUMPKIN TART

175g (6oz) shortcrust pastry
750g (1½lb) pumpkin, peeled and sliced or canned pumpkin purée
50g (2oz) soft light brown sugar
1 tablespoon lemon juice
½ teaspoon ground cinnamon
½ teaspoon ground ginger
2 eggs, beaten
150ml (5fl oz) single cream
50g (2oz) shelled walnuts, chopped

Preparation time: 30 minutes
Cooking time: 1 hour 30 minutes
Oven: 200°C, 400°F, Gas Mark 6
then: 180°C, 350°F, Gas Mark 4
Serves 6

1. Line a 20cm (8 inch) flan ring with the shortcrust pastry. Line the pastry with greaseproof paper or foil and fill with baking beans. Place on a baking sheet and bake in a preheated oven for 15 minutes. Remove the paper and beans and return to the oven for 5 minutes.
2. Meanwhile steam the pumpkin for 1 hour or until tender. Process the pumpkin in a food processor until smooth, or mash and press through a sieve.
3. Put the pumpkin purée in a bowl and stir in the sugar, lemon juice, spices, eggs, cream and half the nuts. Spoon the mixture into the flan case and smooth the surface.

From the left: *Turkish pumpkin tart; Rose petal tart*

4. Reduce the oven temperature and bake the tart for 30 minutes or until set. Sprinkle the remaining nuts on top and serve with whipped cream.

HONEY AND BRANDY ICE CREAM

4 eggs, separated
4 tablespoons warmed clear honey
3 tablespoons brandy
450ml (¾pint) double or whipping cream

Preparation time: 12 minutes plus freezing
Serves 6

A most delicious ice cream, with a warm, velvety flavour.

1. In a bowl beat the egg yolks until light and pale. Gradually add the honey, beating well after each addition. Beat in the brandy.
2. Whip the cream until it stands in soft peaks, then lightly fold into the egg mixture.
3. Whisk the egg whites until stiff, then lightly fold into the mixture.
4. Pour into a lidded plastic or aluminium container and freeze for 2 hours.
5. Remove from the freezer 15 minutes before serving. Serve with Chocolate fudge sauce and brandy snaps.

GINGER ICE CREAM

2 eggs
2 egg yolks
75g (3oz) sugar
450ml (¾pint) single cream
1 teaspoon vanilla essence
200ml (7fl oz) double cream, lightly whipped
50g (2oz) chopped preserved ginger
1 tablespoon preserved ginger syrup

Preparation time: 40 minutes, plus freezing
Cooking time: 25-30 minutes
Serves 6

1. Beat the eggs, egg yolks and sugar until smooth and thick.
2. Heat the single cream to just under boiling point, then pour it on to the egg mixture, beating all the time.
3. Strain the mixture into the top of a double boiler or into a heatproof bowl placed over a pan of simmering water and stir the mixture over a gentle heat until it is thick enough to coat the back of a wooden spoon – about 20 minutes. Cool.
4. Fold in the vanilla essence, lightly whipped cream, chopped ginger and ginger syrup. Pour the mixture into a freezer container and freeze for 2 hours. Beat the ice cream at 30 minute intervals during freezing bringing the ice cream at the sides into the middle.

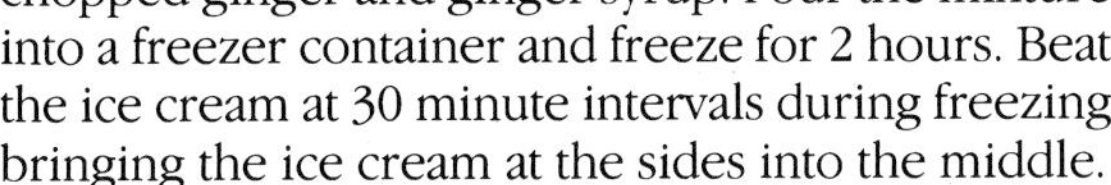

5. Serve with Chocolate fudge sauce, if liked.

From the top: *Ginger ice cream; Chocolate fudge sauce; Honey and brandy ice cream*

CHOCOLATE FUDGE SAUCE

175g (6oz) sugar
1 tablespoon cocoa powder
85ml (3fl oz) water
1 tablespoon butter
½ teaspoon vanilla essence

Preparation time: 5 minutes
Cooking time: 5 minutes

1. Put the sugar, cocoa powder and water in a saucepan and stir over a gentle heat until the sugar is dissolved. Boil gently without stirring to soft ball stage (113-118°C/253-245°F or when a small amount of syrup dropped into iced water forms a soft ball).
2. Remove the pan from the heat and stir in the butter and vanilla essence. Pour the sauce into a warmed jug and serve hot, with ice cream.

Opposite, from the top:
Devils food cake with American white frosting; Almond and pistachio loaf

DEVIL'S FOOD CAKE

4 tablespoons cocoa powder
200g (7oz) sugar
3 tablespoons water
100ml (3 ½fl oz) milk
100g (4oz) butter
1 teaspoon vanilla essence
2 eggs, separated
150g (5oz) plain flour
½ teaspoon cream of tartar
½ teaspoon salt
½ teaspoon baking powder

Preparation time: 30 minutes
Cooking time: 35 minutes
Oven: 190°C, 375°F, Gas Mark 5
Serves 6

A classic American cake, which can be iced with white or chocolate frosting.

1. Butter and lightly dust with flour two round 20cm (8 inch) victoria sandwich tins.
2. Put the cocoa, 3 tablespoons of the sugar and the water into a small saucepan and simmer, stirring with a wooden spoon until smoothly blended. Remove from the heat, stir in the milk and set aside.
3. Cream the butter with one-third of the remaining sugar until light and fluffy. Beat in the vanilla.
4. Add the egg yolks one at a time, beating well between each addition, then beat in the cooled cocoa mixture.
5. Sift the flour with the cream of tartar, salt and baking powder and fold into the chocolate mixture. Whisk the egg whites until stiff, then fold in the remaining sugar and whisk again until stiff. Gently fold the whisked egg whites into the mixture with a large metal spoon.
6. Divide the mixture between both cake tins, spreading it out and smoothing the surface. Bake in a preheated moderately hot oven until a wooden cocktail stick inserted into the centre of the cake comes out clean. Leave to cool in the tins for 5 minutes, then turn on to wire racks to cool completely.
7. Sandwich the cake halves together with American white frosting (see below), ice, and serve.

AMERICAN WHITE FROSTING

450 g (1 lb) granulated sugar
150 ml (¼pint) cold water
2 egg whites

Preparation time: 15 minutes
Cooking time: 20 minutes

1. Place the sugar and water in a heavy-based saucepan and stir over a low heat until the sugar has dissolved. Brush down the sides of the pan with a pastry brush that has been dipped in cold water to remove any sugar that may be clinging to the sides.
2. Bring the sugar syrup to the boil and boil rapidly until it reaches 118°C/245°F (or when a small amount dropped into iced water can be moulded with the fingers into a soft ball which loses its shape when removed from the water).
3. Remove the sugar syrup from the heat and leave to cool until the bubbles on the surface have subsided.
4. Whisk the egg whites until stiff. Slowly pour the hot sugar syrup on to the egg whites, whisking all the time. Pour the syrup in a steady stream directly on to the egg whites that are being whisked.
5. When the frosting is thick enough to stand in peaks with the tips just tipping over quickly ice the cake.

ALMOND AND PISTACHIO LOAF

finely pared rind of 1 orange, cut into matchstick strips, parboiled for 5 seconds and drained
finely pared rind of 1 lemon, cut into matchstick strips, parboiled for 5 seconds and drained
1 tablespoon sugar
5 tablespoons water
100g (4oz) blanched almonds
50g (2oz) blanched pistachio nuts
75g (3oz) sugar
25g (1oz) plain flour
4 tablespoons medium-sweet white wine
3 eggs, separated
½ teaspoon salt
15g (½oz) butter

Preparation time: 40 minutes
Cooking time: 30 minutes
Oven: 180°C, 350°F, Gas Mark 4

1. In a small saucepan combine the orange and lemon peel, sugar and water and bring to the boil. Simmer over a very gentle heat until the liquid is almost reduced and the peel is coated with a thick, syrupy mixture.
2. Pound the nuts in a pestle and mortar to a paste, gradually adding the peel and sugar, a spoonful at a time, or process in a food processor.
3. Add the white wine, a spoonful at a time, alternately with the remaining sugar and flour. Then add the egg yolks, pounding and stirring the mixture to combine well.
4. Whisk the egg whites with the salt until stiff, then fold lightly but thoroughly into the nut mixture, using a large metal spoon.
5. Pour the mixture into a greased 1lb loaf tin. Stand the tin in a dish containing enough hot water to come halfway up its sides, and bake in a preheated moderately hot oven for 30 minutes or until the loaf feels firm to the touch and is cooked through.
6. Leave to cool slightly in the tin, then turn on to a wire rack and leave to cool completely.
7. Serve in slices with single cream.

CHOCOLATE CHIP COOKIES

100 g (4 oz) butter, softened
25 g (1 oz) soft brown sugar
25 g (1 oz) caster sugar
1 egg, lightly beaten
few drops vanilla essence
150 g (5 oz) plain flour, sifted
½ teaspoon bicarbonate of soda
100 g (4 oz) chocolate chips
50 g (2 oz) shelled walnuts, finely chopped

Preparation time: 15 minutes
Cooking time: 15-17 minutes
Oven: 180°C, 350°F, Gas Mark 4
Makes 30

1. Cream the butter with the soft brown sugar and caster sugar together until light and fluffy. Add the egg and vanilla essence and beat until smooth.
2. Sift the flour with the bicarbonate of soda and fold in with the chocolate chips and walnuts.
3. Spoon teaspoons of the mixture on to a lightly greased baking sheet, leaving space in between.
4. Bake in a preheated oven for 15-17 minutes until golden brown. Cool on a wire tray.

PECAN PIE

175 g (6 oz) plain flour
pinch of salt
100 g (4 oz) butter, softened
1 egg yolk
1-3 teaspoons iced water
egg white, beaten
150 g (5 oz) caster sugar
3 eggs, lightly beaten
225 g (8 oz) maple or golden syrup
½ teaspoon vanilla essence
pinch of salt
175 g (6 oz) shelled pecan nuts, chopped

Preparation time: 20 minutes
Cooking time: 50-55 minutes
Oven: 200°C, 400°F, Gas Mark 6
then: 180°C, 350°F, Gas Mark 4
Serves 6-8

1. Sift the flour and salt into a large mixing bowl. Add the butter and rub into the flour until the mixture resembles fine breadcrumbs.
2. Add the egg yolk and sufficient iced water to give a firm dough and knead until smooth. Roll out on a floured board and use to line a 20 cm (8 inch) fluted flan ring. Chill for 45 minutes.
3. Cover the pastry with greaseproof paper and arrange some baking beans on top. Bake blind in a preheated oven for 12-15 minutes until firm.
4. Remove the paper and beans and lightly brush the pastry with beaten egg white. Return to the oven for a further 2 minutes to dry out then remove and cool on a wire tray. Reduce the oven temperature.
5. Make the filling. Mix the sugar and eggs together then stir in the syrup with the vanilla essence. Add the salt and half the pecan nuts.
6. Spoon the filling mixture into the coated flan case, sprinkle the remaining pecans on top, and bake for 35 minutes until firm and golden brown.
7. Cool on a wire tray. Serve with whipped cream.

FRESH FRUIT TARTS

175 g (6 oz) plain flour
pinch of salt
3 tablespoons icing sugar
3 egg yolks
100 g (4 oz) butter, softened
8 tablespoons apple or redcurrant jelly
4 tablespoons Cointreau or other fruit liqueur
350-450 g (12 oz-1 lb) strawberries or raspberries

Preparation time: 25 minutes, plus chilling
Cooking time: 25 minutes
Oven: 200°C, 400°F, Gas Mark 6

1. Sift the flour on to a large board or clean work surface. Make a well in the centre, put the salt, icing sugar and egg yolks into the centre and, using the fingertips, gradually work into the flour.
2. Quickly knead in the butter. Form into a ball, wrap in cling film or foil and chill for 1 hour.
3. Roll out the pastry on a floured board, and use to line eight 7.5 cm (3 inch) tartlet tins. Chill for 30 minutes. Bake blind in a preheated oven for 12-15 minutes until golden brown. Cool on a wire tray and remove from the tins.
4. Put the apple jelly and Cointreau in a small saucepan and stir over a gentle heat until well blended.
5. Brush the base of each pastry case with the jelly glaze. Arrange the fruit on top, and spoon over the remaining glaze. Chill. Serve with whipped cream.

COCONUT BUTTERSCOTCH TART

100 g (4 oz) plain flour
pinch of salt
50 g (2 oz) butter, softened
25 g (1 oz) icing sugar, sifted
1 egg yolk
1 tablespoon iced water
1 egg white, beaten
50 g (2 oz) granulated sugar
300 ml (½ pint) hot water
4 tablespoons golden syrup
125 g (4 oz) creamed coconut
1 level tablespoon cornflour
2 eggs
toasted coconut flakes, to decorate

Clockwise from bottom left: *Coconut butterscotch tart; Chocolate chip cookies; Pecan pie; Fresh fruit tarts*

Preparation time: 20 minutes, plus chilling
Cooking time: 1 hour 10 minutes
Oven: 200°C, 400°F, Gas Mark 6
then: 170°F, 325°F, Gas Mark 3
Serves 4-6

1. Sift the flour and salt into a large mixing bowl. Add the butter and rub into the flour until the mixture resembles fine breadcrumbs.
2. Stir in the icing sugar, yolk and iced water and knead to a firm dough. Wrap in clingfilm or foil and chill for 30 minutes.
3. Roll out the pastry on a floured board and use to line a 20 cm (8 inch) flan tin. Chill for 45 minutes. Cover the pastry with greaseproof paper and arrange some baking beans on top. Bake blind in a preheated oven for 12-15 minutes until the pastry is firm.
4. Remove the paper and beans and lightly brush the base of the pastry with beaten egg white. Return to the oven for 2 minutes to dry out then remove and cool on a wire tray. Reduce the oven temperature.
5. Make the filling. Put the granulated sugar in a small heavy-based saucepan and heat very gently until the sugar has melted and turned golden brown. Do not stir or the sugar will become lumpy.
6. Add 150 ml (¼ pint) of the water, standing well back as it will sizzle furiously. Remove from the heat, stir in the syrup and stir over the heat until blended.
7. Blend the coconut with the remaining hot water and mix in the cornflour. Stir into the pan then gradually bring to the boil, stirring constantly, and simmer for 2-3 minutes.
8. Remove from the heat, cool for 2 minutes then add the eggs and mix well.
9. Pour the filling into the pastry case and bake for 30-35 minutes until set. Cool on a wire tray.
10. Sprinkle with coconut flakes and serve.

HERBS

ANGELICA Ⓑ

Angelica archangelica

This impressive biennial grows to over 180cm (6 feet) in height, with hollow stems, large, indented leaves and greenish-yellow flowers appearing from June to August in its second year. Angelica originated in Iceland, Greenland and northern Russia, but has become naturalized throughout much of Europe, including the UK.
Uses: Leaves, stem and flowers all have a sweet scent and flavour. The stem is the part most often used in the kitchen where its sweetening properties enable the cook to reduce the sugar content. The stem is also candied, for decorating cakes and trifles, and can be bought in this form. The leaves can be chopped and added to salads. Only very young stems should be used; both stems and leaves should be picked in early summer. Young roots and stems can also be cooked and eaten as a vegetable.
To grow: On account of its height, angelica should always be planted at the very back of the herb garden, or separately in a large tub. It likes a light, rich, fairly damp soil, and thrives in semi-shade. It dies after flowering, but its life may be prolonged, either by cutting off the flower heads before they have formed, or by cutting the plant down to ground level in late autumn. Alternatively, if allowed to flower, it will seed itself. Angelica can be grown from seed. Sow in late summer in the position where it is to flower and thin out the seedlings to 15cm (6 inches) apart.

BASIL Ⓐ

Ocimum basilicum

Sweet basil grows about 45cm (18 inches) high, with large, lettuce-green leaves and creamy-white flowers. It originated in India, where it is perennial; in cooler countries like the UK it is best treated as a semi-hardy annual. Bush Basil (Ocimum minimum) is a lower, more compact plant with small leaves, easier to grow. Dark Opal is a decorative red-leafed variety.
Uses: Basil has a unique flavour, closely related to its fragrance. It is lost on prolonged heating, since the oil is volatile, so basil should be used only as a flavouring/garnish, cut into strips and added to hot dishes at the end of the cooking. It should not be bruised except, paradoxically, in the case of Pesto (p. 193), the Genoese sauce. Basil has a special affinity with tomatoes, soft cheeses, pasta, vegetable soups and creamy sauces.
To grow: Basil is delicate, not easily grown from seed. It needs a lot of warmth to bring out its true flavour, and is best grown under glass, or on a sunny window sill, until midsummer, when it can be moved to a sheltered corner of the garden. In autumn it is best moved indoors again, where it will flourish up until Christmas, or later. Flower heads should be picked out as they form.

BAY Ⓟ

Laurus nobilis

Also called Sweet Bay, or Bay Laurel, this must not be confused with the common laurel (Prunus laurocerasus), whose leaves are poisonous. Bay is an evergreen and originated in the Mediterranean. It can be grown as a bushy shrub, trimmed into decorative shapes, or allowed to grow into a tree, when it may reach from 6-18m (20-60 feet). It has glossy dark green leaves, sometimes with wavy edges, followed by small greenish flowers in May and (sometimes) purplish black berries. Bay was used by the Ancient Greeks to crown their heroes.
Uses: The leaves must be subjected to long cooking, when they release their inimitable flavour. It is strong, and often half a leaf is enough to flavour a dish. Bay leaves form part of the classic bouquet garni, and are almost always included in stocks, casseroles, pâtés and *court bouillons.* The leaves can be used fresh or dried, so that they may be left on the tree, or picked at any time. When pruning, whole branches can be cut and hung in the kitchen.
To grow: Bay is a half-hardy plant, and should always be protected from the frost. Bay can be grown from cuttings, but is hard to grow from seed. If grown in a tub, it can be moved indoors in harsh weather.

BERGAMOT Ⓟ

Monarda didyma

This is the Red Bergamot, sometimes called Bee-balm. (There are other varieties, with pink, white, or purple flowers.) It is a beautiful aromatic plant growing 90-120cm (3-4 feet) tall, with highly scented leaves which attract the bees. Crimson flowers appear in July and August, making it a welcome addition to the herb garden.

Uses: Bergamot's culinary uses are few, but its strongly aromatic leaves make it an obvious choice for a scented garden, or bee garden. The leaves can be chopped and added to salads, while the flowers may be crystallized, for decorating iced sponge cakes. They may also be used as a substitute for marigolds.

To grow: Bergamot likes a fairly rich moist soil, so long as it does not become water-logged, in partial or full sun. It can be reproduced by root division, in spring or autumn, and the whole plant should be divided every two or three years.

Bergamot

Borage

BORAGE Ⓐ

Borago officinalis

Borage is an annual, growing between 90-120cm (3-4 feet) high, with large, hairy leaves and bright blue, star-shaped flowers. It grew originally in eastern Europe, but is now naturalized throughout most of Europe and North America.

Uses: Nowadays it is used mainly for its decorative features. Stems complete with leaves and flowers are the traditional garnish for Pimms and other summer cups. Both leaves and flowers have a refreshing, cucumber-like flavour. The young leaves may be added to salads, while the older leaves can be boiled or steamed like spinach, or dipped in batter and deep-fried. The brilliant blue flowers are some of the prettiest for crystallizing for cake decoration; or they can be added to salads.

To grow: Borage likes a light, fairly rich soil and a sheltered, sunny position. Like bergamot, borage attracts bees.

CELERY LEAVES Ⓑ

Apium graveolens

Celery grows wild in most parts of the world. The cultivated variety was introduced to Britain in the late seventeenth century. It is a biennial, growing between 30-45cm (12-18 inches) high, with ridged stems, light green leaves and umbels of yellow flowers.

Uses: Celery leaves are some of the most useful and decorative of herbs. Their essential oil is less volatile than most, so that they can be subjected to heat or dried without losing their flavour. They are used in stuffings, braises and casseroles, and to garnish soups and salads.

To grow: For use as a vegetable, the stalks of most varieties of celery need blanching (see Dandelion, p 139) which means it must be planted in neat rows. For use as a herb this is not necessary, and a few plants should be included in the herb garden, so that a handful of leaves can be picked at will. Celery likes a rich, damp soil. At the end of the first year, dig up all except one or two plants, which should be allowed to self-seed. See also: CELERY SEEDS (p 15).

CHERVIL Ⓐ

Anthriscus cerefolium

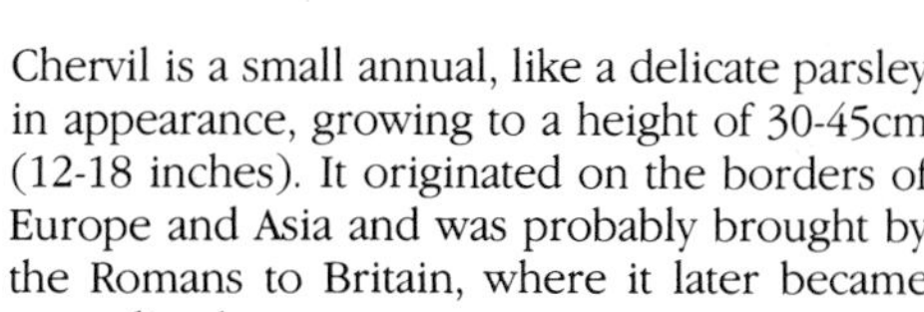

Chervil is a small annual, like a delicate parsley in appearance, growing to a height of 30-45cm (12-18 inches). It originated on the borders of Europe and Asia and was probably brought by the Romans to Britain, where it later became naturalized.

Uses: Chervil has a light, subtle flavour that is equally good alone, or blended with other delicate herbs. It forms part of the classic mixture called *fines herbes*, for use in omelettes and sauces. On its own, chervil is good in bland, creamy soups, with baked or scrambled eggs, pounded into butter for serving with grilled fish, or for flavouring a velouté sauce. Its essential oil is a highly volatile one, so that it must not be subjected to prolonged cooking, or its flavour will be lost. It is best added to dishes once the cooking is over, as a flavouring garnish. Chervil does not dry well, but it can be frozen, either in leaf form, or pounded into a herb butter.

To grow: Chervil likes a light, well-drained soil, in a sheltered, half-shaded spot. It will reproduce itself, if left to self-seed. Chervil leaves can be used when the plant is about 10cm (4 inches) high. Chervil grows well in window boxes and containers and if kept cut well back will make an attractive bushy plant with plenty of leaves.

Celery leaves

Chervil

Chives

CHIVES Ⓟ

Allium schoenoprasum

Chives are perennial, and grow in clumps about 12.5cm (5 inches) high, with dark green tubular leaves and pretty round flowers appearing in early summer. They grow wild throughout most of the northern hemisphere, including parts of the UK. They were probably brought here by the Romans, but the leaves were not much used in cooking until the Middle Ages.

Uses: Chives are the mildest of the onion family, with none of the bitterness of raw onions or the pungency of garlic. They cannot stand heat and must be used as a garnish, added to dishes after cooling. They make the ideal contrast, in flavour and in colour, to pale, creamy dishes like vichy-soisse soup and scrambled eggs. They are good alone, on salads or cream cheeses, or combined with other herbs, as in *fines herbes*. They must be cut with a sharp knife, or with scissors, to avoid bruising. Chives cannot be dried, or even frozen very successfully. They are usually available fresh; otherwise young leaves of spring onions may be used as a substitute, although they have a somewhat coarser flavour.

To grow: Chives like a rich, moist soil in full sun; they also grow well indoors in pots on a sunny window sill. They respond to picking in moderation, but a proportion of fresh leaves must be left, and a dressing of fertilizer given after heavy picking. They should be lifted and divided every two or three years, in spring or autumn, or immediately after flowering.

CORIANDER Ⓐ

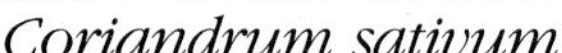

Coriandrum sativum

A hardy annual growing between 45cm (18 inches) and 60cm (2 feet) high, coriander looks much like flat-leafed parsley. To dispel confusion, rub the leaves, for both the leaves and unripe seeds of coriander give off a distinctive, some say unpleasant, smell, which disappears on cooking or drying. Coriander originated on the eastern shores of the Mediterranean, and has been cultivated for centuries throughout Asia. It was brought to Britain by the Romans. It is sometimes called Cilantro, or Chinese parsley.

Uses: The fresh leaves are chopped and added to curries and other spiced dishes, usually towards the end of the cooking, or as a garnish. They are added to stir-fried dishes, or pounded with garlic and chillies in fresh chutneys and curry paste. In the last fifteen years, fresh coriander has reappeared in Greek, Chinese and Indian shops.

To grow: It can be grown either in a sunny spot in the garden, or indoors in pots on a sunny window sill, by planting the whole coriander seeds, which are easily available, being one of the most commonly used in making curries. See also: CORIANDER SEEDS (p 16).

Curry leaves

CURRY LEAVES Ⓟ

Murraya koenignii or *Chălcas koenigii*

These should not be confused with the silvery-grey leaves of the curry plant that is often grown in herb gardens for purely decorative reasons. Curry leaves are small, shiny and evergreen, slightly like small bay leaves. They grow on a tree native to southern Asia.

Uses: Curry leaves are usually chopped and fried in oil, at the start of making curry. They quickly turn brown and become crisp, when the other ingredients are added. The dried leaves may also be ground to a powder and used in making curry powder and paste. They are usually combined with garlic, chillies, ginger, coriander, and sometimes lemon grass. Like bay leaves, they can be used fresh or dried. Curry leaves feature constantly in the cooking of South-East Asia, and in the vegetable dishes of south India. They can be bought either dried or semi-dried in some Indian and Eastern shops. A possible alternative is another leaf from Indonesia, called *daun salam*, also found in Asian shops.

To grow: Not often found in British nurseries, the tree is easily grown and decorative, with an exotic, spicy fragrance.

Coriander

DANDELION Ⓐ

Taraxacum officinale

Wild dandelions grow all over our lands, but the cultivated variety, with its broad leaves and mild flavour, is infinitely superior for eating. The bitterness of wild leaves may be reduced by blanching the whole plant; this is done by covering it with an inverted flower pot, or two slates propped up against each other, for a week to ten days before picking.

Uses: Young dandelion leaves, picked in spring or early summer, may be eaten raw in salads. They can be used alone or mixed with other leaves. (Dandelion and sorrel make a particularly good combination.) The older leaves may be picked later in the year and cooked like spinach. They may be eaten hot, or after cooling, as in Greece, dressed with olive oil and lemon juice. Young dandelion leaves are part of the traditional Provençal mixture of salad leaves called *mesclun* (see Provençal mixed salad (p 188), which is traditionally served with croûtons or a hot bacon dressing.

Dandelion

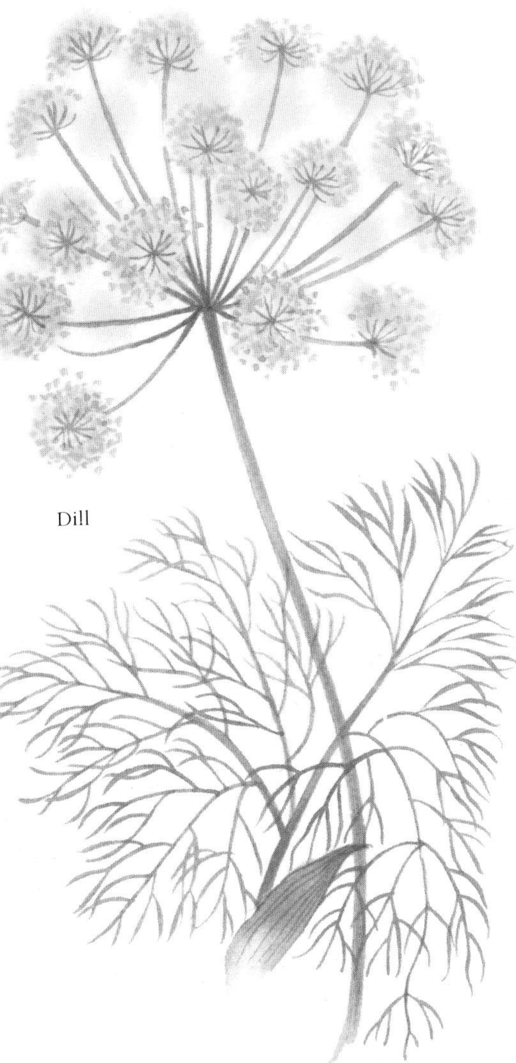
Dill

DILL Ⓐ

Anethum graveolens

A hardy annual growing from 45cm (18 inches) to 90cm (3 feet) high, dill resembles fennel in that both have hollow stems, feathery leaves and umbels of yellow flowers. It is a native of Asia and eastern Europe, but is now naturalized in much of western Europe, although not in the UK.

Uses: Dill leaves have a very volatile essential oil and must not be subjected to prolonged heat, or dried. They are best used as a flavouring/garnish, and freeze well. Dill is widely used in marinades in Scandinavia, central Europe and Russia, as in Gravad lax (p 90), and in soups and sauces, salads, and with potatoes. In the rest of the world dill is little known except as a flavouring for Dill pickles (p 69).

To grow: Dill grows best in a light, medium-rich soil, with plenty of moisture. It should not be transplanted, since this makes it burst into flower. After flowering it is of little use as a herb, since its growth then goes into woody stems. If a few plants are allowed to produce flower heads, however, the herb will self-seed. See also: DILL SEEDS (p 17).

ELDER Ⓟ

Sambucus nigra

This species of elder is a small deciduous tree, or large shrub, native to Europe. (Different varieties are found in Asia, and America.) It has creamy-white flowers which appear in May, followed by purplish-black berries.

Uses: Both elder flowers and berries are used in making wine. The flowers can be used to good effect in the kitchen, for they give a subtle flavour reminiscent of muscat grapes, closely allied to their fragrance. They can be dipped in batter and deep-fried, as is done in Austria, and eaten either as a vegetable, or as a dessert, sprinkled with caster sugar. They can also be infused in a thin syrup, sharpened with lemon juice, for making sorbets, or they can be added to jams and jellies of other fruit in the making: elder has a natural affinity with gooseberries.

To grow: It is rarely necessary to grow elder in the garden, since it abounds in our woods and hedgerows. If you do decide to grow elder, it likes a sunny place in which to grow and will thrive in a good, rather moist garden soil. The bushes should be pruned in early spring or late autumn before growth starts. Elder is not suitable for growing in containers.

Elder

FENNEL Ⓟ

Foeniculum vulgare

Fennel is native to the shores of the Mediterranean and of the UK. It is one of the largest of herbs, often growing over 1.5m (5 feet) high, with woody stems, fine-cut feathery leaves and umbels of yellow flowers. Fennel is very similar to dill in appearance, especially when cut, but with a much stronger and dissimilar flavour.
Uses: The fresh leaves, with their curious taste somewhat like aniseed, are chopped and added to sauces and fish dishes. The digestive properties of fennel have made it a traditional accompaniment to pork and other fatty meat dishes. The leaves do not dry well, and when fresh leaves are not available, it is better to use the seeds as a flavouring agent. In southern France, dried fennel stalks are often laid over barbecues to flavour fish.
To grow: Easily grown, fennel likes a sunny position. It should not be grown close to dill, or they may cross-pollinate. It can be increased by root division, or allowed to self-seed. See also: FENNEL SEEDS (p 17).

GARLIC Ⓟ

Allium sativum

Garlic is a perennial bulb, with leaves growing about 30cm (12 inches) high, and delicate pale flowers. One of the best varieties is the pink-skinned garlic which grows in Provence and Italy, available in early summer as fresh juicy bulbs.
Uses: These are very extensive and defined by personal taste. Garlic may be eaten raw, pounded into pungent sauces like Aïoli (p 192) and Skordalia (p 193), or simmered in water to make the Spanish *sopa del ajo*. Whole bulbs may be divided into cloves and roasted around a joint of lamb, or slivers of garlic inserted into the surface of the meat; the longer garlic cooks, the milder the flavour. A peeled clove may be left to stand in a vinaigrette, then discarded before dressing the salad. Whole cloves may be used to flavour bottles of olive oil or wine vinegar. Garlic butter is the traditional accompaniment to snails, and is delicious when combined with crusty French bread to make garlic bread.
To grow: Garlic is easily grown by dividing into cloves which should be planted 2.5cm (1 inch) deep and 15cm (6 inches) apart, in late winter/early spring. If grown near fruit trees, especially peaches, garlic helps to prevent leaf curl. The cloves will thrive via rich moist garden soil and sunny position, and the plants should be kept well-watered. In late summer, when the tops are down, lift the garlic and leave it to dry out thoroughly under cover.

GERANIUM, SWEET-SCENTED Ⓟ

Pelargonium

Sweet-scented geraniums, or Pelargoniums, to give them their proper name, are half hardy hybrids. They make delightful additions to the herb garden, adding both scent and colour, while their scented leaves may be used in the kitchen. There are numerous different varieties; some of the best from the culinary aspect are as follows: Pelargonium fragrans (nutmeg-scented); P. crispum and P. citriodorum (lemon-scented), P. odoratissimum (apple-scented); and P. tomentosum (peppermint-scented).
Uses: The leaves can be used to flavour a sorbet or granita, by infusing them for 20-30 minutes in a thin sugar syrup. After straining, the syrup is sharpened with lemon juice, and frozen to a mush. For a sorbet, beaten egg whites are folded in halfway through the freezing process. Pelargonium flowers may be crystallized.
To grow: Pelargoniums are easily grown from stem cuttings. These should be about 15cm (6 inches) long, dusted with rooting powder, and planted in pots in potting compost. The best time is March or April, although it can also be done in late summer, or early autumn. They take about six weeks to root. Alternatively, they can be grown from seed, or from root cuttings. Both seed and cuttings do best at a temperature of 12-15°C (55-60°F). Do not let the compost dry out but do not overwater.

GINGER Ⓟ

Zingiber officinale

Ginger is a perennial plant about 90cm (3 feet) high. It grows like a reed and has spiky green leaves and mauve and yellow flowers. Ginger originated in the jungles of tropical Asia, but has been cultivated for centuries in China, India, West Africa and the West Indies. The flavour is contained in the swollen rhizomes, which lie just below the surface of the soil. They are on average about 15cm (6 inches) long, dark to light beige on the outside and a pale yellowy-cream on the inside.

Uses: In the West, ginger is best known in its dried powdered form, as a spice, for flavouring cakes and biscuits, and as one of the constituents of curry powder. In the East, however, it is more widely used fresh; the rhizome is peeled, then sliced, chopped, grated, or ground to a paste and used to flavour dishes of fish, chicken and meat. Ginger gives a fresh, warm taste that blends well with other Eastern flavourings: spring onions, garlic, tamarind, etc. The most tender parts of the rhizomes near the stem are preserved in syrup and sold as the sweetmeat known as stem ginger. The tougher, more fibrous parts nearer the root are sun-dried and sold whole, sliced or ground into a powder. Many English greengrocers, and all Asian shops, sell ginger root.

To grow: Ginger is a tropical plant, and although it can be grown in this country it will not produce rhizomes. See also: GINGER (p 18).

Ginger

HORSERADISH Ⓟ

Cochlearia armoracia

A hardy perennial with wavy, indented leaves and tiny white flowers, horseradish grows 60-90cm (2-3 feet) high, and has a thick, buff-coloured tap root. It originated on the borders of Europe and Asia and has been cultivated in the UK since the sixteenth century.

Uses: The root is grated and used as a condiment, in much the same way as mustard. In the UK it is the traditional accompaniment to roast beef. In Scandinavia it is served with fried or poached fish. When not available fresh, it can be bought ready grated, or in the form of a creamy sauce; much the best produce is one preserved with citric acid, imported from Germany or Scandinavia. Horseradish can be combined with mustard in a sauce for fish, chicken, eggs or vegetables, or with stewed apples in a sauce for duck or goose.

To grow: The horseradish root grows deep and spreads laterally. It likes a light, rich, well-manured soil and an open sunny position. Sections of root can be planted in the spring and dug up the following autumn, by which time they will have grown into a sizeable root. In order to prevent horseradish taking over the garden, like mint, it is best planted separately in an old bucket or large tin can which will contain the roots.

Hops

HOPS Ⓟ

Humulus lupulus

Like other vines, hops are perennial, growing from 5.4-7.5 m (18-25 feet) each season. They die back to ground level each winter, then produce new shoots in the spring. They are native to Europe and western Asia, and grow wild in the UK. During the fifteenth century beer made with hops began to replace ale, and hops were imported from the Continent. In the sixteenth century the cultivation of hops in this country began, and has continued ever since.

Uses: In the UK, hops are used solely for brewing, but in France, Belgium and Germany the young shoots are much esteemed as a vegetable, boiled or steamed, like asparagus. They are served hot, with a melted butter sauce, or with poached eggs; in Germany they are also eaten cold, as a salad. Unless grown in private gardens, hops are unobtainable in the UK, since the ones in general cultivation have been sprayed, and are unfit for consumption.

To grow: Three hop vines, trained up a tripod of 180 cm (6 foot) bamboo poles, make a decorative feature for a herb garden, especially in midsummer when the 'cones' appear. These are the female flowers, or bracts. Hops should be planted in rich soil, in an open sunny spot. They grow swiftly and must be tied in regularly to achieve the desired effect.

Horseradish

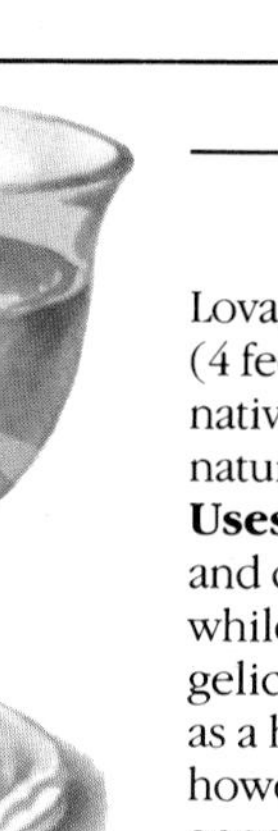
Lemon balm

LEMON BALM Ⓟ

Melissa officinalis

Perennial

Lemon balm is a perennial growing to around 90cm (3 feet), with aromatic leaves which give off a strong lemon fragrance when crushed. It is a native of the Mediterranean and was much grown in Britain in the Middle Ages. It produces small pinkish-white flowers in midsummer.

Uses: The leaves can be chopped and added to stuffings for poultry and game, salads, desserts and fruit cups. They have a flavour somewhat like lemon rind, but more perfumed, and can be used as a substitute for lemon grass.

To grow: Although its culinary uses are few, lemon balm is a pretty plant and eminently suitable for a scented garden, or bee garden. It likes a sheltered spot in partial shade, with fairly rich, moist soil. Propagate by root division in spring or autumn.

LOVAGE Ⓟ

Levisticum officinalis

Lovage is a hardy perennial growing over 120cm (4 feet) high, with large, dark green leaves. It is a native of the Mediterranean but has become naturalized in parts of the UK.

Uses: At one time lovage used to be blanched and cooked like celery, and eaten as a vegetable, while the stems were candied like those of angelica. Nowadays lovage is not much used, even as a herb. It deserves a place in the herb garden, however, for it is a handsome plant and yields a generous supply of leaves with a warm, robust flavour somewhat similar to celery. They preserve their flavour well, both on cooking and drying, so can be used all through the winter in one form or another. The chopped leaves are good alone, or combined with other robust herbs, in stuffings, stews and soups, and in fresh tomato sauce for pasta. They are powerful, however, and must not be allowed to dominate.

To grow: Lovage is a vigorous plant, easily grown, so long as there is adequate space to accommodate it. It likes a fairly rich soil, either in partial shade or full sun, and is best propagated by division in spring or autumn. It dies down to ground level each winter and sends out new shoots in the spring.

Lemon grass

LEMON GRASS Ⓟ

Cymbopogon citratus

Lemon grass is a perennial, native to South-East Asia. It is also found in Africa, South America and Australia. It has pointed aromatic leaves, sharp and spiky, with a slightly swollen leaf base.

Uses: The lower sections of the leaves especially contain an aromatic oil with a strong lemon flavour. Lemon grass leaves are used extensively in South-East Asian curries and spiced dishes, usually in conjunction with garlic, ginger and curry leaves, or fresh coriander. They can be bought fresh from some supermarkets, or dried from Indian shops. They are also available in powdered form, called *sereh*, in Asian shops. The fresh leaves are peeled and sliced, or chopped, while the dried leaf can be tied in a knot and removed after cooking, like a bay leaf. The powdered form is strong and should be used sparingly. Possible substitutes for lemon grass are lemon balm, lemon verbena, or lemon rind.

To grow: Lemon grass is easily grown in pots, if you can manage to get hold of a root.

Lemon verbena

Lovage

LEMON VERBENA Ⓟ

Lippia citriodora

Also called Lemon-scented verbena, this is a pretty shrub with light green leaves and pale flowers in late summer. It is perennial and deciduous, and will grow to 3m (10 feet) or more. A native of South America, it was brought to Europe by the Spaniards.

Uses: It can be used to give a lemon tang to dishes of chicken or fish, stuffings, salads, or desserts, but in moderation, as it has a rather perfumed flavour. The scented young leaves can be blended with mint and made into a refreshing herbal tea to serve hot or cold.

To grow: Grow from cuttings taken in summer. Plant in a sunny, sheltered spot, in a light, well-drained soil. Lemon verbena needs protection from frost, except in very favourable positions. Since it is deciduous, it can be cut back to ground level in winter, and covered with garden compost or bracken. Alternatively, prune in spring.

MARIGOLD Ⓐ

Calendula officinalis

This is the old-fashioned pot marigold, a hardy annual traditionally grown in herb gardens or kitchen gardens. In the Middle Ages marigolds were grown for both culinary and medicinal purposes. A native of southern Europe, the marigold grows wild throughout the British Isles. It produces its single yellow flowers from June until October.

Uses: The flower-heads are used fresh in salads, or dried, in soups and meat stews. They add both flavour and colour and have been used in the past as a substitute for saffron, in rice and fish dishes, cakes and puddings.

To grow: Sow in March or April in drills in light rich soil and a sunny position, and thin out to 30cm (12 inches) to allow them to spread. Marigolds will also self-seed, if some flower-heads are left on the plants.

Marigold

MINT Ⓟ

BOWLES' MINT

Mentha rotundifolia

Largest of all the mints, this grows 1.5m (5 feet) high, with soft, downy leaves.

BLACK PEPPERMINT

M. piperita vulgaris

Decorative, with purple stem, veined leaves and mauve flowers. It grows 90cm (3 feet) high. The leaves have a menthol-scented oil.

CORSICAN MINT

M. requienii

A tiny plant, not more than 2.5cm (1 inch) high. Ideal for paths, with minute mauve flowers, and a peppermint scent when crushed.

EAU-DE-COLOGNE MINT

M. piperita citrata

Also called Orange mint. It has a red stem and red-veined leaves, with a sharp scent, good for pot-pourri.

PENNYROYAL

M. pulegium

Under 5cm (2 inches) high, good for growing between paving stones. Small pink flowers and peppermint scent.

PINEAPPLE MINT

M. rotundifolia variegata

Prettiest of all the mints, this has pale green leaves dappled with cream and white, and a fresh, fruity scent and flavour.

Spearmint

SPEARMINT

M. spicata

The common or garden mint, best known in Britain. It grows 45-60cm (1½-2 feet) high, with smooth, dark green leaves and small white flowers in August.

Uses: Spearmint is the mint most commonly used in the UK, for making mint sauce and jellies, and cooking with garden peas and new potatoes. Bowles' mint has a superior flavour; do not be put off by its hairy leaves. Peppermint is easily recognized by its toothpaste flavour, while Eau-de-Cologne mint and Pineapple mint are rather too perfumed for most tastes to be of any real use in cooking.

To grow: Mint is best planted in the ground in a container – a metal bucket or large tin can – as the roots spread and take over the garden. It is easily grown by planting runners in light, moist soil, in a semi-shaded spot.

MARJORAM, SWEET Ⓐ

Origanum majorana

Three main varieties of marjoram are grown in the UK, but sweet marjoram is the most important for use in cooking. In its native Mediterranean, marjoram is a perennial, but in our harsher climate it is treated as an annual, growing about 30cm (12 inches) high. Pot, or French marjoram (Origanum onites), also native to the Mediterranean, is hardier, and grows as a perennial even in the UK, forming a compact bush up to 60cm (2 feet) high. This is the same herb as the Italian oregano, and the Greek *rigani*, but its flavour varies widely depending on the soil and climate.

Uses: All varieties of marjoram dry well and keep their flavour even when subjected to heat. Sweet marjoram grown in the herb garden is best used fresh, while dried oregano may be bought to give an authentic flavour to Provençal, Italian and Greek dishes. It goes exceptionally well with tomatoes, and is the traditional flavouring for pizzas and Greek salads. Marjoram is an excellent addition to spicy meat dishes. It can be included in meat sauces for pasta, meatloafs and rice stuffings for vegetables. It also combines well with marrow and potatoes.

To grow: Sweet marjoram is delicate and is best sown under glass, then transplanted into a sunny sheltered corner after all danger of frost is over. Pot marjoram is easier to grow, being perennial, and can be increased by root division, but the flavour is slightly inferior.

Sweet marjoram

NASTURTIUM Ⓐ

Tropaeolum majus

The nasturtium is actually a climbing plant, but is usually left to sprawl along the ground. It has round leaves and orange or yellow flowers, with long spurs. It grew first in the forests of South America and was brought to Europe by the Spaniards in the sixteenth century. It is often grown in herb gardens or kitchen gardens, since the leaves, flowers, and seeds can all be used in cooking.

Uses: The leaves have a hot, peppery flavour, and can be added to salads, or bland vegetable soups as a garnish, or very finely chopped and used in sandwiches. The unripe seeds and flower buds may be pickled in vinegar and used as a substitute for capers. The flowers make a pretty addition to a green salad, or can be crystallized for decorating iced cakes.

To grow: Sow nasturtiums in well-drained soil, not too rich, in a sunny position. They grow well in window boxes and other containers.

NETTLE Ⓟ

Urtica dioica

Nettles grow well all over the world, wherever the climate is temperate. They are perennial, growing about 90cm (3 feet) high, with dark green leaves and pendulous, greenish-white flowers. The leaves are covered with fine hairs containing formic acid, which gives them their sting. They spread quickly both by a creeping root system and by seed. Another variety is the Annual nettle (U. urens). The Dead nettle (Lamium album) resembles the true nettle in some ways, although its flower is pure white and is not pendulous, and the leaves have no sting.

Uses: The young shoots of nettles and Dead nettles, picked in spring or early summer, may be cooked and eaten like spinach, provided they have not been sprayed at any stage. Once cooked, nettles lose their sting, but protective gloves must be worn when picking them. They can be served whole or puréed.

To grow: It is rarely necessary to grow nettles specially, since they abound in our woods and hedgerows; indeed, much of the gardener's time is spent uprooting them. It is worth allowing them to grow in one prescribed area, however, so that they can be eaten in the spring.

OREGANO

See Marjoram.

PARSLEY Ⓑ

Petroselinum crispum

A hardy biennial, growing from 15-20cm (6-8 inches) high. Parsley grew first in south-eastern Europe, near the Mediterranean, and was probably brought to Britain by the Romans. It has become naturalized in the UK, but the wild variety closely resembles the poisonous hemlock, and is best left alone. The flat-leafed variety (P. hortense), grown on the Continent and in the Middle East, is hard to distinguish from coriander. Hamburg parsley (P. crispum tuberosum) is grown in central Europe for its root, which is cooked like a parsnip.

Uses: In the UK parsley is used mainly as a garnish, but with its delicious flavour it can be used much more widely in cooking. Parsley forms part of the bouquet garni and *fines herbes* mixture. The essential oil is a volatile one, and except in the case of the bouquet garni, it should be added to food after cooking. Parsley sauce is the traditional English accompaniment to boiled bacon and poached fish. Chopped parsley may be added generously to vegetable soups, fish pies, vegetable purées and salads, while whole sprigs can be deep fried as an elegant and nutritious garnish for fish. Parsley loses its flavour when dried, but may be successfully frozen.

To grow: Parsley is troublesome to grow, being extremely slow to germinate. It should be sown in drills 25cm (10 inches) apart, under 1mm (⅛ inch) fine soil, and thinned out later to 15cm (6 inches). It dislikes cold soil, so should be sown under cloches in spring, or in the open ground from May. An old gardener's tip is to water the drills with boiling water before sowing. Parsley likes a rich, well-drained soil in partial or full sun, and responds to frequent feeding. Although a biennial, it is best treated as an annual, since it produces few leaves in its second year. In hot summers it may even go to seed during the first year.

PURSLANE Ⓐ

Portulaca oleracea

Purslane is an annual, with fleshy stalks and rosettes of green leaves. It spreads over the ground, sending up stalks 15-20cm (6-8 inches) high, with rosettes of leaves on the tips. It originated in India, and although it was widely grown in Britain in the Middle Ages, for use as a salad leaf, it has only reappeared in recent years. It can be bought from Greek and Cypriot shops, where it is sometimes called Continental parsley.

Uses: The tender tips of the stalks may be eaten raw, as a salad, alone or with other leaves. *Salade de pourpier* (purslane salad) is popular in France, and mixed salads containing purslane are widely eaten throughout the Middle East and the Arab countries. Purslane can also be cooked like spinach; in Greece it is cooked with eggs, as a sort of frittata/omelette. A few fresh young purslane leaves can be included in light summer soups. Its sharp clear flavour also blends well with bland ingredients such as cream cheese; a few firmly chopped leaves can be included in creamy dips for crudités.

To grow: Purslane is easily grown from seed in the spring, in a sunny spot. It needs plenty of moisture, but the soil should be well drained.

Purslane

Rosemary

ROSEMARY Ⓐ

Rosmarinus officinalis

Rosemary is a bushy shrub, often growing over 180cm (6 feet) high. It is a perennial, but being delicate, it sometimes fails to survive a hard winter. It has evergreen needles, dark green on top and silvery-grey underneath. It produces light blue flowers in early summer, which attract bees. It is native to the eastern Mediterranean.

Uses: Rosemary's essential oil is a powerful one, not especially volatile. Indeed, its flavour is so robust it can be overpowering, and should be used in strict moderation. Sprigs of the herb must be removed from the dish after cooking, as the needles remain hard and sharp and can be dangerous. Rosemary is best used to flavour roast and stewed mutton and lamb, or in stuffings for strongly-flavoured meat and game.

To grow: Choose a sheltered, sunny spot, preferably against a wall, or in a corner, for rosemary needs all the protection it can get. If grown in a large pot, it can be moved indoors in severe weather. Rosemary makes a good hedge, if clipped back after flowering. The clippings can be dried for use in cooking. Where space is limited, choose an upright variety like Miss Jessup, or a dwarf form like R. lavandulaceus, growing under one foot high. There is also a white-flowered form called R. officinalis alba.

ROCKET Ⓐ

Eruca sativa

Rocket is an annual, related to the mustard family. It is a native of southern Europe and was brought to Britain in the sixteenth century. It was very popular in Britain in Elizabethan times, as a salad plant, and is supposed to have spread rapidly through the ruins of London, immediately after the Great Fire. It is rarely seen nowadays in the UK, although it is still widely cultivated in France, Italy, Greece, Turkey and the USA.

Uses: The young leaves have a warm, peppery flavour, and are delicious in mixed salads. They are also good eaten alone, dressed with oil and vinegar.

To grow: Rocket is easily grown from seed. Sow from April until midsummer, in open ground, and water frequently. If allowed to become dry, the leaves will become rank and sour. Frequent picking encourages new leaf growth. Sadly, seed is hard to find in the UK, but is easily obtainable in France, Italy and the USA. The French name is *roquette*, and the Italian *rugola*, or *ruchetta*.

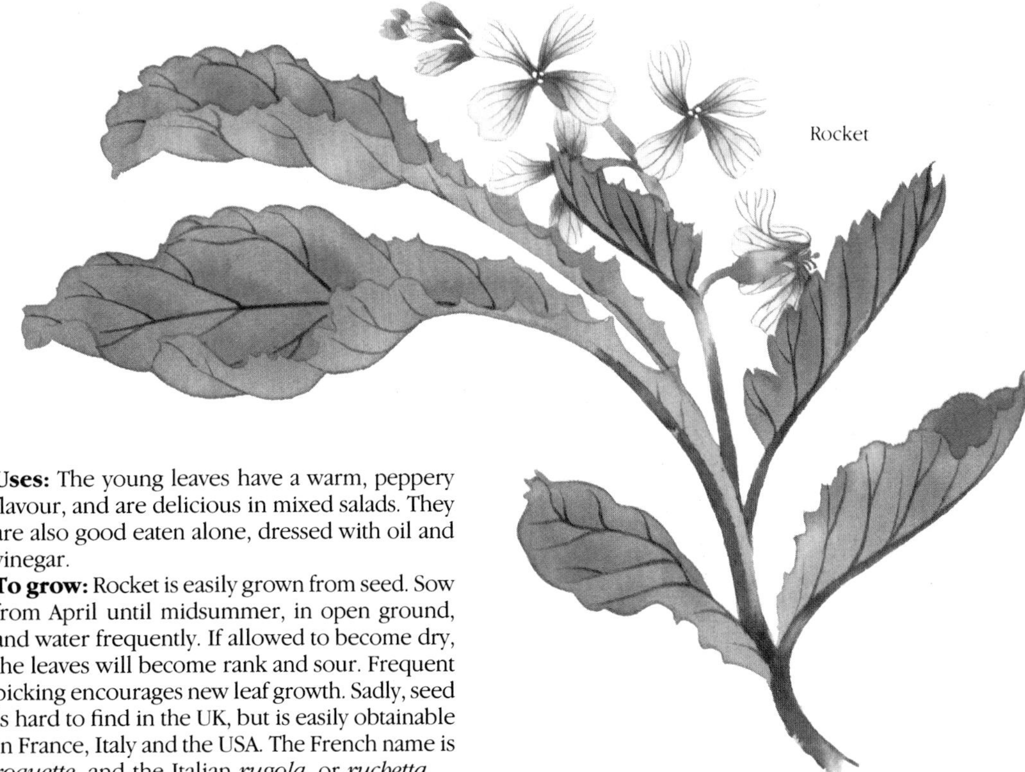

Rocket

SAGE Ⓟ

Salvia officinalis

Sage is a perennial shrub with soft grey leaves, growing about 45cm (18 inches) high. It is native to southern Europe but has been grown in Britain since the fourteenth century. The variety most commonly grown for cooking is the non-flowering broad-leaved sage.

Uses: Sage has an extremely powerful flavour and can be used fresh or dried. It does not lose its taste, even after long cooking, but tends to dominate all others. It is traditionally used to offset fatty meats, such as pork, duck and goose. It is best used with discretion, as in Italy, to flavour dishes of calf's liver or pasta.

To grow: Sage grows well in a sheltered spot, in partial shade. It is only fairly hardy and may need protection during periods of hard frost. The plants should be lifted and divided every two years, after flowering. It is also easily propagated by cuttings taken from mature plants. It can be grown from seeds, but this is a lengthy process, as the plants do not mature until they are two years old. Sage tends to become somewhat straggly in late summer and should be clipped back to a tidy shape after flowering. Red sage can be used for low hedges, as it responds to clipping. Golden sage, purple sage and the variegated tricolour sage make pretty additions to the herb garden.

Sage

Salad burnet

SALAD BURNET

Poterium sanguisorba

Salad burnet is a perennial, growing wild throughout the UK and other parts of Europe. It is a hardy plant growing about 30cm (1 foot) high, with pretty leaflets, nine on each leaf stalk. Small green flowers with red stamens appear in late summer.

Uses: The young leaves have an appealing flavour, fresh and cool, somewhat like cucumber. They do not dry well, nor can they be subjected to heat without losing much of their flavour. They are best used as a garnish, with salads and other cold food. The flavour goes well with iced soups, tomato or cucumber salads and mousses of shellfish or eggs. It also makes a pretty garnish for fruit sorbets.

To grow: Salad burnet is easily grown from seed; sow in spring, in light, well-drained soil, and thin out later to 30cm (12 inches) apart. Alternatively, some of the plants can be allowed to produce flower-heads, when they will self-seed. Although salad burnet is perennial, it is best to keep growing new plants as the young leaves are far more tender than the old ones.

SORREL Ⓟ

Rumex acetosa, R. scutatus

Sorrel, a perennial, grows in clumps. Mature plants reach 45-60cm (18 inches-2 feet) high. It has bright green, sword-shaped leaves, with spikes of reddish flowers. It grows wild in Europe, including the UK, and in Asia. Common sorrel (R. acetosa) is the variety most usually grown in the UK, but French sorrel (R. scutatus) is far superior in terms of flavour.

Uses: Raw, sorrel makes an excellent addition to mixed green salads; a few small leaves should be finely chopped and mixed through, but remember to cut down on the vinegar or lemon juice in the salad dressing. Sorrel can be cooked exactly like spinach, but having a high water content – again, like spinach – it shrinks drastically and one must allow 250g (9oz) per serving. French sorrel has a wonderfully tangy flavour, but like common sorrel has a slightly slimy texture when cooked. This is not noticeable, however, when sorrel is mixed with spinach. It goes well wwith bland foods, in sauces for poached fish, as a base for poached eggs, or in hot or cold soups.

To grow: Sorrel can be grown from seed, or by root division. The plants should be lifted and divided every two or three years, then replanted in a different spot, or the flavour will deteriorate and become coarse. Sow seed in drills in April or May, in a medium-rich soil in a sunny spot, then thin out to about 20cm (8 inches).

Sorrel

Spring onion

SPRING ONION Ⓐ

Allium ascalonicum

Spring onions are simply immature onions, usually a variety called White Lisbon, grown from seed and harvested before the bulb has formed. In the USA they are called scallions, the name by which they were known in medieval and Elizabethan England. A related plant is the so-called Welsh Onion (Allium fistulosum), which is a perennial, and keeps its leaves all through the winter. The leaves are hollow and the bulbs slightly swollen.

Uses: In the UK spring onions are usually eaten raw, in salads, or with bread and cheese. Their strong flavour is milder when cooked, however, and they may be stir-fried or steamed, or used as a garnish. Large spring onions may be substituted for pickling onions, while the leaves may be used instead of chives.

To grow: Both Spring onions and Welsh onions are grown from seed. Spring onions are dug up before they have matured, while Welsh onions are dug up and divided, part used in the kitchen, and the rest re-planted.

SUMMER SAVORY Ⓐ

Satureia hortensis

Summer savory is an annual growing about 45cm (18 inches) high, with narrow green leaves and small pink flowers which appear in July. It is a native of the Mediterranean and was much used in Britain in Roman times. Winter savory (S. montana) is a lower perennial shrub with woody stems and a harsher flavour.

Uses: Savory is much used in France and Germany, rather in the way that sage is used in the UK. It is supposed to have an affinity with bean dishes, and is often used in conjunction with fatty meats, in pork sausages and stuffings. In Provence, a wild savory called *poivre d'ane* is used to flavour a soft cheese made from ewes' milk. Savory has a strong, rather bitter flavour, and should be used in moderation. It needs long cooking to bring out and mellow its true flavour; it also dries well.

To grow: Summer savory can be grown from seed sown in April, in light, rich soil. Thin out later to 20cm (8 inches) and do not be alarmed if it is slow to germinate. Plants will also self-seed, if allowed. Since it dries so well, it is a good idea to pick most of the plants just before they flower, in early July, and dry them for winter use, leaving a few to self-seed.

Sweet cicely

Summer savory

SWEET CICELY Ⓟ

Myrrhis odorata

Sweet cicely is a perennial growing over 90cm (3 feet) high. It has a thick tap-root, hollow stems, and pretty fern-like green leaves. Umbels of lacy white flowers appear in May, followed by shiny brown fruits. It looks rather like a delicate cow parsley. The leaves are aromatic, with a sweet scent reminiscent of aniseed. It grows wild in woods in the north of the UK.

Uses: Like those of angelica, sweet cicely leaves have a natural sweetness and can be used to sweeten puddings that include fruits such as rhubarb, gooseberries, blackcurrants or plums, which may need only a subtle sweetening. They can also be chopped and added to salads and salad dressings.

To grow: Sow from seed in early spring, or propagate by root division; it will also self-seed successfully. Being a native of woodlands, sweet cicely likes moisture and shade.

TARRAGON Ⓟ

Artemisia dracunculus

This is the true French tarragon, not to be confused with Russian tarragon (A.dracunculoides), which looks very similar, but with coarser, virtually tasteless leaves. French tarragon is a perennial, a bushy shrub growing 75-90cm (2½-3 feet) high, with narrow green leaves and spikes of greenish-yellow flowers in July and August.

Uses: French tarragon is one of the subtlest of herbs, and goes well with foods of delicate flavour, such as eggs, fish, chicken and veal, either alone, or mixed with other herbs. It is part of the classic *fines herbes* mixture, and is good used in sauces, and hot or cold soups. French tarragon's essential oil is volatile, but potent; it is lost when dried, but the fresh herb can be cooked, or used as a garnish. Tarragon vinegar, made by steeping the fresh herb in white wine vinegar, can be used to make summery vinaigrettes and marinades.

To grow: In cool climates like that of the UK, French tarragon produces little, if any, seed and must be grown from cuttings or by root division. Even French tarragon can vary greatly in flavour, so it is worth asking a friend with a good plant for a cutting or root. Plants should be lifted every two or three years, then divided and replanted in fresh soil, for the flavour will deteriorate with age. French tarragon is only fairly hardy, and needs some protection from frost. Plant it in a warm, sheltered, sunny spot, in a well-drained, medium-rich soil. Tarragon grows well in containers and during the winter it should be brought indoors.

Violet

VIOLET Ⓟ

Viola odorata

This is the old-fashioned sweet violet which grows wild in the south of the UK and in much of Europe. It is found on the edge of woods and in hedgerows. It grows under 15cm (6 inches) high, with dark green, heart-shaped leaves and purple or white flowers, with a strong, sweet scent. A perennial, it spreads by a system of creeping runners.

Uses: In medieval England, violets were widely used in soups, sauces, salads and desserts. The flowers were candied and used as a sweetmeat, or for decoration. Nowadays they are used almost exclusively in crystallized form for decorating desserts or cakes. The fresh flowers can also be added to salads.

To grow: Propagate by detaching some of the creeping runners and planting in a moist shady position.

Common thyme

Silver posy thyme

Tarragon

THYME

COMMON THYME

Thymus vulgaris

This is the variety of thyme most often cultivated, growing as a bushy shrub about 30cm (12 inches) high, with small, greyish-green, aromatic leaves and tiny mauve flowers in May and June. It is a native of southern Europe and the northern shores of the Mediterranean. There is also a golden variety with variegated leaves (T. vulgaris aureus).

CREEPING AND PROSTRATE FORMS

These include T. serpyllum 'Pink Chintz', T. Doone Valley, T. minimus, T. micromirea and many others. The flowers vary from white to crimson, pale blue to purple and are ideal for carpeting paths, banks and small lawns.

LEMON THYME

T. citriodorus

This variety has a delicate lemon flavour. There is also a golden form (T. citriodorus aureus) and a creeping lemon thyme (T. azoricus).

WILD THYME

T. serpyllum

This pretty low-growing plant grows wild in the UK and over parts of northern Europe. The flavour is inferior to that of common thyme.

Uses: Both common thyme and lemon thyme are very useful to the cook, since they keep their flavour well when dried or after long cooking. Common thyme is good with meat and game, in stuffings, and to flavour tomato sauces for pasta. Lemon thyme goes well with chicken and fish.

To grow: Thyme needs aridity and heat to concentrate its flavour. Thyme can be grown from seed, but it is easier to grow from cuttings, or by root division, in spring or autumn.

WATERCRESS Ⓟ

Nasturtium officinale

Watercress grows wild in the UK and in the rest of Europe, where it can be found on the banks of streams and in low-lying water meadows. It likes to grow with its roots in mud, or under water. A perennial with a spreading root system, watercress has hollow stems growing up to 30cm (12 inches) high, with dark green leaves and tiny white flowers in midsummer. It can be bought all year round, and has been cultivated since the early nineteenth century. The leaves and stems, which are the edible parts, have a peppery flavour. Watercress is rich in iron and vitamin C.
Uses: Too often used merely as a garnish, watercress is a delicious and nutritious plant. It can be eaten raw in salads, or cooked like spinach and puréed. It makes excellent sauces for chicken, veal, or fish. Watercress is traditionally used to make a creamy soup (*potage au cresson*) which can be served hot or cold.
To grow: Since watercress is so easy to buy, it is hardly worth the trouble of growing it. In any case, this can only be done if you have a source of clean, running water nearby, and are prepared to grapple with underwater planting and muddy harvesting. Watercress can be grown from seed, then planted out on the banks of a stream, or portions of the root can be transplanted under running water, in a shallow stream bed. An easier alternative is to grow American land cress (Barbarea praecox); this is similar to watercress, very easy to grow, and a useful source of salad leaves during the winter.

Watercress

Bouquet garni

Fines herbes

BOUQUET GARNI

The classic French flavouring for stocks, soups, stews and *court bouillons*, indeed, almost any dish of fish or meat which requires long slow cooking in liquid, a bouquet garni consists of a bay leaf, a sprig of thyme and three sprigs of parsley. It is always removed after cooking, and is sometimes tied within a celery stalk or wrapped in a piece of muslin for easy removal. Other herbs such as celery, garlic and fennel can be added for specific dishes, but this is the basic mixture.

FINES HERBES

This mixture of herbs is basic to the classic cuisine of France. It consists of equal parts of chervil, tarragon, parsley and chives, although occasionally other herbs are added, for example in southern France basil, fennel, oregano, sage and saffron are often included. Sometimes even chopped truffle is included as well. The well-balanced flavour of *fines herbes* can be best appreciated in an omelette, and the blend is ideal for a herb sauce.

Opposite, clockwise from the top: *Chilled tomato soup; Chilled curried soup; Watercress and ginger consomme; Yogurt gazpacho (recipe p 152)*

WATERCRESS AND GINGER CONSOMMÉ

1 duck, pheasant or chicken carcass
1 onion, unpeeled and quartered
1 large leek, trimmed and halved
1 large carrot, scraped and halved
1 celery stick, halved
1 bay leaf
1 teaspoon salt
6 whole black peppercorns
1.5 litres (2 ½ pints) cold water
TO GARNISH
1 ½ tablespoons finely chopped fresh ginger root
12 small sprigs watercress

Preparation time: 15 minutes
Cooking time: 3¼ hours, plus cooling and chilling overnight

The combination of watercress and ginger gives an unusual hot flavour to this soup.

1. Put the carcass into a large saucepan with the onion, leek, carrot, celery, bay leaf, salt and peppercorns. Pour in the water and bring slowly to the boil, skimming often.
2. When the surface is clear of scum, cover the pan and simmer for 3 hours. Strain and measure the liquid. If necessary, return to the rinsed-out pan and boil rapidly to reduce to 900ml (1½ pints). Leave to cool. Pour into a bowl, cover and chill in the refrigerator overnight.
3. Remove all the fat from the surface of the soup. To serve, reheat gently in a saucepan and taste and adjust the seasoning if necessary. Bring to the boil and add the ginger. Lower the heat and simmer for 30 seconds. Serve garnished with watercress sprigs.

CHILLED TOMATO SOUP

1kg (2lb) tomatoes, skinned and quartered
600ml (1 pint) cold chicken stock
salt
freshly ground black pepper
1 ½ teaspoons caster sugar
1 tablespoon tomato purée (optional)
3 tablespoons orange juice
3 tablespoons finely chopped fresh ginger root
TO GARNISH
1 bunch spring onions, cut into very thin 2.5cm (1 inch) strips
2 tablespoons salad burnet leaves

Preparation time: 10 minutes, plus chilling
Cooking time: 35 minutes

The addition of orange juice and ginger lends extra zest to this beautifully coloured soup which is best made in mid-summer when ripe fresh tomatoes are available. Tomato purée should be added only if you feel the tomatoes used are lacking in flavour.

1. Put the tomatoes into a large saucepan and pour in the stock. Season to taste with salt and pepper, and add the sugar. Bring slowly to the boil, then lower the heat, half-cover the pan and simmer for 20 minutes. Remove from the heat and leave to cool.
2. Pass the tomatoes with the liquid and the tomato pureé (if using) through a medium food mill, or work briefly in a food processor or electric blender and strain through a coarse sieve.
3. Pour the soup into a bowl and stir in the orange juice and ginger. Cover and chill in the refrigerator for 4-6 hours or overnight.
4. Prepare the garnish just before serving. Pour the soup into chilled bowls, scatter the spring onions and salad burnet over the surface and serve.

CHILLED CURRIED SOUP

2 tablespoons sunflower oil
2 shallots, finely chopped
1 stem lemon grass, chopped, or 1 ½ teaspoons chopped lemon balm or lemon verbena
1 teaspoon mild curry powder
1 tablespoon plain flour
900ml (1 ½ pints) hot chicken stock
2 tablespoons lemon juice
150ml (¼ pint) single cream
salt
freshly ground black pepper
1 tablespoon chopped fresh coriander, to garnish

Preparation time: 5 minutes, plus cooling and chilling overnight
Cooking time: 10 minutes

This delicious soup, with its subtle tang of lemon grass, would make an excellent first course for a summer dinner party.

1. Heat the oil in a large saucepan, add the shallots and fry over a gentle heat for 1-2 minutes. Add the lemon grass and fry for 30 seconds, then stir in the curry powder and the flour and fry for a further 3 minutes, stirring constantly.
2. Pour in the stock and bring to the boil, stirring, then lower the heat and simmer for 3-4 minutes. Add the lemon juice and cream and season to taste with salt and pepper.
3. Cook very gently, without boiling, for a further 1-2 minutes, then remove from the heat and pour into a large bowl.
4. Stand the bowl in the sink and pour in very cold water to come halfway up the sides of the bowl. Leave to cool for 15 minutes, stirring often to prevent a skin forming.
5. Cover the bowl and chill in the refrigerator overnight or until completely cold.
6. Remove the soup shortly before serving and work briefly in a food processor or electric blender. Serve garnished with coriander.

YOGURT GAZPACHO

100g (4oz) tomatoes, skinned and finely chopped
50g (2oz) cucumber, peeled and finely chopped
50g (2oz) green pepper, seeded and finely chopped
25g (1oz) fennel, finely chopped
200ml (⅓ pint) plain unsweetened yogurt
200ml (⅓ pint) water
salt
white pepper
1 tablespoon sunflower oil
1 tablespoon lemon juice
3 tablespoons chopped fresh mint
4 ice cubes, to serve
1 sprig mint, to garnish

Preparation time: 20 minutes, plus chilling

This refreshing soup, which is really a liquid salad, is perfect for hot summer days.
1. Put the tomatoes, cucumber, green pepper and fennel into a large bowl.
2. Combine the yogurt and water in a food processor or electric blender. Season to taste with salt and white pepper.
3. Add the oil, lemon juice and mint and process again briefly. Pour the mixture over the vegetables, cover and chill for 2-3 hours. Add the ice cubes just before serving, garnished with mint.

Below: *Lovage soup*

LOVAGE SOUP

50g (2oz) butter
350g (12oz) carrots, scraped and sliced
350g (12oz) Jerusalem artichokes, scraped and sliced
750ml (1 ¼ pints) hot chicken stock
salt
freshly ground black pepper
2 tablespoons chopped fresh lovage, or 2 teaspoons dried lovage
65ml (2 ½fl oz) single cream (optional)
lovage sprigs, to garnish (optional)

Preparation time: 20 minutes, plus cooling
Cooking time: 40 minutes

If you don't have any lovage, you can substitute celery leaves, although you cannot then call it Lovage Soup! An excellent springtime soup.
1. Melt the butter in a large saucepan, add the carrots and fry over a gentle heat for 5 minutes, stirring often.
2. Add the Jerusalem artichokes and fry for a further 5 minutes, stirring often. Pour in the stock, season to taste with salt and pepper and stir in the lovage. Bring to the boil, then lower the heat, cover the pan and simmer for 35 minutes.
3. Remove the pan from the heat and allow to cool for 5 minutes. Pass the vegetables with the liquid through a coarse food mill, or work very briefly in a food processor or electric blender, to achieve a fairly coarse texture.
4. Reheat gently. Add the cream if used and taste and adjust the seasoning. Serve garnished with lovage.

CELERY SOUP

50g (2oz) butter
1 head celery, trimmed and chopped, leaves reserved and finely chopped
1 medium carrot, scraped and sliced
1 medium potato, peeled and sliced
750ml (1 ¼ pints) hot chicken stock
salt
freshly ground black pepper
150ml (¼ pint) single cream

Preparation time: 10 minutes, plus standing
Cooking time: 50 minutes

When using a head of celery, always keep the leaves for garnishes, or to add to salads. They have a distinctive, pungent flavour.
1. Melt the butter in a large saucepan. Add the celery and fry over a gentle heat for 5 minutes.
2. Add the carrot and potato and fry for a further 5 minutes, stirring once or twice.
3. Pour in the stock, season to taste with salt and pepper and bring to the boil. Lower the heat, half-

cover the pan and simmer for 30 minutes.
4. Remove the pan from the heat and leave to cool for 5 minutes. Pass the vegetables with the liquid through a medium food mill, or work in a food processor or electric blender until smooth.
5. Pour the purée into the rinsed-out pan and reheat gently. Stir in the cream, taste and adjust the seasoning, then stir in the celery leaves. Turn out the heat under the pan. Cover the pan and leave to stand for 5 minutes before serving.

CREAMY CHERVIL SOUP

50g (2oz) butter
225g (8oz) leeks, trimmed and sliced
225g (8oz) potatoes, peeled and sliced
225g (8oz) cauliflower, trimmed and coarsely chopped
900ml (1 ½ pints) hot chicken stock
100g (4oz) small carrots, thinly sliced
2 bunches spring onions, white part only
100g (4oz) shelled peas, fresh or frozen
200ml (⅓ pint) single cream
salt
freshly ground black pepper
3 tablespoons chopped fresh chervil

Preparation time: 20 minutes, plus standing
Cooking time: 45 minutes

Chervil is a herb with a fragrant spicy aroma and delicate flavour. On the Continent it is used extensively, especially in France where it often takes the place of parsley. Because its subtle flavour would not stand up to prolonged boiling, it is stirred into the soup once the cooking is over and left to infuse in the hot liquid for 5 minutes. Serve this soup with warm crusty bread.
1. Melt the butter in a large saucepan. Add the leeks and fry over a gentle heat for 5 minutes.
2. Add the potatoes and cauliflower and fry for a further 2 minutes, stirring once or twice.
3. Pour in 600ml (1 pint) of the stock. Bring to the boil, then lower the heat, cover the pan and simmer for 30 minutes.
4. Meanwhile, pour the remaining stock into a small saucepan and add the carrots. Bring to the boil, then lower the heat slightly and cook for 5 minutes.
5. Add the whole spring onion bulbs and the peas. Return to the boil, then lower the heat and cook for a further 5 minutes. Remove from the heat and set aside.
6. Remove the pan containing the leeks and other vegetables from the heat and leave to cool for 5 minutes. Pass the vegetables with the liquid through a medium food mill, or work in a food processor or electric blender until smooth.
7. Return the purée to the rinsed-out pan. Stir in the cream and season to taste with salt and pepper. Stir in the contents of the smaller pan and reheat gently without boiling, stirring once or twice.
8. Stir in the chervil. Turn off the heat under the pan. Cover the pan and leave to stand for 5 minutes before serving.

VARIATION
This soup is also delicious served cold: prepare to the end of stage 7, then cool and chill for 3-4 hours. Add the chervil just before serving.

From the top: *Creamy chervil soup; Celery soup*

GARLIC SOUP

1.2 litres (2 pints) water
1 ½ teaspoons salt
20 garlic cloves, peeled
4 slices French bread
4 eggs (sizes 1 or 2)
freshly ground black pepper
1 ½ tablespoons very finely chopped fresh parsley

Preparation time: 10 minutes
Cooking time: 40 minutes
Oven: 120°C, 250°F, Gas Mark ½

This very simple dish is easy to digest, and is good for anyone who has a cold, or is convalescent.

1. Put the water in a large saucepan and add the salt and garlic. Bring to the boil, then lower the heat and simmer for 30 minutes.
2. Meanwhile, put the bread on a baking sheet and place on the bottom shelf of a preheated oven, to dry out.
3. Remove the garlic with a slotted spoon and discard. Keep the soup on a gentle simmer and break the eggs in one at a time. Poach over a very gentle heat for about 2 minutes, until the whites are set and opaque.
4. Put the slices of bread into warmed individual soup bowls. Lift the eggs out one at a time with a slotted spoon and place one on top of each bread slice. Taste the soup and season to taste with pepper and more salt if needed. Strain the soup over the eggs. Serve garnished with chopped parsley.

Below: *Garlic soup*

MINESTRONE AL PESTO

4 tablespoons olive oil
1 leek, trimmed and chopped
1 celery stick, chopped
1 garlic clove, peeled and chopped
1 carrot, scraped and chopped
2 courgettes, coarsely chopped
100g (4oz) French beans, cut into 1cm (½ inch) lengths
100g (4oz) heart of green cabbage, chopped
1 medium potato, peeled and chopped
1.2 litres (2 pints) hot chicken stock
salt
freshly ground black pepper
40g (1 ½oz) pasta shapes for soup or short-cut macaroni

PESTO

10g (¼oz) basil leaves
25g (1oz) pine kernels
2 tablespoons finely grated Parmesan cheese
2 tablespoons olive oil

Preparation time: 20-30 minutes, plus standing
Cooking time: 1½ hours
Serves 6

There are many variations on minestrone, the famous Italian vegetable soup. This is the Genoese version, made with pesto, the basil sauce which originated in Genoa.

1. Heat the oil in a large flameproof casserole, add the leek and fry over a gentle heat for 3 minutes.
2. Add the celery and garlic and fry, stirring, for a further 2 minutes. Add the carrot and courgettes and fry, stirring, for a further 3 minutes. Finally, add the beans, cabbage and potato and fry, stirring, for a further 5 minutes.
3. Pour in the stock, season to taste with salt and pepper and bring slowly to the boil. Cover the casserole and cook gently for 1 hour, stirring from time to time.
4. Add the pasta and cook for a further 15 minutes, or until the pasta is tender.
5. Meanwhile, make the pesto. Work the basil in a food processor or electric blender until finely chopped, then add the pine kernels and work again.
6. Transfer the mixture to a mortar and pound with a pestle until reduced to a pulp. Add the Parmesan cheese and continue to pound until thoroughly blended. Finally, add the oil, a little at a time, pound-

From the left: *Minestrone al Pesto; Bean soup*

ing between each addition to achieve a creamy paste.
7. Pour the soup into a warmed tureen or clean casserole and stir in the pesto. Leave to stand, covered, for 5 minutes before serving.

BEAN SOUP

350g (12oz) dried cannellini beans, soaked for 3-4 hours, then drained
1.2 litres (2 pints) cold water
salt
3 sprigs savory
3 tablespoons olive oil
2 garlic cloves, peeled and finely chopped
3 tablespoons chopped fresh parsley
freshly ground black pepper
savory sprigs, to garnish (optional)

Preparation time: 5 minutes, plus soaking and standing
Cooking time: 1-1¼ hours

This is a substantial soup. Served with wholemeal bread and followed by a mixed salad, it would make a good supper dish. The soup may be made a day in advance. Prepare to the end of step 4, cover and chill. To serve, heat through gently and garnish with fresh savory sprigs.

1. Put the beans into a large saucepan and pour in the water. Bring slowly to the boil, uncovered, then half-cover the pan and simmer for 30 minutes. Add the salt and savory and simmer for a further 15-30 minutes, until the beans are soft and just beginning to break up.
2. Remove half the beans with a slotted spoon and reserve. Discard the savory and pass the remaining beans with the liquid through a medium food mill, or work in a food processor or electric blender until very smooth.
3. Heat the oil in a small frying pan, add the garlic and fry over a gentle heat until soft and lightly coloured. Stir in the parsley and remove from the heat.
4. Pour the bean purée into a clean saucepan and reheat gently, stirring from time to time. Season to taste with salt and pepper. Gently stir in the reserved whole beans, then the garlic and parsley.
5. Turn out the heat under the pan. Cover the pan and leave to stand for 5 minutes before serving, in warmed soup bowls, garnished with savory sprigs.

From the left: *Catalan eggs; Potato baked eggs*

POTATO BAKED EGGS

4 large potatoes
40g (1 ½oz) butter, diced
2 tablespoons chopped fresh tarragon and chervil, mixed
salt
freshly ground black pepper
4 eggs (size 1 or 2)

Preparation time: 5 minutes, plus cooling
Cooking time: 1¼-1½ hours
Oven: 200°C, 400°F, Gas Mark 6
then: 180°C, 350°F, Gas Mark 4

1. Prick each potato with a fork several times and bake for 1 hour in the centre of the oven. Remove from the oven and reduce the oven temperature.
2. When the potatoes are cool enough to handle, cut a thin slice off the top of each. Scoop out the insides with a teaspoon and pass through a medium food mill into a bowl. Stir in the butter and the mixed herbs and season to taste with salt and pepper. Pile the mixture back into the empty potato skins, making a raised wall of potato round the edge of each to hold the eggs.
3. Arrange the potatoes on a baking sheet and break an egg into each one. Season the eggs with salt and pepper and bake in the oven for 15-20 minutes until the whites are set and opaque. Serve immediately, with a green salad.

VARIATION
Mixed parsley and chives may be substituted for the tarragon and chervil, or 100g (4oz) grated Cheddar cheese may be included in the potato mixture.

CATALAN EGGS

4 tablespoons olive oil
½ Spanish onion, cut into 2.5cm (1 inch) pieces and separated into 'leaves'
225g (8oz) red peppers, cored, seeded and cut into strips
225g (8oz) courgettes, cut into 1cm (½ inch) slices
225g (8oz) tomatoes, skinned and roughly chopped
salt
freshly ground black pepper
¾ teaspoon sugar
1 ½ tablespoons chopped fresh mint
1 ½ tablespoons chopped fresh parsley
4 eggs (size 1 or 2), beaten

Preparation time: 12 minutes, plus cooling
Cooking time: 40 minutes

This is a version of *pipérade*, which is popular around Barcelona. It has more vegetables and less eggs than the French version.
1. Heat the oil in a large frying pan with a lid, add the onion and fry over a gentle heat for about 10 minutes, until softened but not browned.
2. Add the red pepper and fry for a further 10 minutes, stirring from time to time. Add the courgettes and fry for a further 10-15 minutes, stirring from time to time.
3. Add the tomatoes and season with salt and pepper. Stir in the sugar and the herbs. Cover and simmer for 10 minutes, then remove from the heat and leave to cool for 3-4 minutes.
4. Stir the beaten eggs into the vegetable mixture. Return to a gentle heat and cook for 3-4 minutes, stirring constantly, until the eggs have set and the juices are thickened.
5. Remove from the heat and leave to stand, covered, for 5 minutes before serving straight from the pan, with crusty French bread.

From the left: *Watercress Frittata; Mushroom omelette*

MUSHROOM OMELETTE

35g (1 ¼oz) butter
175g (6oz) mushrooms, sliced
2 teaspoons chopped fresh marjoram
5 eggs, beaten
salt
freshly ground black pepper
1 teaspoon very finely chopped fresh parsley, to garnish

Preparation time: 10 minutes
Cooking time: 10 minutes
Serves 2

1. Melt 25g (1oz) of the butter in a small frying pan. Add the mushrooms with the marjoram and fry over a gentle heat for about 5 minutes until softened. Set aside.
2. Season the eggs with salt and pepper. Melt the remaining butter in an omelette pan over a brisk heat, swirling the butter over the base and sides. Pour in the eggs and once the edge starts to set, lift it with a spatula or small fish slice and allow the liquid egg from the centre to run underneath. Cook for a total time of about 45-60 seconds until most of the egg is set.
3. Remove the mushrooms from the pan with a slotted spoon and spread them over one half of the omelette. Cook for a few seconds longer, then fold the omelette over the mushrooms and slide on to a heated serving dish. Garnish with the parsley and serve immediately.

WATERCRESS FRITTATA

40g (1 ½oz) butter
1 bunch watercress, trimmed
5 eggs, beaten
salt
freshly ground black pepper

Preparation time: 3 minutes
Cooking time: 5 minutes
Serves 2

A frittata is like a flat omelette, slightly more solid than the true French omelette.
1. Melt the butter in a frying pan and spread the watercress over the surface of the pan. Fry over a gentle heat for 3-4 minutes, until the watercress is soft.
2. Season the eggs with salt and pepper and pour over the watercress. Once the edge starts to set, lift it with a spatula or small fish slice and allow the liquid egg from the centre to run underneath. Cook for 2-3 minutes until the omelette is well set. Slide the omelette on to a heated serving dish and serve immediately, with a tomato salad.

STEAMED TROUT CHINESE STYLE

2 teaspoons sesame oil
2 teaspoons light soy sauce
1 teaspoon sugar
½ teaspoon salt
sesame oil, for brushing
1 rainbow trout, about 750g (1 ½lb)
8 thin slices fresh ginger root
1 stem lemon grass, chopped (optional)
2 large garlic cloves, peeled and chopped
4 spring onions, sliced

SAUCE

2 tablespoons dry vermouth or sherry
2 tablespoons sunflower oil
1 tablespoon sesame oil
1 tablespoon light soy sauce
4 spring onions, cut into very thin strips, to garnish

Preparation time: 15 minutes
Cooking time: 30 minutes
Serves 2

1. In a cup combine the sesame oil, soy sauce, sugar and salt.
2. Brush the trout inside and out with the mixture. Cut a piece of foil large enough to enclose both trout and brush it with oil. Lay half the ginger, lemon grass, garlic and spring onions on the foil and place the trout on top. Cover the trout with the remaining flavourings and wrap in the foil, sealing it tightly.
3. Bring some water to the boil in a fish kettle or wok with a steaming rack. Lay the parcelled trout on the rack and cover the kettle. Boil steadily for 25-30 minutes, adding more boiling water if needed, until the trout are cooked through.
4. Meanwhile, combine all the sauce ingredients in a small bowl, mixing well with a fork. Unwrap the cooked trout and pour the juices from the foil into the sauce. Using 2 fish slices, carefully transfer the fish to a heated serving dish, discarding the flavourings. Pour the sauce over the trout, garnish with spring onions and serve immediately.

STIR-FRIED SCALLOPS

2 tablespoons sunflower oil
1 small onion, finely chopped
1 ½ teaspoons finely chopped fresh ginger root
1 green chilli, seeded and finely chopped
750g (1 ½lb) scallops, fresh or defrosted if frozen, quartered
5 tablespoons orange juice
2 tablespoons lemon juice
1 tablespoon light soy sauce
2 tablespoons chopped fresh coriander

Preparation time: 10 minutes
Cooking time: 8 minutes

1. Heat a wok or deep frying pan. Add the oil and heat again. Add the onion and stir-fry for 1 minute, then add the ginger and chilli. Stir-fry for 30 seconds, then add the scallops.
2. Stir-fry for a further 3 minutes, then add the orange and lemon juice and soy sauce. Stir-fry for 1 further minute, then add the coriander and stir well. Serve as a first course or as a light main course, with boiled or fried rice.

VARIATION

For a typically Chinese stir-fry replace 250g (8oz) of the scallops with 100g (4oz) uncooked prawns, peeled and deveined and 100g (4oz) squid, cleaned and sliced. Add the prawns and squid to the wok with the scallops and cook as in the recipe above. Just before serving, sprinkle with sesame oil.

From the left: *Steamed trout Chinese style; Stir-fried scallops; Spicy prawns*

SPICY PRAWNS

450g (1lb) peeled prawns, fresh or defrosted if frozen
6 tablespoons lemon juice
6 spring onions, sliced
2 teaspoons finely chopped fresh ginger root
1 stem lemon grass, finely chopped, or 1 teaspoon chopped fresh lemon balm
2 tablespoons chopped fresh mint

TO GARNISH

4 medium lettuce leaves
sprigs of lemon balm or lemon grass

Preparation time: 10 minutes, plus cooling

Serve the prawns as a delicious, easily prepared first course. They look best served in scallop shells, but if these are unavailable, small dishes, bowls or saucers may be used instead.

1. Put the prawns into a bowl and pour over the lemon juice. Stir in the spring onions, ginger, lemon grass and mint. Stir well to mix, cover and chill in the refrigerator for 2-3 hours, stirring once or twice.
2. To serve, lay a lettuce leaf in each of 4 scallop shells and pile the prawn mixture on top. Garnish each portion with a sprig of lemon balm and serve with thinly sliced brown bread and butter.

VARIATION

This is a simple way of making frozen prawns more flavoursome. Quantities may be increased by adding 100g (4oz) lightly blanched petit pois, in which case a few drops of sesame oil could be sprinkled over before serving to enhance the flavour.

Above: *Turbot with horseradish and watercress sauce*
Opposite, from the top: *Steamed sole in Chinese leaves with herb sauce; Monkfish in green sauce (recipe p 162)*

TURBOT WITH HORSERADISH AND WATERCRESS SAUCE

white fish bones and trimmings
1 onion, peeled and halved
1 carrot, scraped and halved
1 celery stick, halved, or 2 tablespoons celery leaves
1 bay leaf
3 parsley stalks
1 teaspoon salt
8 whole black peppercorns
900ml (1 ½ pints) cold water
150ml (¼ pint) dry white wine, or 4 tablespoons vermouth, or white wine vinegar
1.25kg (2 ½lb) turbot, on the bone

SAUCE

150ml (¼ pint) double cream
1 ½ teaspoons watercress leaves
25g (1oz) butter
1 ¼ tablespoons plain flour
2 teaspoons grated horseradish
2 teaspoons Dijon mustard
1 tablespoon fresh orange juice
salt
freshly ground black pepper

Preparation time: 15 minutes
Cooking time: 45 minutes

1. Put the fish bones and trimmings into a large saucepan with the onion, carrot, celery, bay leaf, parsley stalks, salt and peppercorns. Add the water and wine, vermouth or vinegar and bring slowly to the boil. Cover, lower heat and simmer for 30 minutes, then strain.
2. Place the turbot in a large roasting tin and pour in all but 200ml (⅓ pint) of the fish stock and enough hot water to just cover the turbot. Cover with foil and heat until the liquid is barely simmering. Simmer very gently for about 15 minutes, depending on the thickness of the turbot, until the turbot is cooked through and the flesh separates easily from the bone when pierced with a sharp knife. Using 2 fish slices, carefully transfer the turbot to a heated serving dish.
3. Meanwhile, make the sauce; put the cream and watercress into a food processor or electric blender and process until the watercress is finely chopped.
4. Melt the butter in a small saucepan and stir in the flour. Cook for 1 minute, stirring, then remove from the heat and gradually stir in the reserved fish stock. Return to the heat and bring to the boil, stirring, then lower the heat and simmer for 3 minutes, stirring from time to time.
5. Stir in the horseradish, mustard and orange juice. Cook for 1 minute more, then stir in the watercress and cream. Reheat gently and pour a little over the fish. Pour the remaining sauce into a sauceboat. Serve the turbot with new potatoes and spinach, accompanied by the horseradish and watercress sauce.

VARIATION

Hake may be used instead of turbot, for a more economical dish.

STEAMED SOLE IN CHINESE LEAVES WITH HERB SAUCE

2 Dover soles, lemon soles, or plaice, 1.25kg (2 ½lb), skinned and each divided into 4 fillets, with bones and trimmings reserved
1 small onion, peeled and halved
1 carrot, scraped and halved
1 small leek, trimmed and halved
1 celery stick, halved
1 small bay leaf
2 sprigs parsley
1 teaspoon salt
6 whole black peppercorns
65ml (2 ½fl oz) dry white wine
8 Chinese cabbage leaves, blanched and drained

HERB SAUCE

25g (1oz) butter
1 tablespoon plain flour
salt
freshly ground black pepper
150ml (¼pint) single cream
½ tablespoon finely chopped fresh tarragon
½ tablespoon finely chopped fresh chervil
½ tablespoon finely chopped chives
½ tablespoon finely chopped fresh parsley

Preparation time: 12-14 minutes
Cooking time: 40-45 minutes

This recipe would make a refreshingly light main course for a summer dinner party.

1. Make the fish stock: put the fish bones and trimmings into a saucepan with the onion, carrot, leek, celery, bay leaf, parsley, salt and peppercorns. Pour in the wine and enough cold water to cover. Bring to the boil and boil gently, half-covered, for 25 minutes, then strain. Set aside.
2. On a board, carefully spread out the cabbage leaves, being careful not to tear them. Roll up each fish fillet and wrap carefully in a cabbage leaf. Lay the parcels in the top part of a steamer.
3. Pour the fish stock into the bottom part of the steamer and bring to the boil. Lay the sole parcels over it, cover and cook for 10 minutes until cooked through. Remove the top part of the steamer and leave to stand, covered. Strain the stock and measure off 150ml (¼ pint).
4. Make the sauce: melt the butter in a small saucepan, and stir in the flour. Cook for 1 minute, stirring, then remove from the heat and gradually stir in the reserved fish stock. Return to the heat and bring to the boil, stirring, then lower the heat and simmer for 3 minutes, stirring from time to time. Stir in the cream and heat through gently without boiling. Taste and adjust the seasoning, stir in the herbs, and pour into a heated sauce-boat.
5. Arrange the sole parcels on a warmed serving platter and serve immediately with plain boiled potatoes, accompanied by the herb sauce.

MONKFISH IN GREEN SAUCE

40g (1 ½oz) butter
3 tablespoons olive oil
1 medium onion, chopped
50g (2oz) sorrel, chopped
50g (2 oz) spinach, chopped
1 bunch watercress, chopped
2 tablespoons chopped celery leaves
1 tablespoon chopped fresh lovage
750g (1 ½lb) monkfish, cut into 4cm (1 ½ inch) pieces, bones reserved
150ml (¼pint) dry white wine
approximately 150ml (¼pint) hot water
1 bay leaf
salt
freshly ground black pepper
2 tablespoons chopped fresh chervil or dill

Preparation time: 15 minutes
Cooking time: 35 minutes

This is best eaten with a spoon and fork as a main course with plenty of crusty bread.

1. Heat the butter and oil in a flameproof casserole, add the onion and fry over a gentle heat until soft and lightly coloured. Add the sorrel, spinach, watercress, celery leaves and lovage. Cook slowly, stirring often, for 5 minutes.
2. Add the monkfish and cook over a very gentle heat, stirring often, for a further 5 minutes. Pour in the wine and enough hot water just to cover the fish. Add the bay leaf, season with salt and pepper, and lay the monkfish bones on top. Cook briskly for 1 minute, then lower the heat, cover the casserole and simmer for 20 minutes.
3. Discard the monkfish bones and bay leaf, and remove any scum from the surface. Using a slotted spoon, lift the fish into a deep heated serving dish and keep warm.
4. Stir the chervil into the casserole, cover again and leave to stand for 1-2 minutes, off the heat. Pour the sauce over the monkfish and serve in soup plates.

SALMON FISH CAKES

275g (10oz) floury potatoes
75g (3oz) butter, diced
salt
freshly ground black pepper
1 egg yolk (optional)
225g (8oz) cooked salmon, skin and bone removed, flaked and chopped
3 tablespoons chopped fresh parsley
1 teaspoon anchovy essence or ½ teaspoon Tabasco (optional)
1 egg, beaten
dry breadcrumbs, for coating
2 tablespoons sunflower oil
fried parsley sprigs, to garnish (p 189)

Preparation time: 35 minutes, plus chilling
Cooking time: 45 minutes

1. Boil the potatoes in their skins for about 20 minutes or until tender, then drain. As soon as the potatoes are cool enough to handle, peel off the skins. Pass the potatoes through a medium food mill into a large warmed bowl and stir in 50g (2oz) of the butter, seasoning well with salt and pepper.
2. Stir in the egg yolk, if using (this will give a richer mixture), and the salmon. Beat vigorously with a wooden spoon until thoroughly blended, then stir in the parsley and anchovy essence or Tabasco. Shape into 4 large fish cakes, or 8 small ones, and dip first in the egg and then in the breadcrumbs. Chill in the refrigerator for 1 hour.
3. Heat the remaining butter with the oil in a large frying pan. Add the fish cakes and fry over a moderate het for 4-6 minutes on each side, depending on their size. When crisp and golden brown, remove the fish cakes with a fish slice and drain on absorbent paper. Garnish with fried parsley sprigs and serve with a cucumber salad and sauté potatoes.

From the left: *Salmon fish cakes with fried parsley (recipe p 189); Herby fish pie*

HERBY FISH PIE

750g (1 ½lb) potatoes, unpeeled
200ml (⅓pint) milk
50g (2oz) butter
salt
freshly ground black pepper
1 ½ tablespoons chopped fresh dill
1 ½ tablespoons chopped fresh chervil
4 eggs
750g (1 ½lb) haddock fillets, skinned
1 sprig dill, to garnish (optional)

Preparation time: 35 minutes
Cooking time: 50-60 minutes

1. Boil the potatoes in their skins for about 20 minutes or until tender, then drain. As soon as the potatoes are cool enough to handle, remove the skins. Pass the potatoes through a medium food mill or work in a food processor until smooth. Transfer to a clean saucepan and stir over a gentle heat for 2-3 minutes, to dry them out, taking care that they do not catch on the bottom of the saucepan and burn.
2. Heat the milk in a small saucepan with the butter and plenty of salt and pepper. When the butter has melted, gradually stir the mixture into the potato, beating vigorously with a wooden spoon. Stir in the chopped herbs, cover and keep warm.
3. Bring a saucepan of lightly salted water to the boil, then reduce the heat slightly, lower in the eggs and cook for 5 minutes. Plunge the eggs into a bowl of cold water, and shell them as soon as they are cool enough to handle. Slice and set aside.
4. Put the haddock fillets into a large shallow saucepan and pour in enough cold water to just cover. Remove the haddock with a fish slice. Add ½ teaspoon salt to the water and bring to the boil. Return the haddock to the pan and simmer over a very gentle heat for about 8 minutes, until the fish flakes away from the bone easily.
5. Remove the haddock from the pan and when cool enough to handle flake it into a heated 900ml (1½ pint) soufflé dish. Cover with the potato purée, smooth the surface, and arrange the sliced eggs on top. Garnish with dill and serve immediately. The pie should be eaten with a crisp green salad of lettuce, cress and trimmed spring onions.

MIDDLE EASTERN FISH SALAD

1 ½ tablespoons olive oil
1 medium onion, peeled and chopped
2 mackerel, each about 225g (8oz) filleted, skinned and chopped
25g (1oz) blanched almonds, coarsely chopped
½ tablespoon currants
1 pinch of allspice
1 tablespoon chopped fresh coriander
salt
freshly ground black pepper
2 tablespoons chopped fresh parsley
1 ½ tablespoons lemon juice
TO GARNISH
coriander sprigs
lemon wedges

Preparation time: 15 minutes
Cooking time: 15 minutes

This fish salad makes a delicious first course and is best served within 4-5 hours of preparation.

1. Heat the oil in a large frying pan, add the onion and fry over a gentle heat until soft and lightly coloured.
2. Add the mackerel, almonds, currants, allspice and coriander and season to taste with salt and pepper. Cook over a gentle heat for 5 minutes, stirring almost constantly, then stir in the parsley and turn into a shallow serving dish.
3. Leave to cool at room temperature (do not chill). Sprinkle with the lemon juice just before serving. Garnish with coriander and serve with lemon wedges and warm pitta bread.

Below: *Middle Eastern fish salad*

PICKLED HALIBUT

4 halibut steaks, about 175g (6oz) each
salt
2 tablespoons olive oil
1 sachet powdered saffron
3 tablespoons hot water
600ml (1 pint) white wine vinegar
1 tablespoon sugar
6 bay leaves
6-8 sprigs fennel
4 garlic cloves, peeled and chopped
½ teaspoon ground allspice
2 teaspoons whole black peppercorns
25g (1oz) shelled pistachio nuts (about 65g (2 ½oz) unshelled), halved

Preparation time: 10-15 minutes, plus chilling
Cooking time: 10 minutes

This spicy Middle Eastern fish dish can be served as a first course. It needs to be prepared 3-6 days in advance.

1. Rinse the halibut steaks and pat dry, then sprinkle with salt.
2. Heat the oil in a large frying pan, add the halibut steaks and fry over moderate heat for 1-2 minutes, turning once, until lightly browned but not cooked through. Remove from the pan and set aside.
3. Soak the saffron for 10 minutes in the hot water. Put the vinegar in a saucepan and add the saffron water and sugar. Bring to the boil, stirring, and cook for 3 minutes, or until the sugar is dissolved. Set aside.
4. Put 3 bay leaves in the bottom of a deep dish with a lid. Lay 2 halibut steaks on them and cover with half the fennel, garlic, allspice, peppercorns and pistachio nuts. Add the remaining bay leaves, then the remaining halibut steaks, and top with the remaining fennel and spices.
5. Pour over the vinegar to just cover the halibut steaks. Cover with a small plate and weight down with a 750g (1½lb) weight. Cover the dish and chill in the refrigerator for 3-6 days.
6. When ready to serve, lift out the halibut steaks with a fish slice and arrange them on a flat serving dish. Garnish with the bay leaves, fennel and pistachio nuts, and spoon a little of the vinegar over the halibut steaks. Serve with brown bread and butter.

VARIATION
Any firm white fish such as cod or hake may be substituted for the halibut.

From the left: *Pickled Halibut; Stuffed squid*

STUFFED SQUID

150ml (¼pint) hot milk
2 large slices white bread, crusts removed
8 squid, bodies about 10cm (5-6 inches) long
3 tablespoons olive oil
50g (2 oz) butter
3 medium onions, peeled and finely chopped
2 carrots, scraped and finely chopped
2 celery sticks, finely chopped
1 garlic clove, peeled and finely chopped
4 rashers back bacon, rinded and diced
2 tablespoons chopped fresh basil
2 tablespoons chopped fresh parsley
salt
freshly ground black pepper
1 egg yolk
225g (8oz) tomatoes, skinned and chopped
175ml (6fl oz) dry white wine

Preparation time: 30-40 minutes
Cooking time: 50 minutes

1. Pour the hot milk into a shallow dish, add the bread and leave to soak for 10 minutes.
2. Clean the squid: separate the head from the body. Cut across the head just below the eyes, discarding all above that line. Pull the pinkish membrane off the outside of the body, draw back the body pouch, grasp the quill-shaped pen by its tip and gently pull it free. Cut off the side fins and rinse out the body sac. Chop the tentacles and the side fins and set aside.
3. Heat 2 tablespoons of the oil and 40g (1½oz) of the butter in a large frying pan with a lid. Add two-thirds of the onion, all the carrot and celery and fry over a gentle heat for 2 minutes. Add the garlic and cook until softened and lightly coloured.
4. Add the bacon and squid tentacles and fins and cook for a further 4-5 minutes, stir in the basil and parsley and remove from the heat.
5. Squeeze the bread dry and add to the pan. Mix very thoroughly, breaking up the bread with the back of a wooden spoon. Season well with salt and pepper, then stir in the egg yolk to bind.
6. Using a teaspoon, spoon the stuffing mixture into the bodies of the squid, filling them three-quarters full. Secure the opening of each squid with a wooden cocktail stick.
7. Heat the remaining oil and butter in the frying pan, add the remaining onion and fry over a gentle heat for 3-4 minutes. Add the stuffed squid, season with salt and pepper and cover with the tomatoes. Pour in the wine. Cover the pan and simmer gently for 35 minutes. Serve immediately, straight from the pan.

CHERVIL CHICKEN PIE

1 × 2kg (4½lb) roasting chicken
1 onion, peeled and halved
1 carrot, scraped and halved
1 celery stick, halved
1 bay leaf
3 stalks parsley
1 sprig thyme
2 teaspoons salt
8 whole black peppercorns
6 small leeks, trimmed and cut into 2.5cm (1 inch) rings
6 small carrots, cut into 2.5cm (1 inch) slices
100g (4oz) shelled peas, fresh or frozen
225g (8oz) shortcrust pastry, defrosted if frozen

SAUCE

40g (1½oz) butter
2 tablespoons plain flour
150ml (¼ pint) single cream
2 tablespoons chopped fresh chervil

GLAZE

1 egg yolk
1 tablespoon milk

Preparation time: 40 minutes, plus chilling overnight
Cooking time: 2 hours 10 minutes
Oven: 200°C, 400°F, Gas Mark 6
then: 175°C, 350°F, Gas Mark 4

1. The day before serving, put the chicken into a flameproof casserole and pour in enough hot water to cover the legs of the chicken. Bring slowly to the boil, skimming off the scum that rises to the surface.
2. When the liquid is boiling and quite clear add the onion, carrot, celery, bay leaf, parsley stalks, thyme, salt and peppercorns. Cover the casserole and simmer gently for 65 minutes, or until the chicken is cooked through and the juices run clear when the thigh is pierced with a skewer.
3. Remove the chicken and set aside. Boil the stock briskly for 5-10 minutes to reduce. Strain and leave to cool, then leave the chicken and stock overnight in the refrigerator.
4. Next day cook the leeks, sliced carrots and peas in separate saucepans and drain well. Carve the chicken, discarding the skin and bones, and cut the meat into 2.5cm (1 inch) pieces. Arrange the chicken with the vegetables in a greased 900ml (1½ pint) pie dish.
5. Make the sauce: remove and discard the fat from the surface of the stock and measure out 450ml (¾ pint). Heat it in a saucepan and set aside. Melt the butter in a saucepan and stir in the flour. Cook for 1 minute, stirring, then remove from the heat and gradually stir in the stock. Return to the heat and bring to the boil, stirring, then lower the heat and simmer for 3 minutes, stirring from time to time. Stir in the cream and chervil and remove from the heat. Set aside.
6. On a floured surface roll out the pastry to a shape slightly larger than the top of the pie dish. Cut off a strip of pastry all around the edge. Moisten the pie dish rim and press on the pastry strip. Moisten the pastry strip, then cover the pie with the pastry lid, pressing the edges to seal. Knock up and flute the edges and decorate the top with the trimmings cut into decorative shapes. Combine the egg yolk and milk with a fork and brush all over the pastry surface. Make a small hole in the centre of the pastry.
7. Bake for 15 minutes in a preheated oven, then reduce the oven temperature and bake for a further 15 minutes. Serve hot or cold.

CHICKEN PUDDING

350g (12oz) self-raising flour
salt
175g (6oz) shredded suet
200ml (⅓ pint) cold water
1 × 1.5kg (3lb) roasting chicken, skin and bones removed and cut into 2.5cm (1 inch) squares
freshly ground black pepper
2 tablespoons chopped fresh salad burnet
2 tablespoons chopped fresh tarragon
2 tablespoons chopped fresh chervil
1 bunch large spring onions, trimmed of green tops.
2 small leeks, trimmed and thickly sliced
3 small carrots, scraped and thickly sliced
200ml (⅓ pint) chicken stock

Preparation time: 30 minutes
Cooking time: 3 hours if using stock cube

If you have time, use the chicken bones to prepare a home-made stock, this will give the pudding a much better flavour.
1. Grease a 900ml (1½ pint) pudding basin.
2. Make the suet pastry: sift the flour with ¾ teaspoon salt into a mixing bowl and rub in the suet. Using the blade of a knife, stir in enough cold water to make a soft, firm dough. Knead the dough lightly, then cut and reserve one-third.
3. On a floured surface, roll out the larger piece of dough into a circle about 10cm (4 inches) larger than the basin. Sprinkle it all over with flour then fold it in half, then fold again to make a triangle. Put the dough into the basin so that the point touches the base, then open the dough out and use to line the greased basin, easing it in gently to avoid tearing it. Trim the edge.
4. Arrange one-third of the uncooked chicken in the bottom of the basin. Season with salt and pepper and sprinkle with half the mixed herbs. Spoon in half the vegetables, then a further one-third of the chicken. Season again with salt and pepper and sprinkle with the remaining herbs. Spoon in the remaining vegetables and top with the remaining chicken. Season again with salt and pepper, then pour in enough stock to come about two-thirds up the basin.
5. Moisten the rim of the basin. On a floured surface, roll the remaining dough into a circle and use it to

cover the basin. Press the edges together to seal, then trim with a knife.
6. Cover loosely with a pleated and greased circle of foil about 4cm (1½ inches) larger than the top of the basin and tie securely round the edge with string.
7. Stand the basin on a square of cloth and knot the corners over the top to make a handle. Set the basin on an upturned saucer in a large saucepan and pour in boiling water to come halfway up the sides of the basin. Cover, bring to the boil and boil steadily for 3 hours, topping up with more boiling water from time to time.
8. Remove from the heat, uncover and leave until cool enough to handle. Then lift out the basin and untie and remove the cloth. Remove the foil and wrap in a clean tea-towel or table napkin. Serve the chicken pudding straight from the basin, with runner beans or braised fennel.

From the left: *Chervil chicken pie; Chicken pudding*

CHICKEN WITH DILL SAUCE

1×1.5-1.75kg (3½-4lb) roasting chicken
1 onion, peeled and halved
2 cloves
1 carrot, scraped and halved
1 leek, trimmed and halved
1 celery stick, halved
1 bay leaf
3 stalks parsley
1 sprig thyme
1 sprig lovage
1 teaspoon salt
8 whole black peppercorns

SAUCE

25g (1oz) butter
1½ tablespoons plain flour
150ml (¼ pint) double cream
4 tablespoons chopped fresh dill
salt
freshly ground black pepper

Preparation time: 15 minutes
Cooking time: 1-1½ hours

1. Put the chicken into a flameproof casserole into which it will fit snugly. Arrange the vegetables and herbs around it and add the salt and peppercorns.
2. Pour in enough hot water to come halfway up the chicken legs and bring slowly to the boil, skimming off the scum that rises to the surface. When the liquid is boiling and quite clear, cover the casserole and simmer for 1 hour or until the juices run clear when the thigh is pierced with a skewer.
3. Transfer the chicken to a dish and keep warm. Strain and skim the stock and measure out 300ml (½ pint) into a small jug.
4. Melt the butter in a small saucepan and stir in the flour. Cook for 1 minute, stirring, then remove from the heat and gradually stir in the stock. Return to the heat and bring to the boil, stirring, then lower the heat and simmer gently for 3 minutes, stirring from time to time.
5. Put the cream into a food processor or electric blender with the dill and process until the dill is finely chopped. Stir into the sauce and taste and adjust the seasoning.
6. Carve the chicken, removing the skin, and arrange the pieces in a shallow heated serving dish. Pour over the sauce and serve with new potatoes.

Below: *Chicken with dill sauce*

RABBIT IN HERB SAUCE

3 tablespoons olive oil
1 rabbit, jointed into 8
1 medium onion, peeled and chopped
1 garlic clove, peeled and crushed
1×400g (14oz) can tomatoes, drained and chopped
1 tablespoon tomato purée
150ml (¼ pint) dry white wine
½ teaspoon sugar
salt
freshly ground black pepper
3 small sprigs each thyme, marjoram, savory and lovage
1½ tablespoons finely chopped fresh parsley

Preparation time: 10 minutes
Cooking time: 2-2½ hours

1. Heat the oil in a flameproof casserole, add the rabbit pieces and fry over a brisk heat, turning, until lightly browned on all sides. Remove from the casserole and set aside.
2. Add the onion to the casserole and fry over a gentle heat for 2-3 minutes. Add the garlic and continue to fry until soft and lightly coloured.
3. Stir in the tomatoes, tomato purée, wine and sugar. Stir to mix and season to taste with salt and pepper. Return the rabbit pieces to the casserole, tucking the herbs among them. Bring to the boil, cover and simmer for 1½-2 hours until tender.
4. Using a slotted spoon, transfer the rabbit pieces to a heated serving dish and keep warm. Boil the sauce briskly for 2-3 minutes to reduce slightly, then discard the herbs and spoon the sauce over the rabbit pieces. Garnish with chopped parsley and serve with noodles or boiled potatoes.

From the left: *Pheasant with sauerkraut; Rabbit in herb sauce*

PHEASANT WITH SAUERKRAUT

75g (3oz) beef dripping, duck fat or lard
3 medium onions, peeled and chopped
450g (1lb) sauerkraut, drained
900ml (1½ pints) hot chicken stock
75g (3oz) long-grain rice
8 juniper berries, roughly crushed
2 tablespoons roughly chopped fresh lovage
2 tablespoons chopped fresh thyme
1 tablespoon roughly chopped fresh savory
salt
freshly ground black pepper
1 roasting cock pheasant, barded with bacon
50g (2oz) butter, softened
sprigs of thyme, to garnish

Preparation time: 10-12 minutes
Cooking time: 2¼ hours
Oven: 190°C, 375°F, Gas Mark 5
then: 160°C, 325°F, Gas Mark 3

Sauerkraut can be bought in cans or loose from some delicatessens. For a milder flavour, rinse the sauerkraut under cold running water before using, then drain thoroughly.

1. Melt the dripping in a flameproof casserole, add the onions and fry over a gentle heat until soft and lightly coloured.
2. Stir in the sauerkraut and cook over a gentle heat for 10 minutes, stirring from time to time.
3. Pour in the stock and add the rice, juniper berries and herbs. Season to taste with salt and pepper. Bring to the boil, cover the casserole and simmer for 1 hour, adding a little extra stock if necessary.
4. Place the pheasant on a rack in a roasting tin. Spread the butter over the pheasant and roast for 30 minutes in a preheated oven, basting several times.
5. Reduce the oven temperature. Place the pheasant in the casserole and spoon the sauerkraut mixture over it. Cook in the oven for a further 30 minutes.
6. Remove the pheasant and spoon the sauerkraut mixture into a heated shallow serving dish. Carve the pheasant, discarding the bacon and lay on the sauerkraut. Garnish each portion with a sprig of thyme and serve immediately.

Above: *Chicken couscous*
Opposite, from the top: *Turkey skewers (recipe p 172); Spiced lentils Indonesian style (recipe p 184); Spiced chicken*

CHICKEN COUSCOUS

350g (12oz) couscous
450ml (¾pint) cold water
1 × 1.5kg (3½lb) roasting chicken, jointed into 8
1.5 litres (2½pints) hot water
6 small onions, peeled
4 leeks, trimmed and thickly sliced
4 carrots, scraped and thickly sliced
2 celery sticks, thickly sliced
3 sprigs thyme
3 sprigs marjoram
2 sprigs lovage
salt
freshly ground black pepper
4 courgettes, trimmed and thickly sliced
6 tomatoes, skinned and quartered
1 sachet powdered saffron
3½ tablespoons chopped fresh chervil
Serves 8

Preparation time: 15 minutes, plus soaking
Cooking time: 50-60 minutes

This filling dish, of Moroccan origin, is best served in soup plates. In Morocco every housewife has a couscousière, a special pan for making couscous, but a large saucepan or flameproof casserole and a strainer can be used instead.

1. Put the couscous into a large bowl and pour over the cold water. Set aside for 10 minutes until the water is absorbed.
2. Put the chicken pieces into a deep saucepan or flameproof casserole and pour in the hot water to cover. Bring slowly to the boil, skimming off the scum that rises to the surface.
3. When the liquid is boiling and quite clear, add the onions, leeks, carrots, celery, thyme, marjoram and lovage. Season to taste with salt and pepper and bring back to the boil.
4. Tip the soaked couscous into a strainer lined with muslin and set over the chicken, making sure that the strainer does not touch the liquid. Cover and boil gently over a moderate heat for 30 minutes.
5. Remove the strainer of couscous and add the courgettes to the pan. Stir the couscous, breaking up any lumps, then stir in 1-2 tablespoons of the boiling stock to moisten.
6. Replace the strainer of couscous over the chicken, cover the pan and boil gently for a further 10 minutes.
7. Remove the strainer of couscous and add the

tomatoes to the pan. Replace the strainer, cover the pan again and boil gently for a further 5 minutes.
8. Tip the couscous into a heated serving dish, breaking up any lumps with a fork. Remove the chicken pieces from the pan with a slotted spoon and arrange them over the couscous. Sprinkle with ½ tablespoon of the chopped chervil, cover tightly with foil and keep warm.
9. Skim as much fat as possible from the surface of the stock. Stir in the remaining chervil and saffron, taste and adjust the seasoning. Remove from the heat, cover and leave to stand for 5 minutes.
10. Pour the vegetables with the stock into a warmed deep bowl or soup tureen and serve with the chicken couscous, spooning some of the vegetables and stock over each portion.

SPICED CHICKEN

1 × 1.5 kg (3 ¼ lb) roasting chicken, jointed into 8
1 tablespoon plain flour
salt
freshly ground black pepper
6 tablespoons sunflower oil
4 shallots, peeled and finely chopped
2 garlic cloves, peeled and finely chopped
2.5cm (1 inch) square piece of fresh ginger root, finely chopped
2 green chillies, seeded and finely chopped
1 stem lemon grass, finely chopped, or ½ tablespoon finely chopped fresh lemon balm
2 tablespoons fresh lime juice
1 teaspoon sugar
300ml (½ pint) hot water
TO GARNISH
lime slices
sprigs of lemon grass or lemon balm

Preparation time: 15 minutes
Cooking time: 50-55 minutes

1. Sprinkle the chicken pieces with the flour and season with salt and pepper.
2. Heat half the oil in a large frying pan, add the chicken pieces and fry over a brisk heat, turning, until lightly browned on all sides. Set aside.
3. Heat the remaining oil in a flameproof casserole, add the shallots and fry over a moderate heat for 2 minutes, stirring often. Stir in the garlic, ginger, chillies and lemon grass and fry for a further 2 minutes, stirring often.
4. Add the lime juice, sugar and water and simmer for 30 seconds. Add the chicken pieces and cover the casserole.
5. Simmer over a gentle heat for 30-35 minutes, until the chicken is cooked and the juices run clear when it is pierced with a skewer. Garnish each portion with lime slices and a sprig of lemon grass and serve with boiled rice, Spiced lentils (p 184) and a bowl of plain unsweetened yogurt.

TURKEY SKEWERS

1kg (2lb) boneless turkey breasts, cut into 2.5cm (1 inch) squares
3 tablespoons sunflower oil
3 tablespoons dry vermouth
3 tablespoons light soy sauce
1 large garlic clove, peeled and finely chopped
2.5 cm (1 inch) square piece of fresh ginger root, finely chopped
1 stem lemon grass, finely chopped
10-16 bay leaves (optional)

Preparation time: 15 minutes, plus marinating overnight
Cooking time: 10 minutes

Allow 2 skewers per person for a main course. The turkey skewers may also be cooked over a preheated barbecue and served in pockets of pitta bread.

1. Put the turkey pieces into a bowl. Add the oil, vermouth and soy sauce and stir well to mix. Then stir in the garlic, ginger and lemon grass.
2. Cover and leave to marinate overnight in the refrigerator, stirring once or twice.
3. When ready to cook, thread the pieces of turkey on to 8 kebab skewers or wooden saté sticks, including a few bay leaves if liked, reserving the marinade.
4. Arrange the turkey skewers on the grill rack. Place under a preheated grill and cook for 10 minutes, turning frequently and basting with the remains of the marinade. Serve immediately with rice.

DUCK BREASTS WITH HORSERADISH

4 duck breast portions, boned
1 tablespoon sunflower oil
1 large cooking apple, peeled and thickly sliced
2 tablespoons water
3 tablespoons grated horseradish
65ml (2 ½fl oz) soured cream
65ml (2 ½fl oz) plain unsweetened yogurt
1 teaspoon lemon juice
8 leaves batavia, or curly endive, roughly shredded
8 leaves raddicchio, roughly shredded
8 leaves sorrel, cut into strips
8 rosettes lamb's lettuce or mâche, roots removed
8 button mushrooms, trimmed and thinly sliced
8 spring onions, cut into strips and blanched

DRESSING

1 tablespoon lemon juice
1 tablespoon white wine vinegar
2 tablespoons olive oil
2 tablespoons sunflower oil
salt
freshly ground black pepper

Preparation time: 25 minutes, plus cooling
Cooking time: 25 minutes

Batavia, raddicchio, sorrel and lamb's lettuce can be found in summer in specialist greengocers.

1. Brush the duck breasts with the oil.
2. Make the sauce: put the apple with the water into a small saucepan, cover and cook for about 15 minutes until soft, stirring from time to time. Pass through a food mill into a bowl and leave to cool.
3. When the apple purée is tepid, stir in the horseradish, soured cream, yogurt and lemon juice.
4. Arrange the duck breasts skin side up on the grill rack. Place under a preheated grill and cook for 6-8 minutes. Turn and cook for a further 4-5 minutes. Cool.
5. Meanwhile make the salad: arrange the batavia and raddicchio, sorrel, lamb's lettuce, mushrooms and spring onions on 4 plates.
6. Thoroughly combine all the dressing ingredients and spoon over each salad.
7. Using a very sharp knife, cut the cooled duck breasts diagonally into thin slices. Arrange a sliced duck breast in a fan shape on each plate. Spoon a portion of horseradish sauce on to the side of each plate and serve immediately.

BRAISED PARTRIDGES

4 young partridges
salt
freshly ground black pepper
8 large preserved vine leaves, well rinsed
40g (1 ½oz) butter
3 tablespoons olive oil
1 medium leek, trimmed and sliced
3 celery sticks, sliced
1 medium head fennel, sliced
65ml (2 ½fl oz) gin or vodka
2 tablespoons chopped celery leaves
2 tablespoons chopped fresh lovage
1 tablespoon chopped fresh thyme, or 1 teaspoon dried thyme
1 tablespoon chopped fresh marjoram, or 1 teaspoon dried marjoram
1 tablespoon chopped fresh savory
150ml (¼pint) dry white wine, heated
150ml (¼pint) hot chicken stock
1 green pepper, cored and seeded, to garnish
65ml (2 ½fl oz) double cream

Preparation time: 15 minutes
Cooking time: 1½-1¾ hours
Oven: 160°C, 325°F, Gas Mark 3

1. Season the partridges with salt and pepper. Wrap each partridge in 2 vine leaves and tie with fine string to make parcels.
2. Heat the butter and oil in a flameproof casserole, add the leek and fry over a gentle heat for 2 minutes. Add the sliced celery and fennel and fry for a further 2-3 minutes, stirring.
3. Add the gin, celery leaves and the herbs, increase

the heat and boil rapidly, uncovered, until almost all the liquid has evaporated.
4. Add the partridges to the casserole and pour over the wine and stock. Season to taste with salt and pepper and bring to the boil.
5. Cover the casserole and cook in a preheated oven for 1¼-1½ hours (depending on the age of the birds), turning the partridges once or twice.
6. Meanwhile cook the green pepper under a preheated hot grill, turning often, until the skin has charred and blackened. When cool enough to handle, scrape away the skin and cut the flesh into strips. Keep warm.
7. Remove the partridges and unwrap them, discarding the vine leaves but reserving the vegetables and stock. Using a very sharp knife, cut each partridge in half lengthways, discarding the backbone. Arrange the partridges in a heated serving dish, cover and keep warm.
8. Make the sauce: put the vegetables and stock from the casserole into a food processor or electric blender and process briefly, to achieve a fairly smooth texture. Pour into a small saucepan and reheat gently over a low heat.
9. Stir in the cream, taste and adjust the seasoning and pour the sauce over the partridges. Garnish with the green pepper strips and serve immediately with mangetout and new potatoes.

VARIATION

If using old birds, allow an extra 30-45 minutes cooking time. Alternatively, the dish can be made with pigeon, allowing 1¼ hours in the oven for young birds, or 2-2½ hours for old birds.

From the top: *Duck breasts with horseradish; Braised partridges*

MEAT LOAF WITH LOVAGE

750g (1 ½lb) lean minced beef
2 large slices white bread, crusts removed
150ml (¼pint) milk
1 small onion, peeled and finely chopped
2 garlic cloves, peeled and finely chopped
1 tablespoon olive oil
2 tablespoons chopped fresh lovage, or 1 tablespoon dried lovage
½ teaspoon ground allspice
1 teaspoon salt
freshly ground black pepper
butter, for greasing

Preparation time: 15 minutes, plus soaking
Cooking time: 1½ hours
Oven: 180°C, 350°F, Gas Mark 4
Serves 6-8

This recipe comes from Turkey, where allspice is a popular flavouring for meat dishes as well as desserts.

1. Put the minced beef into a large bowl and break up the lumps, using your hands or a wooden spoon.
2. Soak the bread in the milk for 10 minutes, then squeeze dry and add to the beef. Add the onion, garlic, oil, lovage, allspice, and salt and pepper to taste. Knead well with your hands, to mix really thoroughly.
3. Shape the mixture into a rectangle to fit a 22.5×12.5cm (9×4 inch) loaf tin and place in the greased tin. Cover the tin with foil and bake for 1½ hours in a preheated oven.
4. Turn the meat loaf on to a serving dish. Serve hot or cold with plain boiled potatoes and a mixed salad, accompanied by a bowl of plain unsweetened yogurt sprinkled with a little chopped mint.

MEATBALLS IN DILL SAUCE

350g (12oz) minced veal
40g (1 ½oz) fresh white breadcrumbs
1 ½ tablespoons grated onion
1 ½ tablespoons chopped fresh parsley
salt
freshly ground black pepper
1 egg, beaten
900ml (1 ½pints) chicken stock
2 egg yolks
4 tablespoons lemon juice
2 tablespoons chopped fresh dill
lemon wedges, to serve

Preparation time: 15-20 minutes
Cooking time: 35 minutes

Far superior to the more usual meatballs found in every Greek taverna, these are moist and subtly flavoured, served in a lemon and herb sauce.

1. Put the minced veal into a large bowl with the breadcrumbs, onion and parsley and mix well. Season to taste with salt and pepper, then stir in the egg to bind. Using a greased teaspoon, take heaped teaspoons of the mixture and smooth and round the surface, to make about 16 meatballs.
2. Pour the stock into a large saucepan, bring to the boil and gently lower in the meatballs. Bring back to the boil, lower the heat and simmer, half covered, for 20 minutes. Using a slotted spoon, transfer the meatballs to a heated serving dish and keep warm.
3. Strain the stock and reheat in the rinsed-out pan. Beat the egg yolks with the lemon juice in a small bowl, stir in the dill, then beat in 2 tablespoons of the boiling stock. Pour into the hot stock in the saucepan and cook over the lowest possible heat, stirring constantly, for 3 minutes. On no account allow to boil, or the egg yolks will scramble. Taste and adjust the seasoning.
4. Pour the sauce over the meatballs and serve immediately with boiled rice or noodles, lemon wedges and a green salad.

GREEK LAMB

750g (1 ½lb) boneless lamb, cut into 2.5cm (1 inch) cubes
1 medium onion, peeled and thinly sliced
1 carrot, scraped and thinly sliced
1 celery stick, thinly sliced
600ml (1 pint) chicken stock
2 bunches large spring onions, cut into 2.5cm (1 inch) pieces
1 cos lettuce heart, cut across into 2.5cm (1 inch) wedges
1×425g (15oz) can artichoke hearts, drained and quartered

DILL AND LEMON SAUCE

40g (1 ½oz) butter
2 tablespoons plain flour
2 egg yolks
2 tablespoons lemon juice
3 tablespoons chopped fresh dill
salt
freshly ground black pepper

Preparation time: 20 minutes
Cooking time: 1¼ hours

This is a fricassée of lamb, not unlike a *blanquette de veau*, but the use of dill makes it typically Greek.

1. Put the lamb, onion, carrot and celery into a flameproof casserole and pour in enough stock to just cover. Bring slowly to the boil, skimming off the scum that rises from the surface. When the liquid is boiling and quite clear, cover the casserole and simmer for 1 hour.
2. Add the spring onions to the casserole and return to the boil. Cook over a moderate heat for 5 minutes.
3. Add the lettuce wedges and the artichoke hearts.

Return to the boil and simmer for 2 minutes. Using a slotted spoon, transfer the meat and vegetables to a heated serving dish and keep warm.
4. Strain the lamb stock into a bowl and stand in enough cold water to come halfway up the sides and leave for 5 minutes, to cool slightly. Then skim off the fat and measure out 400ml (14fl oz) stock.
5. Melt the butter in a saucepan and stir in the flour. Cook for 1 minute, stirring, then remove from the heat and gradually stir in the stock. Return to the heat and bring to the boil, stirring, then lower the heat and simmer for 3 minutes, stirring from time to time.
6. Beat the egg yolks with the lemon juice in a small bowl, stir in the dill, then beat in 2 tablespoons of the hot sauce, until thoroughly blended. Pour into the hot sauce in the pan and cook over the lowest possible heat, stirring constantly, for 3 minutes. On no account allow to boil, or the egg will scramble. Taste and adjust the seasoning.
7. Pour the sauce over the lamb and vegetables, turning gently to mix. Serve with boiled rice or roast potatoes and a mixed salad.

From the left: *Meat loaf with lovage; Meatballs in dill sauce; Greek lamb*

PARSLEYED CALF'S LIVER

2 tablespoons plain flour
salt
freshly ground black pepper
4 large thin slices calf's liver, about 100g (4oz) each
25g (1oz) butter
2 tablespoons olive oil
2 garlic cloves, peeled and finely chopped
1-2 tablespoons white wine vinegar
4 tablespoons dry white wine
2 tablespoons chopped fresh parsley

Preparation time: 5 minutes
Cooking time: 12 minutes

The combination of calf's liver and parsley makes a particularly healthy and delicious dish, rich in iron and Vitamin C.

1. Spread the flour out on a large flat plate and season with salt and pepper. Dip the liver slices in the seasoned flour to coat thoroughly.
2. Heat the butter and oil in a frying pan and add 2 liver slices. Fry over a moderate heat for about 2 minutes on each side or until the liver is still slightly pink in the centre.
3. Transfer the fried liver to a heated serving dish and keep warm. Fry the remaining liver in the same way and transfer to the serving dish.
4. Add the garlic to the pan and cook over a gentle heat, stirring often and adding a little more butter or oil if necessary, for about 1½ minutes. Add the vinegar and wine and swirl round the pan for 1-2 minutes. Stir in the parsley and pour the mixture over the liver. Serve immediately with broad beans and steamed cauliflower florets.

VARIATION
Calf's liver has an especially delicate flavour, but it is expensive. Lamb's liver may be used instead, for a more economical dish.

PORK FILLET WITH BASIL

1 large pork fillet, about 450-500g (1-1¼lb), cut into thin slices
25g (1oz) butter
1 tablespoon olive oil
2 teaspoons plain flour
150ml (¼pint) dry white wine, heated
150ml (¼pint) hot chicken stock
150ml (¼pint) single cream
½ teaspoon Dijon mustard
salt
freshly ground black pepper
2 tablespoons fresh basil, cut into thin strips

Preparation time: 5 minutes
Cooking time: 15-20 minutes

For a special occasion, escalopes of veal may be substituted for the pork fillet.

1. Lay the pork fillet slices on a sheet of cling film on a board, cover with another sheet of cling film and beat them out with a mallet or rolling pin until very thin.
2. Heat the butter and oil in a large frying pan, add half the pork slices and cook for 3-4 minutes on each side, until cooked through and golden brown. Transfer to a heated serving dish and keep warm. Fry the remaining pork fillet slices in the same way and transfer to the serving dish.
3. Sprinkle the flour into the pan and cook gently for 1 minute, stirring. Remove from the heat and gradually stir in the wine and stock. Return to the heat and cook briskly for about 3 minutes, until reduced by about half. Lower the heat and stir in the cream and mustard to blend thoroughly. Simmer over the lowest possible heat for a further 1-2 minutes. On no account allow to boil, or the sauce will curdle. Sea-

son to taste with salt and pepper, stir in the strips of basil and pour over the pork fillet slices. Serve immediately with finely pared carrot strips, that have been blanched for 1 minute, and spinach.

PORK CHOPS WITH JUNIPER

4 tablespoons olive oil
4 pork chops, about 225g (8oz) each
2 shallots, peeled and chopped
1 garlic clove, peeled and chopped
8 juniper berries, roughly crushed
225g (8oz) tomatoes, skinned and roughly chopped
4 tablespoons gin or vodka
120ml (4fl oz) chicken stock
½ tablespoon chopped fresh thyme or ½ teaspoon dried thyme
salt
freshly ground black pepper

Preparation time: 10 minutes
Cooking time: 30 minutes

1. Heat the oil in a deep frying pan with a lid. Add the pork chops and fry over a brisk heat for 3-4 minutes on each side to brown, then remove and keep warm.
2. Add the shallots to the pan and fry over a gentle heat for 2 minutes, then add the garlic and cook for 1 further minute.
3. Stir in the juniper berries and tomatoes and cook for 2-3 minutes, stirring. Then add the gin and boil rapidly over a brisk heat until reduced by half. Pour in the stock and stir in the thyme. Season to taste with salt and pepper.
4. Return the pork chops to the pan, cover and simmer for 15-20 minutes, adding a little extra stock if necessary, until the chops are cooked through.
5. Serve the pork chops with buttered cabbage and baked potatoes if liked.

From the left: *Parsleyed calf's liver; Pork fillet with basil; Pork chops with juniper*

OX TONGUE WITH GREEN SAUCE

1 ox tongue, salted
1 large onion, peeled and halved
1 large carrot, scraped and halved
1 celery stick, halved
3 sprigs parsley
1 bay leaf
6 whole black peppercorns
GREEN SAUCE
1 egg yolk
1 tablespoon Dijon mustard
1 teaspoon sugar
salt
freshly ground black pepper
2 garlic cloves, peeled and crushed
½ Spanish onion, peeled and finely chopped
4 tablespoons chopped mixed fresh herbs (parsley, chives, chervil, tarragon and dill)
3 tablespoons white wine vinegar
150ml (¼ pint) olive oil
2 hard-boiled eggs, chopped
green salad vegetables, to garnish

Preparation time: 30 minutes, plus soaking
Cooking time: 3½ hours

1. Put the tongue in a large bowl, pour in fresh cold water to cover and leave to soak for 4 hours.
2. Drain the tongue and put it into a saucepan that fits it as closely as possible. Place the onion, carrot, celery, parsley, bay leaf and peppercorns around the tongue. Bring slowly to the boil, skimming off the scum that rises to the surface. When the liquid is boiling and quite clear, cover the pan tightly and simmer for 3 hours.
3. Meanwhile, make the sauce: put the egg yolk, mustard, sugar, and salt and pepper to taste into a food processor or electric blender and process until blended. Then add the garlic, onion and herbs, and process again until smooth. Then add the vinegar and oil in a steady stream through the lid, while still processing. Finally, add the hard-boiled eggs and process again briefly. Pour the sauce into a jug.
4. Remove the cooked tongue from the pan and set aside for a few minutes, until cool enough to handle. Remove the skin and any pieces of bone and gristle near the root. Using a very sharp knife, carve the tongue into neat slices. Arrange the slices on a serving platter and garnish with salad vegetables. Serve with a beetroot and potato salad, accompanied by the green sauce.

Below: *Ox tongue with green sauce*

ROAST LAMB WITH GARLIC AND ROSEMARY

1 leg of lamb, about 2.5-2.75kg (5½-6lb)
1 large garlic clove, peeled and cut into slivers
1 small branch rosemary
freshly ground black pepper
150ml (¼ pint) red wine, heated
1 sprig rosemary, to garnish

Preparation time: 3 minutes
Cooking time: 2¼-2½ hours, plus standing
Oven: 180°C, 350°F, Gas Mark 4

Rosemary is the traditional flavouring for lamb. Unlike many herbs, its flavour can easily become overpowering, so use it with caution.
1. Make a series of small slits in the surface of the lamb with the point of a small sharp knife, and stick a sliver of garlic in each one.
2. Put the lamb in a roasting tin with the rosemary and cook in a preheated oven for 1 hour.
3. Pour the wine over the lamb and cook for a further 1¼-1½ hours, basting two or three times, until the lamb is cooked but still slightly pink in the centre.
4. Transfer the lamb to a carving dish, cover loosely with foil and allow to stand for 20 minutes. Drain off the fat from the tin, discard the rosemary, and stir the juices for 1-2 minutes over a gentle heat, using a wooden spoon to scrape the base and sides of the tin. Strain the gravy into a heated sauceboat.
5. Garnish the lamb with a sprig of rosemary and serve carved into slices, with sliced boiled potatoes, and Mushroom purée (p 188), accompanied by the gravy.

From the left: *Roast lamb with garlic and rosemary; Rack of lamb with garlic cream; Mushroom purée (recipe p 188)*

RACK OF LAMB WITH GARLIC CREAM

1 head garlic divided into unpeeled cloves
150ml (¼pint) milk
1 best end of neck of lamb, trimmed for roasting
65ml (2½fl oz) dry white wine, heated
150ml (¼pint) hot chicken stock
½ teaspoon plain flour
65ml (2½fl oz) soured cream
salt
freshly ground black pepper

Preparation time: 15 minutes
Cooking time: 45-55 minutes
Oven: 200°C, 400°F, Gas Mark 6
Serves 3

This dish should be made with plump juicy cloves of garlic, preferably the fresh pinkish Provençal garlic that can be bought in early summer. The exact cooking time for the meat will depend on how the rack has been trimmed: some butchers will do this in the French manner, taking away all the fat and cleaning the bones entirely, while others leave on more, giving a thicker joint that takes longer to cook through.

1. Put the cloves of garlic into a small saucepan with the milk. Bring to the boil and cook gently for 3 minutes then drain, discarding the milk.
2. Put the lamb into a roasting tin and arrange the garlic cloves around it. Wrap pieces of foil around the end of each bone to prevent them charring and roast for 40-50 minutes in a preheated oven by which time the joint should still be slightly pink in the centre.
3. Transfer the garlic cloves to a small plate and crush with a fork. Discard the skins. Transfer the lamb to a heated carving dish and keep warm.
4. Drain off the fat from the roasting tin. Add the wine, stock and crushed garlic to the meat juices in the tin and stir over a moderate heat, using a wooden spoon to scrape the base and sides of the tin, for 2-3 minutes, then remove from the heat.
5. Mix the flour into the soured cream, beating until smooth. Add to the garlic sauce, little by little, whisking vigorously with a small whisk.
6. Simmer the sauce over the lowest possible heat for 2-3 minutes. On no account allow the sauce to boil, or it will curdle. Taste and adjust the seasoning.
7. Carve the lamb into cutlets and serve with baby carrots, accompanied by the sauce.

From the left: *Neapolitan beef; Beef olives with marigolds*

NEAPOLITAN BEEF

2 tablespoons olive oil
1.5kg (3lb) good-quality braising beef in one piece, cut into very thin slices
2 garlic cloves, peeled and finely chopped
3 tablespoons chopped fresh parsley
½ tablespoon dried oregano, or 2 tablespoons chopped fresh marjoram
salt
freshly ground black pepper
2×400g (14oz) cans tomatoes, roughly chopped

Preparation time: 10 minutes
Cooking time: 1¾ hours
Oven 160°C, 325°F, Gas Mark 3
Serves 6

Oregano is probably the most popular of all herbs in Italy. Fresh oregano is hard to find here, so use fresh marjoram, which is very similar and more readily available, or dried oregano.

1. Spoon the oil over the base of a wide flameproof casserole and arrange the beef slices on the bottom.
2. Sprinkle the garlic, parsley and oregano or marjoram over the beef and season with salt and pepper. Pour in the tomatoes with their juice and bring quickly to the boil.
3. Cover the casserole and cook in a preheated oven for 1½ hours, or until the beef is tender.
4. Using a fish slice, arrange the beef slices on a heated serving platter and spoon the sauce over them. Serve immediately with a mixed salad.

BEEF OLIVES WITH MARIGOLDS

4 thin slices beef topside, about 100g (4oz) each
50g (2oz) shredded suet
25g (1oz) fresh white breadcrumbs
2 rashers streaky bacon, rinded and diced
½ teaspoon grated orange rind
2 tablespoons chopped fresh parsley
2 tablespoons marigold petals
salt
freshly ground black pepper
1 egg, beaten
40g (1½oz) butter
1 medium onion, peeled and thinly sliced
1 medium carrot, scraped and thinly sliced
1 small leek, trimmed and thinly sliced
1 celery stick, thinly sliced
½ tablespoon plain flour
300ml (½ pint) hot beef stock

Preparation time: 25-30 minutes
Cooking time: 1¾ hours
Oven: 160°C, 325°F, Gas Mark 3

Marigolds always had a place in the medieval English herb garden, and were often used to flavour and garnish meat dishes. The beef olives may be served straight from the casserole, or on a bed of mashed potatoes, with the vegetables spooned round them in a ring, and the sauce handed separately in a heated sauceboat.

1. Lay the beef slices on a sheet of cling film on a board, cover with another sheet of cling film and beat them out with a mallet or rolling pin until very thin. Trim each beef slice to a neat rectangular shape, reserving the trimmings.
2. Make the stuffing: finely chop the beef trimmings and put them in a bowl with the suet, breadcrumbs, bacon, orange rind, half the parsley and half the marigold petals. Stir well to mix and season to taste with salt and pepper. Stir in the egg to bind then spread a portion of the stuffing on each beef slice, dividing it equally between them. Roll up and tie securely in 2 or 3 places with fine string.
3. Melt the butter in a flameproof casserole, add the onion, carrot, leek and celery and fry over a gentle heat, stirring from time to time, until very lightly coloured.
4. Using a slotted spoon, remove and reserve the vegetables, and add the beef olives to the casserole. Fry over a brisk heat for 3-4 minutes, turning often, until browned all over.
5. Remove the beef olives from the casserole and stir the flour into the juices. Pour in the stock and stir well until blended. Season to taste with salt and pepper.
6. Return the vegetables to the casserole and arrange the beef olives on top. Cover the casserole and cook in a preheated oven for 1½ hours or until the beef olives are tender.
7. Discard the string from the beef olives, sprinkle with the remaining parsley and marigold petals and serve immediately with the vegetables.

TAMARIND VEAL

1 medium onion, peeled and roughly chopped
2 garlic cloves, peeled and roughly chopped
1 green chilli, seeded and chopped
1cm (½ inch) square piece fresh ginger root, chopped
1 stem lemon grass, sliced
½ tablespoon curry leaves
½ teaspoon ground turmeric
3 tablespoons sunflower oil
2.5cm (1 inch) square piece tamarind
65ml (2½fl oz) hot water
750g (1½lb) pie veal, trimmed and cut into 4cm (1½ inch) cubes
4 tablespoons chicken stock
1 tablespoon light soy sauce
2 tablespoons chopped fresh coriander
2 tablespoons chopped spring onions

Preparation time: 20 minutes, plus soaking
Cooking time: 1¾ hours

This is a dry curry dish, so do not expect a lot of sauce when the veal is cooked. If you prefer mild curries, halve the chilli quantity.

1. Put the onion, garlic, chilli, ginger, lemon grass and curry leaves into a food processor or electric blender and process until reduced to a fine pulp. Stir in the turmeric.
2. Heat the oil in a flameproof casserole and add the spice mixture. Cook over a gentle heat for 15 minutes, stirring often.
3. Meanwhile, soak the tamarind in the hot water for 10 minutes, then mash it to a paste and pass it through a medium food mill or coarse strainer.
4. Add the veal to the casserole and stir well to coat with the spice mixture. Add 2 tablespoons of the tamarind liquid with the stock and soy sauce. Bring to the boil, lower the heat, cover the casserole and simmer gently for 1½ hours, stirring from time to time, or until the veal is tender and cooked through.
5. Sprinkle with the coriander and spring onions. Serve immediately with a salad such as Avocado salad with coriander (recipe overleaf) and rice. As the curry is very dry, it can be accompanied by a bowl of plain unsweetened yogurt if liked.

From the bottom: *Tamarind veal; Avocado salad with coriander (recipe overleaf)*

AVOCADO SALAD WITH CORIANDER

2 large ripe avocados, peeled, stoned and diced
350g (12oz) tomatoes, skinned, seeded, drained and chopped
2 bunches spring onions, sliced
dash of Tabasco sauce (optional)
1 tablespoon lemon juice
1 tablespoon fresh lime juice
2 tablespoons sunflower oil
2 tablespoons chopped fresh coriander
salt
freshly ground black pepper
lime slices, to garnish

Preparation time: 20 minutes

This salad should be served on its own as an hors d'oeuvre or vegetable course.

1. Combine the avocados, tomatoes and spring onions in a bowl.
2. Add the Tabasco sauce, if using, the lemon and lime juices, oil and coriander. Stir lightly but thoroughly to mix well and season to taste with salt and pepper. Garnish with lime slices and serve.

CELERY RÉMOULADE

2 hard-boiled egg yolks
2 egg yolks
1 tablespoon Dijon mustard
pinch of salt
freshly ground black pepper
2 tablespoons white wine vinegar
2 tablespoons tarragon vinegar
300ml (½ pint) sunflower oil
150ml (¼ pint) soured cream
2 heads celery, trimmed and cut into matchstick strips, with leaves reserved

Preparation time: 15 minutes
Cooking time: 12 minutes (for the hard-boiled eggs)

Serve this rich celery dish as a starter, with melba toast, or as part of a selection of salads for a party.

1. Make the rémoulade sauce: put the hard-boiled egg yolks into a bowl and mash well with a fork. Using a wooden spoon, beat in the raw egg yolks and continue to beat to make a smooth paste. Beat in the mustard and season with salt and pepper.
2. Add the vinegar very gradually, beating well between each addition until thoroughly blended. Add half the oil drop by drop, as if making mayonnaise. Add the remaining oil in a steady trickle, stirring constantly.
3. Fold in the soured cream and taste and adjust the seasoning if necessary. Add the celery strips and stir well to mix.
4. Turn the Celery rémoulade into a serving dish and garnish with the celery leaves.

EGGS IN A FIELD

75g (3oz) sorrel leaves, cut into very fine strips
6 eggs, hard-boiled, shelled and halved lengthways
150ml (¼ pint) mayonnaise
65ml (2½fl oz) single cream
65ml (2½fl oz) plain unsweetened yogurt
1 teaspoon lemon juice
TO GARNISH
1 tablespoon chopped summer savory
1 sprig summer savory

Preparation time: 10 minutes

1. Spread the sorrel over a flat serving dish. Lay the eggs cut side down on the sorrel.
2. In a small bowl mix together the mayonnaise, cream and yogurt, beating well until smooth and thoroughly blended. Stir in the lemon juice.
3. Spoon the mixture over the eggs and garnish with the savory. Serve at room temperature or lightly chilled, with melba toast.

From the left: *Celery rémoulade; Eggs in a field; Tomatoes with horseradish sauce; Tomato and basil salad*

TOMATOES WITH HORSERADISH SAUCE

750g (1lb) small tomatoes, skinned
150ml (¼pint) mayonnaise
65ml (2½fl oz) soured cream
65ml (2½fl oz) plain unsweetened yogurt
2 teaspoons lemon juice
4 tablespoons grated horseradish
1½ tablespoons chopped fresh dill
1 sprig dill, to garnish

Preparation time: 10-12 minutes
Cooking time: 1 minute

Use the tiny cherry tomatoes, if available, in this dish.

1. Pile the tomatoes in a pyramid on a flat dish. In a bowl combine the mayonnaise with the soured cream and yogurt, then stir in the lemon juice, horseradish and dill.
2. Spoon the horseradish sauce over the tomatoes just before serving and garnish with the dill sprig.

TOMATO AND BASIL SALAD

750g (1½lb) large ripe tomatoes, sliced
freshly ground black pepper
½ teaspoon sugar
3 tablespoons olive oil
1 tablespoon white wine vinegar
2 tablespoons fresh basil, cut into thin strips
1 sprig basil, to garnish

Preparation time: 10 minutes, plus standing

Basil and tomatoes together make one of the most delicious combinations. For a summer lunch dish, add 175g (6oz) thinly sliced mozzarella cheese.

1. Arrange the tomato slices neatly overlapping on a large flat serving dish. Season with plenty of pepper and sprinkle over with the sugar.
2. Combine the oil and vinegar and spoon evenly over the tomatoes. Leave to stand for 1 hour. Just before serving, scatter the basil over the tomatoes. Serve garnished with a basil sprig.

From the top: *Spiced lentils Indonesian style; Stir-fried courgettes with herbs and spices*

STIR-FRIED COURGETTES WITH HERBS AND SPICES

750g (1 ½lb) large courgettes, peeled, and cut into 2.5cm (1 inch) chunks
salt
3 tablespoons sunflower oil
1 tablespoon chopped curry leaves
3 spring onions, sliced
1 garlic clove, peeled and chopped
1 tablespoon chopped fresh ginger root
1 tablespoon chopped fresh coriander
1 teaspoon light soy sauce
2 tablespoons chicken stock or hot water

Preparation time: 15 minutes, plus draining
Cooking time: 10-12 minutes

1. Put the courgettes into a colander and set over a large plate. Sprinkle the courgettes with the salt and leave to drain for 30 minutes, then pat dry with a cloth or absorbent paper.
2. Heat a wok or deep frying pan, add the oil and heat again. Add the curry leaves and fry for 1-2 minutes. until they turn brown, then add the spring onions, garlic, ginger and coriander. Stir-fry over brisk heat for 1-2 minutes.
3. Add the courgettes and stir-fry for a further 2 minutes, then cover the wok and simmer for a further 2 minutes over a gentle heat. Add the soy sauce and stock and stir-fry for 30 seconds. Turn the courgettes into a warmed serving dish and serve immediately as an accompaniment to curried poultry, fish or veal.

VARIATION
Vegetable marrow, peeled, seeded and cut into 2.5cm (1 inch) cubes, may be substituted for the courgettes.

SPICED LENTILS, INDONESIAN STYLE

225g (8oz) orange, green or brown lentils
900ml (1 ½pints) cold water
3 tablespoons sunflower oil
½ teaspoon mustard seeds
½ tablespoon chopped curry leaves
1 medium onion, peeled and finely chopped
2 green chillies, seeded and finely chopped
1 garlic clove, peeled and finely chopped
½ teaspoon salt
1 stem lemon grass, peeled and sliced, or ½ teaspoon chopped lemon balm or lemon verbena
2 tablespoons chopped fresh coriander

Preparation time: 15 minutes
Cooking time: 50-60 minutes

This dish will thicken up if left to stand, so it should be served as soon as it is made. If you do not like very hot food, use only 1 green chilli.
1. Pick over the lentils, put them in a colander and rinse well under cold running water. Put them into a saucepan and pour in the water. Bring slowly to the boil, then lower heat and simmer gently until soft, about 20 minutes for orange lentils, about 35 minutes for green or brown. Drain.
2. Meanwhile, heat the oil in a frying pan, add the mustard seed and curry leaves and fry for 2 minutes, until the seeds start to sputter and the leaves turn brown. Add the onion and fry over a gentle heat for about 5 minutes until the onion is soft and lightly coloured.
3. Stir in the chillies, garlic, salt and lemon grass and fry for a further 8-10 minutes, stirring often.
4. Add the lentils and stir well to mix. Reheat gently, stirring all the time. Stir in half the coriander and turn the spiced lentils into a warmed serving dish. Sprinkle with the remaining coriander and serve immediately, with Spiced chicken (p 171) or a selection of Indian vegetarian dishes.

SHALLOTS IN DILL SAUCE

350g (12oz) shallots, peeled and left whole
450ml (¾pint) chicken stock
salt
freshly ground black pepper
25g (1oz) butter
1 tablespoon plain flour
65ml (2 ¼fl oz) single cream
2 tablespoons chopped fresh dill
sprigs of fresh dill, to garnish

Preparation time: 25 minutes
Cooking time: 40 minutes

1. Put the shallots into a small saucepan and pour in the stock to cover. Season lightly with salt and pepper and bring to the boil. Lower the heat and simmer gently, half-covered, for 15-30 minutes, or until the shallots are tender when pierced with a fine skewer. Drain, reserving the stock, transfer the shallots to a warmed serving dish and keep warm.
2. Measure out 150ml (¼ pint) of the stock. Melt the butter in the rinsed out pan and stir in the flour. Cook for 1 minute, stirring, remove from the heat and gradually stir in the stock. Return to the heat and bring to the boil, stirring, then lower the heat and simmer for 3 minutes, stirring from time to time.
3. Stir in the cream and heat through gently without boiling. Stir in the chopped dill and pour the sauce over the shallots. Garnish with sprigs of fresh dill and serve immediately, with one or two other vegetables, as an accompaniment to poultry, game, veal or fish dishes.

From the top: *Shallots in dill sauce; Savory beans*

SAVORY BEANS

100g (4oz) dried cannellini beans soaked for 2-3 hours, then drained
salt
225g (8oz) French beans, cut into 2.5cm (1 inch) pieces
225g (8oz) shelled broad beans, fresh or frozen
2 tablespoons olive oil
3 shallots, peeled and chopped
1 garlic clove, peeled and chopped (optional)
1 ½ tablespoons chopped fresh savory
freshly ground black pepper
2 tablespoons chopped fresh parsley
1 sprig fresh savory, to garnish

Preparation time: 15 minutes plus soaking
Cooking time: 45-60 minutes

1. Put the cannellini beans into a large saucepan and pour in fresh cold water to cover. Bring to the boil, then lower the heat and simmer for 30 minutes. Season with salt, then cook for a further 15 minutes or until tender.
2. Meanwhile cook the French beans and broad beans in separate saucepans of slightly salted boiling water for 4-5 minutes or until just tender, then drain.
3. Heat the oil in a frying pan, add the shallots and fry over a gentle heat for about 10 minutes until soft and golden. Stir in the garlic, if using, and the savory, and fry for a further 2 minutes, stirring constantly.
4. Drain the cannellini beans and turn them into a warmed serving bowl. Stir in the French beans and the broad beans and season to taste with salt and pepper. Add the shallots, savory, garlic and fresh parsley and stir well to mix. Garnish with a sprig of savory, and serve immediately with plainly grilled meat or poultry.

From the top: *Herb fritters; Herb and flower salad*
Opposite, from the top: *Turkish mixed salad; Middle Eastern salad; Crushed wheat salad*

HERB FRITTERS

FRITTER BATTER
100g (4oz) plain flour, sifted
pinch of salt
2 tablespoons sunflower oil
150ml (¼ pint) tepid water
1 egg white
24 large borage leaves, or 24 sprigs parsley, coriander, chervil, tarragon, salad burnet or mint
vegetable oil

Preparation time: 10 minutes plus resting
Cooking time: 10-15 minutes

1. Sift the flour with the salt into a large mixing bowl and gradually beat in the oil using a wire whisk. Slowly add the water, beating all the time, until the batter is the consistency of fairly thick cream. Set aside in a cool place for 1 hour.
2. Just before using the batter, beat again thoroughly. Whisk the egg white until stiff, then lightly fold in.
3. Make sure the herbs are absolutely dry. Pour enough oil into a deep saucepan to come one-third of the way up the sides. Heat to 180°C/350°F or until a cube of bread browns in 40 seconds.
4. Dip the herbs into the batter, shake off the excess, and drop into the hot oil, a few at a time. Fry for 2-3 minutes, turning once, then using a slotted spoon remove and drain on crumpled absorbent paper. Transfer to a heated serving dish while frying the next batch. Use to garnish savoury dishes.

HERB AND FLOWER SALAD

1 round lettuce, crisp inner leaves only
8 sprigs chervil, torn into small pieces, or 8 leaves sorrel, cut into thin strips
1 handful nasturtium flowers, marigolds or primroses, divided into petals or left whole
DRESSING
salt
freshly ground black pepper
½ tablespoon white wine vinegar
½ tablespoon lemon juice
3 tablespoons sunflower oil

Preparation time: 10 minutes

1. Lay the whole lettuce leaves in a bowl and scatter the chervil or sorrel over. Reserve a few nasturtiums, marigolds or primroses for a garnish and scatter the rest over the salad.
2. Mix the dressing: put salt and pepper in a small bowl and add vinegar and lemon juice. Stir well, then add the oil and whisk until blended. Just before serving, pour it over the salad and toss lightly. Scatter the reserved flowers over the top before serving.

TURKISH MIXED SALAD

50g (2oz) rocket, shredded
1 bunch spring onions, thinly sliced
½ cucumber, peeled and chopped
1 green pepper, seeded and chopped
225g (8oz) tomatoes, skinned, seeded, and chopped
2 tablespoons chopped dill
DRESSING
1 tablespoon lemon juice
2 ½ tablespoons olive oil

Preparation time: 15 minutes

1. Pile the shredded rocket into a salad bowl, and scatter the remaining ingredients over it.
2. Combine the dressing ingredients in a small jug and pour over the salad and mix thoroughly. Serve with simple dishes of grilled meat or fish.

MIDDLE EASTERN SALAD

1 pitta bread, lightly toasted and cut into 2.5cm (1 inch) squares
1 bunch spring onions, chopped
1 small cucumber, peeled and chopped
225g (8oz) tomatoes, skinned and chopped
1 garlic clove, peeled and crushed
1 cos lettuce heart, sliced
50g (2oz) purslane (tops only) or watercress leaves
4 tablespoons chopped fresh parsley
4 tablespoons chopped fresh mint
salt
freshly ground black pepper
65ml (2 ½fl oz) olive oil
65ml (2 ½fl oz) lemon juice

Preparation time: 15 minutes, plus standing
Cooking time: 1 minute

This is best served as a starter, or as part of a light vegetarian meal.

1. Arrange the pieces of pitta bread in a salad bowl. Cover with the spring onions, cucumber, tomatoes and garlic.
2. Leave for 10 minutes to allow the bread to absorb the juices, then add the lettuce, purslane or watercress, parsley and mint. Season to taste with salt and pepper, then combine the oil and lemon juice and pour evenly over the salad. Toss well and serve immediately while the vegetables are still crisp.

CRUSHED WHEAT SALAD

100g (4oz) crushed wheat or burghul
2 bunches spring onions, chopped
225g (8oz) tomatoes, skinned, chopped, and drained
50g (2oz) chopped fresh parsley
4 tablespoons chopped fresh mint
4 tablespoons olive oil
3 tablespoons lemon juice
salt
freshly ground black pepper

Preparation time: 15 minutes, plus soaking
Cooking time: 1 minute

This very healthy salad, rich in Vitamin C, is a variation of the Middle Eastern *tabbouleh*. Be sure to buy crushed wheat or burghul, as it is called in the Middle East: cracked or kibbled wheat will not do.

1. Put the crushed wheat into a bowl and pour in fresh cold water to cover. Leave for 30 minutes, then drain and squeeze dry between your hands.
2. Put the crushed wheat into a bowl and add the spring onions, tomatoes, parsley and mint. Stir well to mix, then stir in the oil and lemon juice and season to taste with salt and pepper. Serve with cold meats, or with grilled kebabs, instead of rice.

A SIMPLE PIZZA

25g (1oz) butter
2 tablespoons olive oil
1 medium onion, peeled and chopped
350g (12oz) tinned tomatoes, coarsely chopped
1 garlic clove, peeled and chopped
salt
freshly ground black pepper
¼ teaspoon sugar
½ tablespoon chopped fresh marjoram or 1 teaspoon dried oregano
½ tablespoon chopped fresh lovage or 1 teaspoon chopped dried lovage
½ tablespoon fresh thyme or 1 teaspoon dried thyme
225g (8oz) Mozzarella cheese, coarsely grated
350g (12oz) self-raising flour
50g (2oz) butter
1 egg
approx. 120ml (4fl oz) milk

Preparation time: 25 minutes, plus cooling
Cooking time: 45 minutes
Oven: 200°C, 400°F, Gas Mark 6

This is not a true pizza, which has a base of bread dough, but a quickly made alternative.

1. Heat the butter and oil in a heavy based pan and gently cook the onion until it is soft and transparent.
2. Add the tomatoes with their juice, garlic, salt and pepper, sugar, and chopped herbs. Simmer gently, uncovered, stirring occasionally for about 25 minutes until quite thick. Leave to cool for 1 hour.
3. To make the base, sift the flour and a pinch of salt into a bowl. Lightly rub in the butter.
4. Beat the egg with the milk and blend into the mixture to give a soft dough which leaves the sides of the bowl cleanly. If necessary add a drop more milk. Turn out on to a floured surface and knead once or twice, then roll out into a circle about 25cm (10 inches) in diameter.
5. Lay the dough in a greased pizza pan or shallow flan ring, or on a flat baking sheet. Spoon the topping over the base, leaving a 2.5cm (1 inch) edge all around. Scatter the cheese over the filling, and bake on the top shelf of the oven for 15 minutes, until golden brown around the edges and puffy.

PROVENÇAL MIXED SALAD

1 slice dry white bread, 1cm (½ inch) thick
1 large garlic clove, peeled and halved
50g (2oz) each of as many of the following as are available: lamb's lettuce, rocket, dandelion leaves, lettuce leaves, inner leaves of curly endive, thoroughly washed and dried
3½ tablespoons olive oil
1 tablespoon white wine vinegar
salt
freshly ground black pepper

Preparation time: 12-15 minutes
Cooking time: 20-30 minutes
Oven: 110°C, 225°F, Gas Mark ¼

This popular salad, called *mesclun* in Provence, was originally made with a mixture of tiny wild green leaves, gathered by the local country people and brought to the markets in sacks. It is usually served as a first course in the restaurants of the region.

1. Make the garlic croûtons: dry the bread for 20-30 minutes in the preheated oven, then rub each side with the cut garlic clove. Cut the bread into small squares.
2. Pile the salad leaves loosely in a bowl. Combine the oil and vinegar and season to taste with salt and pepper. Pour over the salad, toss well and mix in the croûtons. Serve immediately.

MUSHROOM PURÉE

150ml (¼ pint) milk
¼ bay leaf
1 slice onion
salt
freshly ground black pepper
pinch of freshly ground nutmeg
75g (3oz) butter
450g (1lb) mushrooms, roughly chopped
1 tablespoon plain flour
2 tablespoons chopped fresh savory, salad burnet or lovage
150ml (¼ pint) double or whipping cream
TO GARNISH
sprigs of fresh savory, salad burnet or lovage
sliced mushrooms (optional)

Preparation time: 10 minutes
Cooking time: 25 minutes, plus infusing

This creamy purée is like a cross between a sauce and a vegetable dish, and goes particularly well with roast meat recipes such as Roast lamb with garlic and rosemary (p 178). The purée will not keep well and should be eaten as soon as it is made.

1. Put the milk into a small saucepan with the bay leaf, onion, salt and pepper and nutmeg. Bring slowly to the boil, then remove from the heat, cover and leave to infuse for 20 minutes. Strain the milk, discarding the flavourings.
2. Melt 50g (2oz) of the butter in a saucepan, add the mushrooms and cook over a gentle heat for about 10 minutes, stirring from time to time, until softened. Raise the heat and cook briskly for 2-3 minutes, to allow the excess liquid to evaporate. Set aside and keep warm.
3. Reheat the strained milk. Melt the remaining butter in a small saucepan and stir in the flour. Cook for 1 minute, stirring, then remove from the heat and gradually stir in the milk. Return to the heat and

From the top: *Provençal mixed salad; A simple pizza*

bring to the boil, stirring, then lower the heat and simmer for 3 minutes, stirring from time to time.
4. Add the sauce to the mushrooms, stirring lightly to mix. Return to the boil and add the savory, then lower the heat and cook very gently for 3 minutes, stirring almost constantly. Stir in the cream and reheat gently without allowing to boil. Stir in the nutmeg and season to taste with salt and pepper.
5. To serve, pour into a warmed serving dish and garnish with savory sprigs and sliced mushrooms.

VARIATION
For a pasta sauce add 2 tablespoons chopped parma ham, a crushed garlic clove and a tablespoon of chopped parsley to the purée.

FRIED PARSLEY

12 large sprigs parsley
vegetable oil

Cooking time: 5-6 minutes.

1. Heat the oil in a deep saucepan to 160°C/325°F or until a cube of bread browns in 50 seconds. Drop in 4 sprigs of parsley and fry for 30 seconds on each side. (The parsley will turn bright green almost immediately and become very crisp).
2. Using a slotted spoon, remove the parsley and drain on absorbent paper while frying the next batch. Serve with Salmon fish cakes (p 162).

HORSERADISH SAUCE

150ml (¼pint) plain unsweetened yogurt
150ml (¼pint) thick mayonnaise
2-3 tablespoons grated horseradish
1-1½ tablespoons lemon juice

Preparation time: 8 minutes

Traditionally served with hot or cold roast beef, horseradish sauce is also good with smoked or fresh fish. In Scandinavia it is a usual accompaniment to fried sole or plaice.

1. Put the yogurt into a bowl and beat with a wooden spoon until smooth. Add the mayonnaise and stir very thoroughly to mix.
2. Add horseradish to taste, then stir in the lemon juice to taste. The sauce should have a sharp flavour; add slightly more lemon juice if it is to be served with fish.

From the left: *Horseradish sauce; Horseradish and apple sauce*

HORSERADISH AND APPLE SAUCE

2 Bramley cooking apples, about 350g (12oz), peeled, cored and thickly sliced
3 tablespoons water
150ml (¼pint) soured cream
3-4 tablespoons grated horseradish
2-3 teaspoons lemon juice

Preparation time: 12-15 minutes, plus cooling
Cooking time: 6-8 minutes

An unusual sauce from Scandinavia, where it is served with hot or cold roast duck or goose. It is also good with roast pork.

1. Put the apples in a saucepan with the water, cover and cook over a gentle heat, stirring occasionally, until soft. Pass the apples through a food mill and set aside for about 20 minutes to cool.
2. Stir in the soured cream and add horseradish to taste. The sauce is best served at room temperature.

PARSLEY SAUCE

25g (1oz) butter
1½ tablespoons plain flour
300ml (½pint) hot chicken stock
4 tablespoons single cream
salt
freshly ground black pepper
4 tablespoons chopped fresh parsley

Preparation time: 5 minutes
Cooking time: 12 minutes

Generous quantities of chopped green parsley give this sauce a delightfully fresh appearance and fragrant aroma. Parsley emphasizes other flavours with overpowering them and can therefore be used in fairly large quantities, unlike other, more overpowering herbs. This old-fashioned sauce is delicious with boiled beef or gammon, or poached chicken, or fish.

1. Melt the butter in a small saucepan and stir in the flour. Cook for 1 minute, stirring, then remove from the heat and gradually stir in the stock. Return to the heat and bring to the boil, stirring, then lower the heat and simmer for 3 minutes, stirring from time to time.
2. Stir in the cream and season to taste with salt and pepper. Stir in the parsley. Serve the parsley sauce hot, with boiled beef, gammon steaks or poached chicken.

VARIATION

For a parsley sauce that goes particularly well with fish, use 3 tablespoons chopped fresh parsley and 1 hard-boiled egg, finely chopped and substitute fish stock for chicken. This version is excellent to serve with smoked fish such as haddock.

From the left: *Parsley sauce; Mint sauce; Mushroom sauce*

MUSHROOM SAUCE

350g (12oz) mushrooms, quartered
450ml (¾pint) chicken stock, heated
2 tablespoons chopped salad burnet, or 1 tablespoon chopped savory
salt
freshly ground black pepper
65ml (2½fl oz) soured cream

Preparation time: 10 minutes
Cooking time: 20 minutes

1. Put the mushrooms into a saucepan with the stock, and bring to the boil, then lower the heat and simmer for 10 minutes, half covered.
2. Add the salad burnet and season to taste with salt and pepper. Simmer for a further 5 minutes, then stir in the soured cream (do not allow to boil, or the sauce will separate).
3. Purée briefly in a food processor or electric blender, and serve hot, with roast chicken or game.

MINT SAUCE

4 tablespoons finely chopped fresh mint
1 teaspoon sugar
2 tablespoons lemon juice
1 tablespoon white wine vinegar
4 tablespoons boiling water

Preparation time: 10 minutes plus cooling

1. Put the mint and sugar in a mortar and pound with a pestle until thoroughly blended, or process briefly in a food processor or electric blender.
2. Add the lemon juice, vinegar and finally boiling water. Stir well to mix, then set aside for 30 minutes to cool. Serve with roast lamb.

AÏOLI (FRENCH GARLIC SAUCE)

4 garlic cloves, peeled and chopped
2 egg yolks
pinch of salt
300ml (½ pint) olive oil
1½ tablespoons white wine vinegar

Preparation time: 20-25 minutes

This Provençal sauce is traditionally served with poached chicken or fish, accompanied by a large platter of boiled vegetables. It is also good with hard-boiled eggs, boiled potatoes, or a mixture of raw and cooked vegetables. It should ideally, be made in a mortar and pestle, although a food processor may be used instead.

1. Put the garlic in a mortar and pound with a pestle until reduced to a pulp, or crush the garlic, then pound it with the back of a wooden spoon in a bowl. Add the egg yolks and continue to pound until thoroughly blended.
2. Add the salt, then start to add the oil very gradually, drop by drop, beating constantly with a wooden spoon. Once half the oil is used up, add the remainder a little more quickly, in a slow trickle, beating constantly.
3. When all the oil is absorbed, gradually add the vinegar, stirring constantly until well blended. Serve the Aïoli in a bowl.

YOGURT SAUCE WITH HERBS

1 large garlic clove, peeled and crushed
pinch of salt
150ml (¼ pint) plain unsweetened yogurt
freshly ground black pepper
½ tablespoon each chopped fresh tarragon, chervil, chives and parsley
½ tablespoon chopped fresh herbs, to garnish

Preparation time: 12 minutes, plus chilling

This sauce is subtly flavoured with the classic *fines herbes* mixture.

1. Put the garlic into a bowl, add the salt and mash together with a fork, to make a paste. Gradually beat in the yogurt.
2. Taste and adjust the seasoning, then stir in the herbs, cover and chill in the refrigerator for at least 1 hour. Serve the yogurt sauce with grilled lamb chops, chicken pieces, or fish steaks, or with baked stuffed vegetables, sprinkling over the chopped herbs for garnish just before serving.

VARIATION

Instead of the mixed herbs, use 2 tablespoons chopped fresh mint, or 2 teaspoons dried mint, and 2 tablespoons grated cucumber. Serve with roast or grilled lamb, or meatballs.

SKORDALIA (GREEK GARLIC SAUCE)

2 large slices stale white bread, crusts removed
4-6 tablespoons cold water
½ garlic bulb, peeled and chopped
1 large potato, boiled
150ml (¼ pint) olive oil
1-2 tablespoons lemon juice
1 tablespoon single cream, top of the milk, or evaporated milk (optional)

Preparation time: 20-25 minutes plus soaking
Cooking time: 20 minutes

This pungent sauce, irresistible to garlic-lovers, is good served with fried fish, hard-boiled eggs or vegetable fritters. In Greece, where cream does not exist, a little evaporated milk is sometimes added at the end, to improve the colour. Single cream or top of the milk may be used instead. If at any stage the sauce starts to separate, beat in 1 tablespoon warm water to reconstitute it.

1. Soak the bread in the water for 10 minutes. Meanwhile put the garlic in a mortar and pound with a pestle until reduced to a pulp, or crush the garlic, then pound with the back of a wooden spoon in a bowl. Press the potato through a food mill or mash it with a fork and add to the garlic. Blend thoroughly.
2. Squeeze the bread dry and add to the garlic mixture. Pound until thoroughly blended to a thick paste, then start to add the oil, very gradually, drop by drop, beating constantly with a wooden spoon. When the oil is absorbed, stir in the lemon juice and the cream, if using.

PESTO

15g (½oz) fresh basil, leaves only
1 garlic clove, peeled and chopped
pinch of salt
50g (2oz) pine kernels
4 tablespoons grated Parmesan cheese
6 tablespoons olive oil
sprigs of basil, to garnish

Preparation time: 15 minutes

This is the basil sauce, as made in Genoa, that is also found in and around Nice, and in Provence. In Italy it is made with a mixture of cheeses: half Parmesan, and half sardo, a hard cheese from Sardinia. Since Sardo is not always available in this country, all Parmesan may be used instead.

1. Put the basil into a food processor or electric blender and process until finely chopped. Add the garlic, salt, pine kernels and Parmesan and process until reduced to a smooth paste.
2. Tip the paste into a mortar or heavy bowl, and gradually beat in the olive oil using either a pestle or heavy wooden spoon. Serve the pesto spooned over pasta, and garnished with a sprig of basil, or stirred into a thick vegetable soup (see Minestrone al Pesto p 154). Pesto is also delicious with jacket-baked potatoes.

Opposite, from the top: *Aioli; Skordalia; Yogurt sauce with herbs*
From the top: *Herby tomato sauce (recipe overleaf); Pesto*

HERBY TOMATO SAUCE

2 tablespoons olive oil
1 large onion, peeled and chopped
2 large garlic cloves, peeled and crushed
2×400g (14oz) cans tomatoes, roughly chopped
1 small bay leaf
1 tablespoon chopped fresh lovage or ½ tablespoon dried lovage
1 tablespoon chopped fresh marjoram or ½ tablespoon dried oregano
1 tablespoon fresh thyme or ½ tablespoon dried thyme
1 ½ teaspoons sugar
salt
freshly ground black pepper
sprig of thyme, to garnish

Preparation time: 12 minutes
Cooking time: 1¼ hours

This is based on the Italian pizziola sauce, traditionally flavoured with oregano. Including lovage and thyme as well gives it a warm, extra spicy flavour.

1. Heat the oil in a large saucepan, add the onion and cook gently for about 10 minutes until soft but not browned. Add the garlic and cook for a further 2 minutes.
2. Add the tomatoes, herbs and seasonings. Bring to the boil, then lower the heat and simmer, very gently, half-covered, for 1 hour, stirring occasionally.
3. Remove and discard the bay leaf. Taste and adjust the seasoning if necessary. Leave the sauce to cool for a few minutes, then purée briefly in a food processor, or electric blender, or pass through a coarse food mill. Reheat the sauce gently, and serve with pasta or grilled steaks, garnished with a thyme sprig.

VARIATION

Fresh tomatoes, when plentiful and cheap, may be substituted for canned. Use 1kg (2lb) fresh tomatoes, skinned and roughly chopped, and flavour the sauce with 1½ tablespoons tomato purée as well.

Below, from the left: *Mint, parsley and sage herb butters*

Above: *Herb stuffing used to stuff the chicken breast and to make stuffing balls*

HERB BUTTER

75g (3oz) unsalted butter, softened
3 tablespoons chopped fresh parsley
1 garlic clove, peeled and crushed
1 tablespoon lemon juice
salt
freshly ground black pepper

Preparation time: 10 minutes, plus chilling

1. Cream the butter in a food processor or electric blender, or in a bowl using a wooden spoon. Add the parsley, garlic and lemon juice and cream again. Season to taste with salt and pepper.
2. Wrap the herb butter in cling film and chill in the refrigerator for about 20-30 minutes until firm. Unwrap and shape the butter into a neat roll about 2.5cm (1 inch) wide, wrap again in cling film, and chill in the refrigerator until hard. Cut into thick slices and serve with grilled steaks, sole or plaice.

VARIATIONS
Substitute the same amount of fresh tarragon, chervil, or dill for the parsley, or use 2 tablespoons chopped fresh mint, or 1 tablespoon chopped fresh sage. For a mixed herb butter, use ½ tablespoon each tarragon, chervil, chives and parsley.

HERB STUFFING

50g (2oz) butter
100g (4oz) shallots, peeled and chopped
225g (8oz) fresh white breadcrumbs
1 teaspoon salt
1 teaspoon black peppercorns, roughly crushed
1 teaspoon juniper berries, roughly crushed
4 tablespoons chopped fresh parsley
2 tablespoons chopped celery leaves
1 egg, beaten

Preparation time: 15 minutes
Cooking time: 4-5 minutes

The quantities given here are sufficient to stuff a large chicken or capon; they can be increased or decreased as necessary.
1. Melt the butter in a frying pan, add the shallots and fry over a gentle heat until soft and lightly coloured.
2. Put the breadcrumbs into a large bowl and stir in the onions with the butter. Add the salt, peppercorns, juniper berries and herbs. Add the beaten egg and stir to mix very thoroughly.

VARIATION:
Extra herb stuffing may be shaped into balls, placed on a baking sheet and roasted for 30 minutes.

COMPOTE OF PEARS

4 large Williams pears, peeled, cored and quartered
2 tablespoons sugar
½ tablespoon chopped sweet cicely

Preparation time: 10 minutes, plus 1 hour cooling
Cooking time: 5-10 minutes

Sweet cicely is a sweet, anise-flavoured herb that grows easily from February to November. Its main contribution to cooking is that its natural sweetness allows the cook to reduce sugar quantities. Its fresh aromatic flavour can be added to all manner of sweets, trifles, fruit salads and summer cocktails.

1. Pour a little cold water into a large, heavy-based saucepan to just cover the bottom and lay the pears in it. Add the sugar and bring to the boil, then lower the heat, cover the pan and simmer gently until the pears are tender when pierced with a skewer.
2. Carefully transfer the pears to a serving dish. Stir the sweet Cicely into the syrup, pour over the pears and set aside to cool for 1-2 hours. Serve with thick cream or yogurt.

BLACKCURRANT COMPOTE

450g (1lb) blackcurrants, stringed and topped and tailed
4 tablespoons sugar
1 tablespoon chopped fresh lemon balm or lemon verbena
lemon balm sprigs, to decorate

Preparation time: 3 minutes, plus cooling
Cooking time: 6 minutes

In the summer the cool fragrant flavours of lemon balm and lemon verbena can be included in numerous fruit drinks and desserts. The deliciously-scented young leaves can also be used in sauces and dressings instead of lemon rind.

1. Pour a little cold water into a large, heavy-based saucepan just to cover the bottom, then add the blackcurrants, sugar and lemon balm or verbena. Bring to the boil, cover the pan and simmer gently, for about 3 minutes, until the blackcurrants start to burst.
2. Spoon the blackcurrants into glasses and set aside for 1-2 hours to cool. Decorate each glass with a lemon balm sprig and serve with thick cream or plain unsweetened yogurt.

VARIATION

Blackcurrants and lemon balm or verbena can also be combined to make a delicious creamy summer pudding. Whip 150ml (¼ pint) double cream until thick but not dry. Beat 150ml (¼ pint) plain unsweetened yogurt until smooth. Beat 2 egg whites until stiff then lightly fold them into the cream. Then fold in the yogurt. Stir in 2 tablespoons of caster sugar, then mix in 500g (1lb) prepared blackcurrants. Stir in 1 tablespoon chopped fresh lemon balm or lemon verbena leaves and serve. For extra colour, use a combination of red and blackcurrants.

MIXED MELON SALAD

1 small Ogen melon, peeled and cut into 2.5cm (1 inch) cubes
1 small honeydew melon, peeled and cut into 2.5cm (1 inch) cubes
1 slice watermelon, peeled and cut into 2.5cm (1 inch) cubes
juice of 2 limes
juice of 1 small orange
1-2 tablespoons caster sugar (optional)
½-1 tablespoon finely chopped fresh mint

Preparation time: 15 minutes, plus chilling

A refreshing fruit dish with a slightly tart flavour which would make a perfect ending to a rich meal or an ideal starter to a summer breakfast. The melon skins may be reserved and used to make Melon rind pickle (p. 68).

1. Put the melon into a bowl, pour over the fruit juices and stir well to mix. Sweeten with a little sugar if liked.
2. Stir in the mint and chill for 1-2 hours before serving.

VARIATION

When watermelon is out of season, 225g (8oz) hulled raspberries can be used instead to give colour contrast. For special occasions the melon flesh can be cut with a melon baller and the fruit salad served in the scooped out honeydew melon shell.

RHUBARB COMPOTE

750g (1 ½lb) rhubarb, cut into 2.5cm (1 inch) pieces
4 tablespoons sugar
young angelica leaves
1 teaspoon chopped crystallized angelica

Preparation time: 8 minutes
Cooking time: 5-10 minutes

1. Pour a little cold water into a large, heavy-based saucepan to just cover the bottom. Add the rhubarb, sugar and fresh angelica. Bring to the boil, then lower the heat, cover the pan and simmer gently until the rhubarb is tender, stirring once or twice.
2. Spoon the rhubarb into individual glasses and cool for 1-2 hours.
3. Decorate with angelica leaves and crystallized angelica over just before serving at room temperature or chilled with cream.

From the left: *Compote of pears; Blackcurrant compote; Mixed melon salad; Rhubarb compote*

FLOWERY SPONGE CAKE

175g (6oz) self-raising flour, sifted
1 teaspoon baking powder
175g (6oz) soft margarine, at room temperature
175g (6oz) caster sugar
3 eggs (size 1 or 2), beaten
2 teaspoons lemon juice
margarine, for greasing

BUTTERCREAM FILLING

75g (3oz) unsalted butter, at room temperature
100g (4oz) icing sugar
1 tablespoon lemon juice

ICING

175g (6oz) icing sugar, sifted
1-1½ tablespoons lemon juice, warmed

DECORATION

crystallized flowers and leaves
angelica stems

Preparation time: 30-45 minutes, plus cooling overnight
Cooking time: 30-35 minutes
Oven: 180°C, 350°F, Gas Mark 4

In keeping with its delicate summer mood, the cake should be served with crustless cucumber sandwiches and a fragrant tea such as jasmin or Earl Grey. Alternatively a tisane, made by infusing dried lime flowers or dried lemon balm leaves in boiling water may be served. This cake would look pretty on a summer tea table.

1. Grease two 17.5cm (7 inch) sandwich tins and line them with non-stick silicone paper or greased greaseproof paper.
2. Put the flour with the baking powder into a large mixing bowl and add the magarine, sugar and eggs. Beat with an electric hand beater or rotary whisk until all the ingredients are thoroughly combined, then beat in the lemon juice. Turn the mixture into the prepared sandwich tins and smooth the surface with a palette knife.
3. Bake the cakes for 25-30 minutes in the centre of a preheated oven or until a warmed fine skewer inserted into the middle comes out clean.
4. Leave the cakes to cool slightly in the tins, then turn out on to a wire rack and leave for about 8 hours or overnight to cool completely.
5. Make the filling: put the butter and sugar into a bowl and cream together with a wooden spoon until light and fluffy. Beat in the lemon juice. Spread one of the cakes with the buttercream filling and place the other cake on top.
6. Make the icing: put the icing sugar into a bowl and gradually mix in just enough lemon juice to give a spreading consistency. Using a palette knife dipped in water, spread the icing over the top of the cake and leave to set for 2-3 hours.
7. Decorate the top of the cake with Crystallized flower and angelica stems, using tweezers to arrange them in the pattern of your choice.

VARIATION

The sponge cake mixture can be used to make individual cakes. Line a bun tin with paper cases and put teaspoons of the mixture in each one, taking care not to overfill. Lightly smooth the surface of each one with a palette knife and bake in an oven preheated to 180°C, 350°F, Gas Mark 4, for 20-25 minutes until well risen and firm to the touch. Cool in the tin on a wire rack.

The cakes may be decorated in a variety of ways. They may be iced with the Buttercream filling. Make up according to the recipe for Flowery sponge cake and if liked divide it into two small bowls, tinting one portion pink or green with a few drops of food colouring. Spread a layer of buttercream over the top of each cake and decorate with piped shells, stars or a border of contrasting buttercream, using a greaseproof paper icing bag fitted with a medium star nozzle. Complete the decoration with Crystallized flowers. More simply, make up the Icing according to the recipe and spread a little over the top of each cake. Allow to dry then decorate with Crystallized flowers as liked.

To make butterfly cakes, cut a slice off the top of a cake and cut the slice in half. Pipe buttercream filling on top of the cake and position the halves of the slice on top. Decorate with Crystallized flowers. More simply, pipe the top of the cakes with uncoloured buttercream filling and decorate with Crystallized flowers.

CRYSTALLIZED STEMS AND FLOWERS

a few young angelica stems, or a handful of violets, nasturtiums and pelargoniums, or borage or bergamot flowers
1 egg white
pinch of salt
25g (1oz) caster sugar

Preparation time: 20-25 minutes, plus overnight drying

These make the prettiest of all decorations for an iced sponge cake, or for scattering over a cold mousse, fool or sorbet. Pick the stems or flowers at their freshest and best, preferably on a dry sunny morning, after the dew has evaporated (the flowers must be absolutely dry). The crystallized stems or flowers are best used the day after making, but can be kept for a day or two, stored between layers of greaseproof paper in an airtight tin.

1. Put the egg white on a flat plate and beat it lightly using a flat-bladed knife: do not allow it to get frothy.
2. Using tweezers, dip the stems or flowers first into the egg white, then into the sugar. Use a very fine paint brush to get the sugar into the folds of the flowers. Shake off the excess sugar, then lay the stems or flowers on a wire rack and leave them to dry in a warm room for about 8 hours or overnight.

Opposite: *Flowery sponge cake and individual cakes decorated with Crystallized stems and flowers*

PLANNING A HERB GARDEN

1. Clematis
2. Spearmint
3. Marjoram
4. Lemon Thyme
5. Lily *(L. regale)*
6. Chervil
7. Chives
8. Lovage
9. Dill
10. Pansies
11. Common Thyme
12. Rosemary
13. Marigolds
14. Parsley
15. Tarragon
16. Border carnation
17. Basil

One basic decision has to be made before even starting to plan a herb garden: is it to be formal or informal? Your decision will be guided partly by the space at your disposal, and partly by personal preference. There is little point in planning a formal garden within an irregular-shaped piece of land, or on uneven ground. A garden based on geometric designs demands a square, or at least rectangular, plot, and one that is perfectly flat: the garden of a small terrace house would be ideal. In fact the idea of imposing intricate geometric designs on herbs, surely the most vigorous and unruly of growing plants, may not seem entirely appropriate, yet no one would deny that herbs do look at their best growing near stone, or set against a formal hedge of clipped box or yew. Perhaps a design based on a square or rectangle, intersected with paths of stone or brick, is the perfect compromise. Once this formal design has been achieved, the herbs may be allowed to grow naturally, mingling with each other in an unforced manner. This also solves the problem of maintenance, as truly formal herb gardens must be rigorously kept up if they are to look their best. In these garden plans, the herbs have been selected specifically for culinary purposes, although many have a decorative value too. The smallest plans restrict the choice to seven or eight favourites, largely the delicate summer herbs that are less easy to buy fresh – chervil, basil, tarragon and dill – and that form the basis of summer cooking.

When siting the herb garden, remember that a sunny, sheltered spot is imperative, for almost all herbs need a few hours of sunshine each day, and dislike the wind. The herb garden should be as close to the kitchen as possible, for easy access is vital if the herbs are to be used to any great extent in cooking.

Once this has been established, a few other points should be borne in mind:

1. Plants that spread or cross-fertilize
Mints have a spreading root system that tends to take over the garden, and they cross-fertilize with each other when grown too close. Horseradish also has a creeping root system, and like mint should be planted in a container of some sort, either above or below the ground. Fennel and dill tend to cross-fertilize with each other, and should be ket apart.

2. Patterns of growth
Most herbs are perennial, but some are annuals, or best treated as such. (This applies to many of the biennials, which produce woody stems and flowerheads only during the second year.) Perennials and annuals should be mixed, when height permits, in

order to avoid ugly gaps in winter. Try also to place evergreens judiciously for the same reason, to provide interest during the dormant season.

3. Contrasts in leaf, shape and colour

Much of the charm of herbs lies in the diversity of their leaves, and best use should be made of these whenever possible. Soft, downy, round leaves should be planted next to spiky needles; pale, dappled shades of white and cream against dark glossy evergreens; shiny purples and bronzes adjacent to furry silvery-greys.

4. Inclusion of flowers

Most of the visual interest of herbs lies in their leaves; with a few obvious exceptions, like bergamot, borage, rosemary and chives, their flowers are undistinguished and the herbs are pickled before they have a chance to bloom. You may wish to add a few flowers, which from medieval times have been traditionally included in herb and kitchen gardens. In the Middle Ages border carnations (called gilly flowers), lilies, marigolds and violets were included. Roses were often planted in the monastic herb gardens of medieval France, and lavender earned its place as a herb for strewing on floors, and for scenting linen. More recent horticultural developments also seem appropriate today in the herb garden, for example sweet-scented geraniums and nasturtiums, whose leaves and flowers can be used in the kitchen, and pansies, a hybrid of the old-fashioned violet, which was often candied for decoration. Vines or hops seem appropriate in a walled garden, as do old-fashioned climbing roses, honeysuckle, or clamatis.

5. Inclusion of vegetables

It is hard to draw any clear line between vegetables and herbs. Celery can be included, for the sake of its leaves, as can spring onions and garlic as well. If there is room, one might be tempted to include more; globe artichokes add interest to any bed, as do ornamental cabbages, on a smaller scale.

The semi-formal garden needs paths, both for the sake of the overall design, and for practicality. Any bed over 90 cm (3 feet) wide also needs stepping-stones set within it, for the herbs to be within easy reach. The stones will soon be hidden from sight by the herbs themselves, but their position is easily memorized, for use in muddy weather. Ideally, paths and stepping-stones should be of grey York stone – old flag-stones or paving stones are ideal – or of old brick. Pockets of low herbs may be grown among them, in small gaps, or in the joins. Since both stone and brick are expensive, cheaper alternatives may have to be considered; concrete may be set in slabs, to resemble stone, or blocks of composition or synthetic stone may be used. An alternative is to make paths of creeping herbs, and to set pieces of stone within them, at intervals of about 45 cm (18 inches), so that they are usable even in wet weather. There are many prostrate herbs suitable for paths – various mints, thymes, and camomile - but they must be enclosed in some way to stop them encroaching on the beds. Small pieces of slate, set on edge, or small stones make a decorative border that takes the minimum of space.

In any formal design a centrepiece is required, as a focal point. There are many possibilities, depending on the available space, the aspect and personal preference. An irregular shape would offset the formality of the general design well. Any small tree would look good: a fruit tree grown on the least vigorous root stock, a (weeping) willow-leaf pear, a mulberry, medlar or quince. For a smaller space, a weeping standard rose would be suitable, or a honeysuckle or clematis trained as a standard.

A small statue would also look elegant as a centrepiece, or an urn filled with ivy-leafed geraniums or nasturtiums, trailing over the edge. For those who prefer a strictly geometric design, an ornamental bay tree can be grown in a tub, clipped into a pyramid shape. If the garden is itself enclosed within a wall, as in a town garden, a seat may be placed at the end; if set within a larger garden, however, as in the country, it is better to leave it open, to allow the paths to continue to the outer world.

TOP ROW, FROM THE LEFT: Basil, Chervil, Dill, Tarragon. Bottom row, from the left: Marjoram, Chives, Thyme.

LEFT HAND TUB, CLOCKWISE FROM TOP LEFT: Basil, Rosemary, Marjoram, Chervil. RIGHT HAND TUB, CLOCKWISE FROM TOP RIGHT: Dill, Thyme, Chives, Tarragon.

STORING HERBS

Freezing home-grown herbs

Most of the herbs that do not dry well can be frozen. This applies to all the delicate annuals; chervil, dill and basil, as well as to chives, parsley and tarragon. It is very simple to do; in the case of large-leafed herbs like basil, simply pick the leaves off the stalks and pack, twelve at a time, into small polythene bags, label, and freeze. With small-leafed herbs like tarragon, chervil and dill, it is better to freeze small sprigs, also packed into bags. Chives are packed in bunches, and parsley heads loosely bundled into larger polythene bags.

Chopped parsley and *fines herbes* can be pounded into butter, flavoured with lemon juice, and frozen in rolls (see below, centre), for serving with grilled food. Large amounts of basil may be made into pesto (p 193) and frozen, for eating with pasta and minestrone through the winter. Aromatic herbs like marjoram and thyme are useful combined with tomatoes – also at their cheapest in late summer – and made into a concentrated herby tomato purée, for enriching sauces for pasta.

A sweet syrup, flavoured with elder flowers, scented geranium leaves, or young blackcurrant leaves, may be frozen for making desserts. Make by infusing a handful of flowers, or leaves, in a thin sugar syrup for 30 minutes, then strain, cool, and freeze. Use as a base for making sorbets.

Preserving home-grown herbs in oil and vinegar

Before the days of home freezers, basil was sometimes preserved in olive oil and salt. This is not very satisfactory, for it becomes slimy. For those without freezers, I would suggest using it to flavour olive oil, for use in salad dressings and vegetable dishes. The same technique can be used to flavour white wine vinegar, using tarragon or salad burnet instead of basil. Garlic can also be used to make a flavoured oil, while elder flowers make a delicious perfumed vinegar. The herbs can be left as sprigs, chopped or crushed before immersing in oil or warmed vinegar. Close tightly, and stand for two weeks, shaking every two or three days, before straining and re-bottling. Six tablespoons chopped herbs, or 4 cloves garlic, or 6 elder flower umbels will flavour 1 pint of olive oil or vinegar.

Harvesting home-grown herbs

All herbs should be harvested at the same moment in their life cycle, after the flower buds have formed, and before they burst into bloom. They can of course be picked at other times, but this is when the main crop should be taken, when the foliage is at its most abundant, and the flavour most intense. After flowering, most of the strength goes into producing seeds, and – in some cases – woody stems, and the flavour grows weaker. This also applies to biennials in their second year of growth.

Choose a warm, dry day for harvesting and be sure to pick the herbs in the morning, after the dew has evaporated, and before the sun has reached its zenith. Annuals are best demolished and dug up, since there is little point in leaving bare, unsightly stems. Most biennials can be treated in the same way, although a few plants can be left to self-seed. In the case of perennials, the picking must be done with care, so as not to denude the plant, and weaken it. At least one-third of the leaves must be left unpicked. Herbs that need pruning, such as bay, rosemary, and lemon verbena, will probably have already supplied enough leaves for household use at the time of pruning, which is usually done in early spring.

Drying home-grown herbs

The traditional method of storing home-grown herbs for winter use is by drying, but this is only effective in the case of a few plants whose essential oils are not too volatile to survive the drying process. Woody perennials like rosemary, bay and thyme dry well, but as they are evergreen, the leaves may equally well be left on the shrub, and picked as needed through the winter. Both bay and rosemary require pruning to keep in shape, as does lemon verbena, and the clippings can be dried and hung in the kitchen. Most annuals are not worth drying, since their essential oils are volatile, and the flavour is lost; this applies to chervil, dill, chives, basil and parsley, as well as to the perennial tarragon. The herbs that dry best are lovage, marjoram, mint, sage and savory. In the Arab countries home-dried mint is used in preference to fresh, in dishes of cucumber and yogurt, while the Greeks use dried oregano all summer long in their salads of tomatoes, black olives and feta cheese.

The best way to dry herbs is to lay them in a single layer, on a ventilated rack covered with a piece of muslin, in a dry, airy room. Leave them until completely dry: this may take anything from two days for delicate leaves like mint, to a week for woody herbs like rosemary. The process can be accelerated slightly by placing the rack in an airing cupboard or on a night storage heater. Branches of rosemary and bay may be hung singly (see right), and left to dry naturally. The disadvantage of drying herbs in bunches, which was common at one time, is that the air does not always penetrate right into the centre.

Once dried, the herbs become brittle. In almost all cases the leaves should be rubbed off the stalks and packed into jars. There is no need to reduce the leaves to powder, as is usually done commercially. A few, like rosemary and thyme, may be left on sprigs, for easy removal after cooking, and packed in plastic bags. If the dried herbs are stored in plain glass jars or plastic bags, they must be kept in cupboards, away from the light. Coloured glass or china jars may be left in the daylight. All containers must be carefully labelled.

Herbs dried at home have more flavour than bought ones; even so, their flavour will not last very long and they are best used within six months. As herbs keep longer in unopened jars than once they have been exposed to the air, small jars are preferable to large ones.

LIST OF SUPPLIERS

Nowadays herb plants are fairly easy to obtain, but if you have problems obtaining any of the herbs mentioned in this book, it might be worth contacting the following suppliers, all of whom operate a mail order service.

Down to Earth Seeds,
Streetfield Farm,
Cade Street,
Heathfield,
East Sussex,
TN21 9BS
Tel: 04352 3964

Herb seeds.
Catalogue on request.

Hollington Nurseries,
Woolton Hill,
Newbury,
Berkshire
Tel: Highclere 253908

Herb plants and seeds.
Send S.A.E. for list.

Suttons Seeds Ltd,
Hele Road,
Torquay,
Devon,
TQ2 7QJ

Herb seeds.
Catalogue on request.

Heches Herbs,
St. Peter in the Wold,
Channel Islands
Tel: 0 481 63345

Herb plants.
List on request.

Wells and Winter,
Mere House,
Near Maidstone,
Kent
Tel: 0622 812491

Herb plants.
Send S.A.E. for list.

INDEX

T

U

V

W

Y

ACKNOWLEDGEMENTS

Photography: Laurie Evans and Charlie Stebbings
Photographic styling: Lesley Richardson and Liz Allen-Eslor
Preparation of food for photography: Caroline Ellwood, Allyson Birch, Anne Ager and Jacqui Hine
Illustrations:. Claire Davies, Jenny Mitchell, Delyth Jones and Jill Tomblin

The publishers would like to thank the following companies for the loan of props for photography: Elizabeth David, 46 Bourne Street, London SW1; Putnams, 72 Mill Lane, London NW6; David Mellor, 4 Sloane Square, London SW1.

The publishers would also like to thank Hollington Nurseries, Woolton Hill, Newbury, Berks, for their help in supplying herb plants for photography